Oxford

Also in the series:

Buenos Aires by Nick Caistor
Prague by Andrew Beattie
Berlin by Norbert Schürer

Oxford

Martin Garrett

Interlink Books

An imprint of Interlink Publishing Group, Inc.
Northampton, Massachusetts

First published in 2016 by
INTERLINK BOOKS
An imprint of Interlink Publishing Group, Inc.
46 Crosby Street, Northampton, Massachusetts 01060
www.interlinkbooks.com

Library of Congress Cataloging-in-Publication Data

Garrett, Martin.
Oxford / by Martin Garrett.
    pages cm -- (Interlink cultural guides)
First US edition published in 2015 by Interlink Books.
ISBN 978-1-56656-087-0
1. Oxford (England)--History. 2. Oxford (England)--Description and
travel. I. Title.
DA690.O98G27 2015
942.5'74--dc23
                          2015014309

Cover Images: © Darrell Godliman; Oxford Punts © Paula Stanley |
Dreamstime.com

Printed and bound in United States of America

Contents

To Helen

Preface

"It didn't look wonderful today. Some days Oxford just looked like an elitist mausoleum." So says a character in Marilyn French's *The Bleeding Heart* (1980). But most days it does look wonderful to most people—golden stone, curving High Street, wooded hills—and usually it is nothing like a mausoleum. Its elite students shout, cycle, study, party, perform music, go to lectures, play soccer, and punt and row. Perhaps you are more likely to overhear philosophical discussions than in most cities, but the talk is surrounded by the multiple, very un-mausoleum-like activities of two universities—Oxford and Oxford Brookes—and a busy, expanding city of shopping and business developments, markets, science and technology companies, and a City Farm.

My own experience is as an undergraduate and doctoral student at St. Edmund Hall in the University of Oxford, living in college, off Iffley Road and in North Oxford (near Port Meadow). I lived in Oxford—in Headington—for another eleven years, involved in teaching, research, cycling, and walking up and down Headington Hill, taking my children to nursery and primary school, the sandpit on Shotover, Cutteslowe Park, Blenheim, and the Cotswold Wildlife Park near Burford. Then we moved to Cambridge—a city in many ways more like Oxford than anywhere else, but very different nevertheless. (Oxford and Cambridge have been compared to Rome and Venice and claimed, with admittedly decreasing applicability, as opulent and austere, artistic and scientific, Cavalier and Roundhead.) As an outsider gradually becoming an insider, I wrote *Cambridge: A Cultural and Literary History* (Interlink, 2004). I continued to have many connections with Oxford. I thought longingly of writing about it one summer's day as I walked through the Parks and on northwards through the grassy meadows by the Cherwell. (People often don't realize that Oxford has even more expansive and various green spaces than Cambridge.) Later I got the chance to do it.

Writing about the city involved going back to familiar places and seeing them in a new light, and discovering many new places, stories, history, and paintings. The muddy Thames towpath, Brasenose Wood on the lower slopes of Shotover in spring, cows in Christ Church Meadow, open-air plays, long-gone Indian restaurants, the grasshopper (perhaps less distinctively Oxonian) who traveled on our car-bonnet from Headington to the station, the smell of coffee and sawdust in the Covered Market: there were endless memories and associations. But much had been built and done and written in and about Oxford since I lived there. The radically remodeled Ashmolean Museum has opened, the Radcliffe Observatory quarter is still being developed, and cafés and restaurants have filled in the once quiet, slightly bleak south side of the High Street. There are many new books and websites, new fictional detectives detecting in Cowley and drinking in Broad Street, new archaeological discoveries (see p.193).

Resources for finding out more about Oxford include Stephanie Jenkins' always accurate and perceptive *Oxford History* at oxfordhistory.org.uk. Oxford University provides a wealth of information at www.ox.ac.uk; more detailed material is contained in the readable and absorbing volumes of the *History of the University of Oxford* (general editor T. H. Aston, 1984-94). Christopher Hibbert's *Encyclopaedia of Oxford* (1988) has articles on everything from Academic Dress to Brewing to the Ring Road. John Dougill gives an authoritative survey in *Oxford in English Literature: the Making, and Undoing, of the 'English Athens'* (1998). There are several very useful and incisively written books by Geoffrey Tyack, including his *Blue Guide: Oxford and Cambridge* (1995) and *Oxford: an Architectural Guide* (1998).

Whatever its intrinsic beauties and virtues, Oxford is important to me personally as the place where I met my wife, Helen, who read English at St. Hilda's. This book is dedicated to her with continuing love and thanks. I have drawn gratefully on the Oxford memories of her late father, Roy Foster (see p.206). Many thanks also to Ed Taylor-Garrett for drawing the maps and Philip Garrett for taking the photograph of Minster Lovell dovecote. Thanks also to those good listeners Christine L. Corton, Jennifer M. Fellows, Delwen Foster, and Robert Inglesfield; and to James Ferguson for all his excellent suggestions and hard work on this and my other books published by Signal.

Martin Garrett, Cambridge 2014

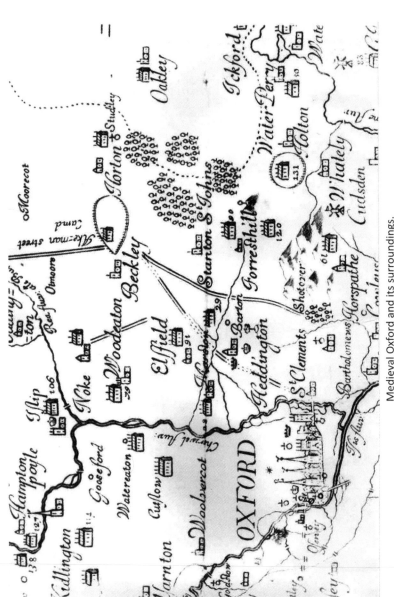

Medieval Oxford and its surroundings.

1 | Contours
How Oxford Grew

The "spires, domes, freestone-work" of the city gleam like points of light from topaz in Thomas Hardy's *Jude the Obscure*, and after dark there is "a halo or glow-fog overarching the place." It is guarded by "gentle battlements of silvergrey" whose "leafage" is "filled with nightingales and memories" for the narrator of Henry James' "A Passionate Pilgrim." It, or she, spreads "her gardens to the moonlight and whispers from her towers the last enchantments of the Middle Age," claims Matthew Arnold in *Essays in Criticism*. Everything is so beautiful that "One almost expects the people to sing instead of speaking" (W. B. Yeats, letter to Katharine Tynan). But why are these poetical bricks and mortar where they are?

Oxford can be described, more prosaically, as occupying a gravel terrace or spit between the flood-plains of the Thames or Isis and its tributary the Cherwell. It is, as *Bradshaw's Hand-Book for Tourists in Great Britain and Ireland* put it in 1873, "situated on a gentle eminence in a rich valley between the rivers . . . and is surrounded by highly cultivated scenery—the prospect being bounded by an amphitheater of hills."

The hills form the much-photographed backdrop to the city. In the "rich valley" there are some traces of prehistoric and Roman settlement: Bronze and Iron Age defenses and farming on Port Meadow, Roman burials near the present University Museum. (To the east, in the areas later called Headington, Rose Hill, and Cowley, there were very active Roman-period kilns; the Ashmolean Museum shows a selection of their products including a white ware crucible found in Between Towns Road and a grinding bowl from Rose Hill.)

The site was attractive for its central position on the tracks, and then the roads, linking the Midlands with Winchester and the port of Southampton. The crossing from which Oxford takes its name enabled people to drive oxen—and no doubt much else—across the Thames. The first reference to "Oxenaforda" is in about 900; John Blair in *Anglo-Saxon Oxfordshire* suggests that "it could have been so called because only long-legged beasts were able to use it." The ford was roughly where Folly Bridge is now. Substantial settlement began in the eighth century. A roughly rectangular *burh* or fortified town was laid out in the reign of King Alfred, probably in the 790s. (Alfred did not, of course, found the university as some chroniclers later claimed—mainly in order to make Cambridge seem ridiculously recent—any more than one Mempric, King of the Britons, founded the town in 1009 BCE.) Even before the *burh*, probably in the mid-eighth century, a market-town had developed around the monastic foundation of St. Frideswide. Her church was on or near the site of the twelfth-century Augustinian abbey of St. Frideswide and, later, of Christ Church.

Within the rectangle was a grid-pattern of streets around Carfax—the *quatre voys* or crossroads at the topographical and human center of Oxford. In *Jude the Obscure* it is Fourways,

> where men had stood and talked of Napoleon, the loss of America, the execution of King Charles, the burning of the Martyrs, the Crusades, the Norman Conquest, possibly of the arrival of Caesar. Here the two sexes had met for loving, hating, coupling, parting; had . . . cursed each other in jealousy, blessed each other in forgiveness.

St. Martin's Church, the official focus of civic life, was built at Carfax in the early eleventh century, rebuilt in the early 1820s, and demolished in 1896. The so-called "Carfax Conduit" does survive, but elsewhere. From 1617 water was piped from springs on Hinksey Hill to this elaborate, once gilded cistern and monument, with heraldic beasts and figures of Julius Caesar, James I, and other worthies. It became (like St. Martin's) a traffic hazard and in 1787 was removed to Earl Harcourt's estate at Nuneham Park, now university property.

The main survival from Anglo-Saxon Oxford is the evidently defensive structure at the other end of one of the old grid-streets (now Cornmarket Street) from Carfax: the tower of St. Michael at the North Gate, built in strong, rough coral rag in the mid-eleventh century. Originally Oxford was on the frontier between the kingdoms of Wessex and Mercia; later, the tower may, John Blair suggests, have been part of a residence of the Earl of Mercia or his representative. After the Norman Conquest authority was asserted instead from Oxford Castle, in the west of the city. The city walls, rebuilt in the thirteenth century, follow the line of earlier defenses; well preserved stretches can be seen in New College garden, at the back of Merton and Corpus, and in the garden of Morton's Café in Broad Street. None of the city gates survive. The north gate was by St. Michael's; the east roughly where the Eastgate Hotel is now; the south across St. Aldate's Street (next to the surviving wall in Brewer Street and leading towards the causeway and bridges which had superseded the ford). The west gate was near the Castle, roughly where Castle and Paradise Streets now join.

In the late twelfth century individual teachers and students in Oxford began to coalesce into a university. Oxford was becoming known as a legal as well as a clerical center—most study, initially, was of civil or canon law—and further impetus was provided after 1193 by wars which cut English students off from Paris, the most prestigious university of the day. Possibly, V. H. H. Green suggests in his history of the university, another attraction was low property and rental prices following a decline in the local clothing industry. By 1201 there was a "Master of the Oxford Schools" and from 1214 a Chancellor. (At this point the university was effectively re-established after a prolonged dispute with the town which nearly destroyed it: see p.57.)

Numerous halls of residence were built or adapted; by the early fourteenth century student numbers had reached perhaps two thousand and there were at least 120 halls. In the late thirteenth century colleges—Merton, Balliol, and University—were also established. (Seven more followed between 1314 and 1458.) They were, on the whole, much wealthier than the halls through endowments, regulated themselves by detailed statutes, and were mainly graduate institutions. They functioned both as educational establishments and as places where mass was said regularly in order to lessen the time the souls of their benefactors must spend in Purgatory. Particularly after the Reformation, the colleges' emphasis became more secular, they admitted undergraduates, and they incorporated many of the former halls. Teaching in the early centuries took place in a variety of "schools," mostly near St. Mary the Virgin, north of the High Street.

All this university activity did not, however, lead to rapid expansion of the city. Some colleges—Magdalen and St. John's, for instance—grew up outside the walls, but housing and commerce remained mostly within. Oxford gained its royal charter in 1199 but declined in importance as a market-town during the fourteenth century. Colleges bought up land whose owners died in the Black Death, and during the Reformation acquired former ecclesiastical property or re-used the stone and timber. The first significant building away from the traditional center—to the north, on Woodstock Road—was the Radcliffe Infirmary of 1759–67. Development and rebuilding continued, particularly on the western edge, but it was not until the nineteenth century that expansion really began, as housing developed near the railway stations and canal and moved out beyond the boundaries of the inner city: east along Iffley and Cowley Roads, south along Abingdon Road, west along Botley Road. Often rather grander residences went up in North Oxford—Woodstock and Banbury Roads—from the 1850s. Cowley grew rapidly with the motor industry after World War I, and Headington was disfigured, at least for John Betjeman, by "untidy speculative buildings" and "blaring arcades of shops" (*An Oxford University Chest*, 1938). When deprived areas of the city such as St. Ebbe's were bulldozed and redeveloped in the 1960s, people who lived there were resettled in estates like the one at Blackbird Leys, near Cowley (begun in 1957).

With much of the gravel terrace filled, building began to extend onto some of the hills—up Morrell Avenue towards Headington and up Cumnor Hill from Botley, for example. But woodland survives, nourished by the acidic soil of Shotover Hill and Boars Hill. Wytham Woods, owned by the university since 1943, are preserved for environmental research. And a few miles further north are attractive fragments of the once enormous Wychwood Forest, still in places as "tousled, tangled, and remote" as it was for John Piper (*Oxfordshire*, 1953 edition).

River and Canal

> Never in his life had he seen a river before—this sleek, sinuous, full-bodied animal, chasing and chuckling; gripping things with a gurgle and leaving them with a laugh, to fling itself on fresh playmates that shook themselves free, and were caught and held again. All was a-shake and a-shiver—glints and gleams and sparkles, rustle and swirl, chatter and bubble. The Mole was bewitched, entranced, fascinated. By the side of the river he trotted as one trots, when very small, by the side of a man, who holds one spellbound by exciting stories.

Mole's adventure in *The Wind in the Willows* reflects Kenneth Grahame's experience of the Thames, mainly downstream of Oxford at Cookham Dene. The river also provided Grahame with an escape from the harsh environment of St. Edward's School in Oxford in the 1860s and 1870s: he would wander by "the cool secluded reaches of the Thames . . . remote and dragon-fly haunted, before it attains to the noise, ribbons, and flannels of Folly Bridge."

There has been much joyous "messing around in boats" on the Thames (sometimes called, in its Oxford phase, the Isis). But for many centuries it was primarily a working river. Fishermen and millers built weirs, locks, and dams, and merchants and boatmen, sometimes with official backing, tried to remove or redesign these obstacles to navigation. There were periods when you could sail as far as London—mainly, it seems, in the thirteenth century and again from 1635. (Successful work to clear the river followed an Act of Parliament in 1624.) Stone, malt, and coal were some of the main goods transported. But that there was much else is clear from the inventory of the stock owned by Thomas West at his death in 1573, printed by Mary Prior in *Oxoniensia* in 1981. West, who lived in Wallingford and could take a barge as far upstream as Culham, near Abingdon, dealt mainly in timber, coal, and corn. (In Oxford his coal was bought by two smiths with the proto-Dickensian names Winckle and Cagbred.) But the inventory also lists eighteen yards of Genoa fustian cloth, lace, three dozen horse-bells, plated and zinc-alloy candle-sticks, five hundred "sixpenny nails," 4000 hob-nails and some 21,000 pins "of all sorts," many different varieties of thread, a half-hogshead of vinegar, Psalmbooks and grammars, silk buttons, trenchers, ink-horns, knives, and knitting-needles.

Oxford's other river the Cherwell, a tributary of the Thames, must always have been more peaceful—a Rat and Mole sort of water-way with overhanging trees and drifting weeds. Thomas Warton defends it stoutly in his "Ode IX: the Complaint of Cherwell": big sister Isis may "pace sublime, a stately queen," yet "Mine is the gen-tle grace, the meek retiring mien." But in 1790, the year of Warton's death, a more practically useful stretch of water was attracting most people's attention. The completion of the Oxford Canal that year extended the commercial reach of Oxford. It linked the coalfields of the Midlands with the city and the Thames, greatly reducing the price of coal. (Before this it had usually traveled from Newcastle to London by sea and then up the river.) In the early nineteenth century new canals made possible other useful routes to the Thames from the West Country and Wales. Hayfield, Worcester Street, and New Road wharfs were established. Canal boatmen and their families soon joined the communities of river bargemen and fisher-men long established on Fisher Row (the subject of Mary Prior's authoritative study of 1982) and Folly Bridge. But the success of the canal, mainly because of the coming of the railways, was relatively short-lived. *Jackson's Oxford Journal* on 26 March 1853 summed up the decline in terms of "the heavy-good train, whirling onwards at the rate of *12* or *14* miles an hour, whistling in derision as it passes by the Thames and Canal navigations, and by its speed mocking the drowsy barge." The revenue of the Oxford Canal fell from £86,600 in 1838 to £56,000 in 1848 and £24,700 in 1858. Steady decline continued. In 1954 the Canal Basin, long disused, was finally filled in and Nuffield College built on part of the site. In the early twen-tieth century James Elroy Flecker, in his poem "Oxford Canal," still sees signs of industrial activity: a barge, a working sawmill, a cart rattling down to a wharf, and workmen clanging over an iron foot-bridge. But already he is in a land "Half town and half country" which can at times be eerily quiet: "nothing makes me so afraid as the clear water of this idle canal on a summer's noon."

Road and Railway

Until the nineteenth century Oxford remained mostly within its medieval boundaries. But road improvements in the late eighteenth century began, like the canals soon afterwards, to open up communications with other parts of the country. Magdalen Bridge was rebuilt in the 1770s and travelers proceeded towards London by a new, direct route up Headington Hill. (The previous route, more laboriously, had gone along Cheney Lane and Old Road and over Shotover Hill.) Other roads were upgraded, New Road was built in west Oxford, and two of the narrow city gates—North and East—were demolished. Stage-coaches could now reach London in a day, a feat first accomplished in the 1660s, and in six hours or less by about the 1820s.

In about 1830, William Tuckwell recalled in his *Reminiscences of Oxford* coaches and waggons coming into the city along the Henley Road traveled between cornfields and meadows until "At once, without suburban interval, you entered the finest quarter of the town, rolling under Magdalen Tower." Stage-coaches stopped, whether you arrived from the Henley and London direction or down St. Giles', at the Angel, Mitre, or Star. Tuckwell is nostalgic for a world in which distinctively-named stage-coaches sped in and out of town: "Tantivy, Defiance, Rival, Regulator, Mazeppa [named, a little disconcertingly, after the poem by Byron in which a man is bound, naked, to a wild horse by his lover's husband], Telegraph, Rocket ..., Dart, Magnet, Blenheim, and some thirty more; heaped high with ponderous luggage and with cloaked passengers, thickly hung at Christmas time with turkeys, with pheasants in October." These vehicles contributed also to the pre-railway soundscape of the town, dominated otherwise by the bells of churches and colleges: "picked buglers," as they came into Oxford, played "the now forgotten strains of ... 'I'd be a Butterfly', 'The Maid of Llangollen', or 'Begone, dull Care.'" The drivers, too busy for bugling, were notice-able nevertheless: "queer old purple-faced many-caped" figures, "Cheeseman, Steevens, Fowles, Charles Homes, Jack Adams, and Black Will" the bigamist—he had one wife in Oxford and another in London.

The Rocket, apparently, got from Oxford to Birmingham in seven hours. Railways, of course, made possible much faster journeys. The Great Western Railway had reached Oxford in 1844, delayed for some years by opposition from the Oxford Canal Company and the university, and the London and North Western Railway in 1851. The present station is on the same site as the GWR's. The LNWR station, at Rewley Road—later belonging to London Midland and Scottish and on the site of the Saïd Business School—closed down in 1951. But with Morris and Company flourishing in Cowley, the main emphasis of local transport switched once more to the roads. Express coaches to London were introduced. Perhaps the most sig-nificant change came with the building of the M40, which linked Oxford to London from 1974 and to Birmingham from 1991.

But roads have not always improved travel; in Oxford, Matthew Arnold's "home of lost causes," John Ruskin conceived a character-istically idealistic plan for a road in the village of Ferry (now North) Hinksey. It was to be built by the honest labor of undergraduates, wielding pick-axes and spades instead of wasting their energies on sport and other unworthy amusements. One of the more im-probable to turn out was Oscar Wilde of Magdalen. The resulting structure was much more successful as a social experiment than as a road. But "the young men have done no mischief to speak of," the surveyor was able to report.

2 | **The Urban Map**
Oxford Old and New

entral Oxford contains peaceful quadrangles, noisy main streets, shops, museums, restaurants, churches, and kebab-vans. This chapter begins with one of the most interesting and distinctive smaller streets in Oxford and then focuses on some of the diverse suburbs and surroundings.

Merton Street: Merton and Corpus Christi Colleges

Merton Street contains, in a small space, even more fine stone and historical connections than most of Oxford. (Other interesting streets range from New College Lane—the "grim ravine" of Max Beerbohm's *Zuleika Dobson*—to Broad Street with, at its grand east end, its porticoes, statues, and cream, golden, yellow, and gray stone.)

On the north side of the road, starting from the High Street, you first pass part of the Examination Schools, T. G. Jackson's mighty Jacobean-revival building of 1876–8 in Clipsham stone; its style, according to John Ruskin, is "as inherently corrupt as it is un-English." Its size is intended both to reinforce the dignity of learning and to accommodate large numbers of candidates in popular subjects. Following the cobbled street round the corner you come upon many other stone buildings including the Weldon stone former lodge of the Warden of Merton, a work by Basil Champneys of 1908 in Elizabethan style. More to the liking of pur-ists is the slate-roofed Postmasters' Hall, the mainly sixteenth- and seventeenth-century "ancient stone house opposite to the forefront of Merton College" where the Oxford antiquary Anthony Wood (1632–95) was born, lived, and died. (Postmasterships are under-graduate scholarships at Merton, endowed in the 1380s.) Next is Beam Hall, a partly fifteenth-century academic hall taken over by Corpus Christi College in 1553. Behind these buildings are a Real Tennis Court (first mentioned on this site in 1595) and a network of

Merton College, Oxford (1771) by Michael "Angelo" Rooker (Google Art Project)

houses, accommodation blocks, and small gardens belonging mainly to Corpus, Merton, and University Colleges. The narrow Magpie Lane—known, less salubriously, as Grope or Gropecunt Lane in the thirteenth century—goes through to the High Street with a view up to the spire of St. Mary the Virgin. At the lane's corner with Merton Street is "an exuberantly detailed block of buildings designed by T. G. Jackson for Corpus in 1884–5" (Geoffrey Tyack in the revised *Blue Guide to Oxford and Cambridge*).

The walls and main buildings of Merton and Corpus Christi Colleges dominate the other side of the street. Merton, founded by Walter de Merton in 1264, has some of the earliest remaining college buildings in Oxford. The great hall (thirteenth-century with later restorations) still has its early oak door. Two sides of Mob Quad, built in two stages in the late thirteenth and late fourteenth centuries, house the Old Library. The upper floor preserves the late sixteenth-century bookshelves which—an innovation at the time—replaced the earlier book-chests.

From the beginning Merton was a rich and powerful institution, as its sizeable chapel suggests. The choir was built in 1290–4, the transepts or ante-chapel were added more gradually in the fourteenth and fifteenth centuries, and the whole was crowned by the tower eventually completed in 1450. There is a fine medieval east window. The stalls and roof (painted by J. H. Pollen in 1849–51) are part of William Butterfield's extensive restoration. The ante-chapel contains memorials to such noted Mertonians as Sir Henry Savile (1549–1622), Warden of Merton and Provost of Eton. Beneath the trumpeting figure of Fame is the upright half-figure of Sir Henry, gowned and with his hand on a thick gold-bordered volume. He is flanked by statues of four of the worthy ancients he edited, translated, or expounded: St. John Chrysostom, holding a book; Ptolemy, bearded and turbaned like one of the Magi; Euclid in a hat like a Cardinal's; and Tacitus, in a rough seventeenth-century version of a toga, again armed with a book. Beneath these figures are detailed painted views of both Merton and Eton. At the bottom is the globe, with labels, likely to appeal to the learned, for the Tropic of Capricorn, Java, and Madagascar. It is a triumphantly secular monument. (Savile was, a Merton fellow told John Aubrey, "too much inflated with his learning and riches.")

The ante-chapel also has brasses, Nicholas Stone's marble and alabaster memorial to Savile's friend and fellow bookman Sir Thomas Bodley—the pilasters represent books—and a green marble font presented by Tsar Alexander I, who visited Merton in 1814. A glass chalice is engraved by Laurence Whistler in memory of T. S. Eliot, who was a graduate philosophy student at Merton in 1914–15. The words "the fire and the rose are one" ("Little Gidding") are accompanied by a large rose which seems at once to emit flames and to become them.

In 1515 Merton sold land at the west end of Merton Street to Richard Foxe, Bishop of Winchester and a powerful royal counselor. Here in 1517 Foxe founded Corpus Christi College, an institution intended to promote the "new learning" of scholars like Erasmus—a place, as the bishop saw it, "wherein scholars, like ingenious bees, are by day and night to make wax to the honour of God, and honey dropping sweetness to the profit of themselves and of all Christians." The front quadrangle, stone where others are grass, like a small piazza, might seem a rather forbidding enclosure. But the stone is golden, at least when the sun shines; bamboo and other carefully deployed shrubs and plants now soften the hard edges; and the sundial of 1581 in the middle, crowned by the college emblem of the pelican, provides a visual focus. Another sixteenth-century survival is the hammerbeam roof of the hall. Beyond the front quadrangle is the small, intimate chapel, with late seventeenth-century woodwork. Memorials to two Presidents, John Rainolds and John Spenser (died 1607 and 1614), dominate the small space as Rainolds in particular must have dominated the college. He was a Puritan leader, prominently involved in the Hampton Court conference of 1604 and, at the end of his life, in the committee which translated the Old Testament Prophets for the Authorised or King James Bible. Rainolds looks suitably austere compared with his suaver contemporaries next door in Merton. He is congratulated here on his Erudition, Piety, and Incomparable Integrity.

Beyond the front quad are smaller, greener areas and the slope up to one of the clearest views of Christ Church Cathedral. You can also look out on the green expanse of Christ Church Meadow. On the sandy paths by the Meadow—at the back of Merton and Corpus, along part of the old city wall—there is a sense of being on an edge, a shore. Merton Street, with its interestingly worked stone and complex history, seems far away.

North Oxford

These are not houses but flights of fancy. They are three storeys high and disguise themselves as churches. They have ecclesiastical porches instead of front doors and round norman windows or pointed gothic ones, neatly grouped in threes with flaring brick to set them off. They reek of hymns and the Empire, Mafeking and the Khyber Pass, Mr Gladstone and Our Dear Queen. They have nineteen rooms and half a dozen chimneys and fire escapes. A bomb couldn't blow them up, and the privet in their gardens has survived two World Wars.

So Penelope Lively introduces *The House in Norham Gardens* (1974), her novel about Clare Mayfield, a fourteen-year-old growing up in the sprawling house of her unworldly but wise great-aunts in the "inner" North Oxford of Norham Gardens, other streets near it, and the University Parks it overlooks. The rarely used dining-room is still dominated by the portraits of the aunts' formidable anthropologist father and their mother (by Sargent) in "red silk to the floor, most elegantly curved fore and aft." The dress and much else is still to be found in a chest in the attic; the house is cluttered, fascinatingly for Clare, with her great-grandfather's papers and the ceremonial spears and shield he brought back from New Guinea. (The novel skillfully blends modern concern over the removal of the sacred shield from its people and context—communicated to Clare partly through dreams—and the more everyday adolescent anxieties and questions she is learning to solve.)

Oxford and suburbs

Ed Taylor-Garrett

Already in 1974 the house, in bad repair and occupied, not by "a fat busy Victorian family" with servants but by a girl and two old ladies, is "a fossil, stranded among neighbours long since chopped up" into smaller units. Increasingly the larger North Oxford residences have either been divided or taken over by language schools, colleges, and university departments. The original families for whom they were built, mainly from the 1860s onwards, were from the expanding mid-Victorian "professional" classes—doctors, clergy, or people successful in trade. After 1877, when the university at last decreed that dons could marry without losing their jobs, academic families followed. Neo-Gothic and neo-Jacobean homes proliferated. The young John Betjeman cycled happily past the mansions of Norham Gardens, the classical villas near North Parade and the Italianate villas in Park Town (as distinguished in his *An Oxford University Chest*, 1938; Samuel Lipscomb Seckham's Park Town, begun in 1853, preceded much of North Oxford). From the Dragon, the preparatory school which opened in 1877 and moved to a green site by the River Cherwell in North Oxford in 1895, and later from Magdalen College, Betjeman wandered in this paradise for the sort of Victorian architecture he loved against the fashion. It was "a home of married dons, dons' widows, retired clergymen, retired dons . . . theological seminaries, bicycle sheds, ladies' colleges, tea-parties, perambulators."

North of inner North Oxford is Summertown, in the eighteenth century an open area notorious for its highwaymen, from the 1820s a village and now a pleasant suburb with shops, restaurants, offices, and houses along a very broad stretch of Banbury Road. It still feels quite like a village.

Cowley Road: florists, grocers, tattooists

It is lined with businesses that seem to represent every nation on earth. Among them are Jamaican, Bangladeshi, Indian, Polish, Kurdish, Chinese, French, Italian, Thai, Japanese, and African restaurants; sari shops, cafés, fast-food outlets, electronics stores, a florist, a Ghanaian fishmonger, pubs, bars, three live-music venues, tattoo parlours, betting-shops, a Russian supermarket, a community centre, a publisher, the headquarters of an international NGO . . . two mosques, three churches, a Chinese herbalist, a pawn shop, a police station . . . an independent cinema, call centres, three sex shops, numerous grocers, letting agencies, a bingo hall, and a lap-dancing establishment.

So James Attlee sums up the diversity of Cowley Road in *Isolarion: a Different Oxford Journey* (2007), his W. G. Sebald-like account of a personal pilgrimage into his own diverse local area.

Housing along the road between Oxford city-center and Cowley developed gradually from the mid-nineteenth century onwards. The population became increasingly ethnically mixed after the late 1950s, as workers and then families arrived mainly from the Caribbean, India, Pakistan, and Bangladesh. Other groups continued to come, enriching the place explored and championed by Attlee and more practically surveyed by Annie Skinner in *Cowley Road: a History* (revised edition 2008). Both authors find Cowley Road tolerant, welcoming of diversity, and often given an unfairly bad press in comparison with the rest of the city.

One building off Cowley Road, Bartlemas Chapel, is connected with a much earlier period. This church—originally twelfth-century, several times rebuilt—is all that is left of a leper hospital, placed as always well out of the city. Here for Jan Morris (*Oxford*) "All is fragrant and meditative, and seems peopled by gentle ghosts. It is an ivory enclave, fastidiously preserved." Medieval pilgrims came here to get the benefit of relics including Edward the Confessor's comb and St. Bartholomew's skin. These objects were brought out, says Anthony Wood, "at high and select times . . . And happy did he account himself that could come near, either to touch or kiss them." The holy skin helped with leprosy. The royal saint's comb, logically enough, cured headaches.

Iffley: jazzy monsters

The carefully restored Romanesque church at Iffley, near the Thames just downstream of Oxford, survives in "an oasis of cottages and chestnut trees, billowing with springtime blossom," says Simon Jenkins in *England's Thousand Best Churches*. Jenkins celebrates the detailed carving, "the chunky, barbaric richness of door and window surrounds ... with zigzag and beakhead over roll-moulding, creating a jazzy effect of monsters with huge beaks biting into long rolls of bread." The outer arch of the west doorway is carved with the symbols of the Evangelists (lion, eagle, man, and ox) and signs of the Zodiac. The scenes on the capitals of the south doorway are fighting horsemen and—ingeniously fitted in—a female centaur breast-feeding her child. The two seem almost to collide in mid-gallop as the mother, hair and tail streaming behind her, deftly lowers her loaded bow with one hand and holds her breast with the other.

The interior has an aisle-less nave, a substantial late twelfth-century font in black, gray, and white marble, and a southwest window with glass by John Piper, installed in 1995—another version of the Nativity in Magdalen ante-chapel (see p.113).

Headington

Headington Hill, beloved of descending cyclists, ascended regularly on television by Inspector Morse's Jaguar, helps maintain Headington's separate identity. There are parks on each side of the road: Headington Hill Park and the much larger South Park. South Park is popular for summer picnics, winter tobogganing—some enthusiasts even bring skis—firework displays, and the view down to the spires of the city. In June 1933 its grassy and wooded slopes were the setting for an ambitious production of *A Midsummer-Night's Dream* by the German director Max Reinhardt, using a temporary lake, boar-hounds, and a considerable number of electric lamps. In 2001 Radiohead gave a concert here which raised £145,000 for local charities.

Most of the buildings of Oxford Brookes University are at the top of the hill and along London Road towards Headington.

Brookes has expanded rapidly in recent years, and for a few hundred yards the main road feels almost like part of the campus. In 1992 it took out a long lease on Headington Hill Hall, built in the 1850s as the home of one branch of the wealthy Morrell brewing family, and bought by the City Council in 1958. (In the Morrells' heyday, the grounds included both the parks.) Before Oxford Brookes, from 1959, the tenant had been the notorious publisher, politician, and crook Robert Maxwell, who used the site both as the headquarters of Pergamon Press and as a luxurious, heavily fortified family residence. John Henry Brookes (1891–1975), after whom the university is named, was a very different character, honored on the blue plaque at his home at 195 The Slade, Headington, as "Artist, craftsman, inspirational educator." Brookes became Principal of Oxford Art School in 1928 and then, following a merger, of the Oxford Schools of Technology, Art, and Commerce in 1934. The schools were scattered on many different sites and it was Brookes who was mainly responsible for bringing them together at the top of the hill in the mid-1950s. The College of Technology, as it was called from 1956, became Oxford Polytechnic in 1965, and Oxford Brookes University in 1992.

Before the students, prosperous Oxford citizens followed the Morrells' example and settled in Headington. Often they came in search of the healthy air that was considered to circulate on its heights. This also attracted invalids and convalescents, and most of the city's hospitals are now here. The Wingfield, which opened in 1872, became the Nuffield Orthopaedic Hospital in 1950, and the Churchill was founded in 1940. The Osler Pavilion opened in 1927 and became the Osler Hospital in 1954. On the same site, the John Radcliffe Hospital, known at least initially as JR2 to distinguish it from the old Radcliffe Infirmary, was built mainly between 1968 and 1979. Not far from here is the Croft—stone-walled lanes and some of the stone houses built by the prosperous settlers—and St. Andrew's church, Old Headington, with its fine chancel arch of about 1150.

A later monument is the fiberglass shark (John Buckley's "Untitled, 1986") which plunges into the roof of 2 New High

Street, Headington. It seems playfully incongruous in an ordinary suburban street. Its more serious intention is to commemorate the atom-bombing of Nagasaki, when no-less ordinary streets were suddenly obliterated.

Headington Quarry and Shotover

"The Quarry of Headington, scarce two miles from Oxford, supplies us continually with a good sort of stone and fit for all uses but that of fire. In the quarry it cuts very soft and easy and is worked accordingly for all sorts of building, very porous and fit to imbibe lime and sand, but hardening continually as it lies to the weather." So observes Robert Plot in *The Natural History of Oxfordshire* (1677). There had been quarries in the area since at least the fourteenth century, and according to the *Victoria County History* thirty-nine were still active in 1907. By the early seventeenth century the workers had formed their own community, east of Headington. It was small and close and came to be dominated by a few families including the Coxes and the Coppocks. (Widow Coxe already had an ale-house in Headington in Plot's day; Cox's and Coppock's Alleys are on the site of tracks which once ran between quarries.) Quarry supplied the stone for many Oxford college buildings, beginning with the bell-tower of New College, built in Headington hardstone in 1396–7. It was not until several centuries later that it became apparent that Headington freestone, which was used most often by the colleges, crumbles and needs to be replaced; this realization led to a gradual decline in quarrying here from the eighteenth century. The area is full of reminders of the past: blocks of good stone in walls and houses; dips and hollows like Quarry Hollow children's play area; slopes and unexpected changes of level.

Holy Trinity church was built in Quarry in 1848–9 by Sir George Gilbert Scott. Now that stone is no longer being extracted, worked, and transported nearby, it is a very peaceful place. A path leads into the graveyard from Quarry Road; the other entrance is near the village school and the Masons' Arms. C. S. Lewis worshipped in the church and is buried in the graveyard. (The slab is inscribed with words from *King Lear*: "Men must endure their going hence, even as their coming hither.") Inside the church, a Narnia window by Sally Scott (1991) shows snowy mountains, Aslan as the sun, the winged horse Fledge, and the castle Cair Paravel.

Lewis had enjoyed a close, possibly sexual, relationship with Janie Moore (died 1951), the mother of a friend killed in World War I; from 1930 they, her daughter, and Lewis' brother lived in a house near Quarry and on the wooded lower slopes of Shotover Hill (once part of the much larger Shotover Forest). At the Kilns, now in Risinghurst but then very countrified, Lewis walked in the woods, planted trees, and swam regularly in the pond—an old clay-pit from the site's brickmaking days. Beyond the pool he could climb up "a steep wilderness broken with ravines and nooks of all kinds" running onto "a little cliff topped by a thistly meadow, and . . . a thick belt of fir-trees." The Kilns is owned by the C. S. Lewis Foundation and can be visited by appointment.

Jericho

Jericho takes its name from the seventeenth-century Jericho House, later the Jericho Tavern in Walton Street, rebuilt in 1818. The original tavern was outside the city walls and was regarded as a place of refuge for travelers arriving after the gates were closed; possibly "Jericho" arose from a (jocular?) connection with the walled biblical city of Joshua: 6. It was once a busy industrial area, with wharfs for unloading coal, boatyards, timber-yards, and, from 1825, the foundry which later became Lucy's Eagle Ironworks. Lucy's produced agricultural machinery, ornamental ironwork, lamp-posts, and, at the end of the nineteenth century, cast-iron library shelving.

In the twentieth century Lucy's moved into electrical engineering and machine tools. It stopped production in 2005; the buildings were demolished in 2007 and replaced by apartments. Most of Jericho is now residential. A plan to demolish the whole area in 1962, run a main road through it, and build offices and parking lots was defeated by local people led by the Vicar of St. Barnabas. The terraces of carefully restored nineteenth-century brick houses are now valuable property. Near the canal, on foggy mornings or evenings, the streets—traffic allowing—can be almost eerily quiet. Even more peaceful is St. Sepulchre's Cemetery, off Walton Street through iron gates and a gatehouse of 1865, a green enclave among tall modern buildings. Snowdrops, bluebells, and other plants—sixty-five species, a notice tells us—are allowed to flourish in areas of uncut grass.

The cemetery opened in 1850. Among the first people buried here was John Wilson, "44 Years Porter of Worcester College." The more famous included Benjamin Jowett, Master of Balliol, in 1893, and Thomas Combe, senior partner in Oxford University Press, in 1872. It was money (£6000) and support from Combe and his wife, Martha (1806–93), which built the best-known landmark in Jericho, St. Barnabas Church (1869–72). The exterior, built by Arthur Blomfield in stone-rubble faced with cement, is deliberately plain—designed to save money for the rich Anglo-Catholic interior. Outside, St. Barnabas "on its marshy site next to the Oxford Canal," evokes for Geoffrey Tyack "the melancholy glories of Torcello and Ravenna." The distinctive, rather ugly flat roof of the pale campanile replaced the original pyramidical roof on grounds of safety in 1893. The interior inspires that of St. Silas—in the district of "Beersheba"—in Thomas Hardy's *Jude the Obscure.* Here, late at night, Sue Bridehead tortures herself, and Jude, with her belief that her misfortunes are a divine judgement for having left the man she does not love, Jude's former mentor Phillotson:

> High overhead, above the chancel steps, Jude could discern a huge, solidly constructed Latin cross—as large, probably, as the original it was designed to commemorate. It seemed to be suspended in the air by invisible wires; it was set with large jewels, which faintly glimmered . . . as the cross swayed to and fro in a silent and scarcely perceptible motion. Underneath, upon the floor, lay what appeared to be a heap of black clothes, and from this was repeated the sobbing that he had heard before. It was his Sue's form, prostrate on the paving.

Port Meadow

> This meadow is two and a half miles in circumference and much more suited for a race-course than the one at Epsom, though it is somewhat marshy. Many booths had been set up, where beer was sold, each of which had its sign, a hat, a glove, and suchlike. Nearly all the people from the town were there and also many strangers, some riding, some driving, some in boats.

So a German scholar visiting Oxford in 1710, Zacharias Conrad von Uffenbach, records the horse-races in Port Meadow, the 440-acre expanse of rough grass and thistle by the Thames west of Oxford. Uffenbach spent a day carefully observing the event but would not go back: "When one has seen this sport once or twice, it ceases to have any particular attraction; one must be an Englishman, in fact a regular knacker, to take delight in forcing on these poor animals" (W. H. and W. J. C. Quarrell's translation).

The races gradually declined in frequency and popularity in the nineteenth century. A less ambitious and more animal-friendly version, however, was revived on Wolvercote Common, at the north end of Port Meadow, in the 1980s. Skating—gliding or tumbling as in a scene from Avercamp or Brueghel—is also popular when the Meadow floods in winter. Its more usual occupants are horses, grazing or cantering about, and cows, standing stolidly in the shallows. The livestock are the property of either the Commoners of Wolvercote or the Freemen of Oxford: Port Meadow has been common pasture since Saxon times. (From much earlier there are traces of Bronze Age ring-ditches and Iron Age farms.) The most controversial human activity in the vicinity has been the building of higher than expected accommodation blocks for graduate students in Roger Dudman Way, southeast of Port Meadow. Diarmaid MacCulloch feels moved, reluctantly, to condemn the university in which he is Professor of Church History for perpetrating "a visual disaster on one of the world's historic landscapes. It is like building a skyscraper beside Stonehenge" (letter to *The Oxford Times*, 7 February 2013).

The meadow leads onto the ruins of Godstow nunnery, traditionally the burial place of Henry II's lover, Rosamund Clifford or "Fair Rosamund." According to the chronicler Hoveden (as translated from Latin by John Stow) in 1191, two years after Henry's death, the Bishop of Lincoln was aghast when he came upon her tomb in the middle of the chancel of the abbey church, "covered with a pall of silk, and set about with lights of wax." He had "the Harlot" removed "lest Christian religion should grow in contempt" and as a warning to women against "unlawful and advouterous [adulterous]" contact with men. But apparently the nuns put her back. In later centuries the ruins were occupied by cattle and horses; chicken-runs are recorded in 1909. Here and by Godstow lock Matthew Arnold's less domesticated "black-winged swallows haunt the glittering Thames."

Beyond Godstow is the seventeenth-century Trout Inn, the "pleasant house, with its shady alleys, waterside bowers, and rustic bridge" of Fred S. Thacker's *The Stripling Thames* (1909). Across the river from Port Meadow at Binsey is another well known pub, The Perch. The felling of a line of poplars by the river near here inspired Gerard Manley Hopkins' "Binsey Poplars": a passionate lament for the passing of his "aspens dear, whose airy cages quelled/ . . . in leaves the leaping sun." But there are still poplars here and the city whose "brickish skirt" Hopkins feared would overwhelm such landscapes still seems fairly distant.

Osney

Osney (or Oseney) Abbey, the large and powerful monastery of Augustinian canons to the west of Oxford, was founded, initially as a Priory, in 1129. Legend has it that it owes its beginnings to a gang of clamorous magpies. Walking in the meadows, Editha, wife of the local magnate Robert d'Oilly the Younger, wondered why the birds were so noisy. Her chaplain Radulph, with that unhesitating insight into the ways of the unseen allegedly possessed by many a saintly medieval churchman, explained that they were souls in purgatory. If a monastery were built on the spot, their suffering could be relieved through prayer, and so Editha persuaded her husband to build one.

The Abbey flourished for four centuries. D'Oilly had endowed it with land, property, and income from the castle mills. Its church was over 300 feet long, had two towers and many chapels, and survived the Dissolution of the Monasteries to become, in 1542, the first Oxford Cathedral. But the abbey buildings decayed rapidly when the see moved, in 1546, to what became Christ Church. What was left of the west tower was demolished in 1650. All that remains of the Abbey now is one small fifteenth-century structure in Mill Street. Mill Street Cemetery is on the site of part of the abbey church.

Modern Osney Island (or Osney Town) developed many years later on what had been meadows belonging to the monastery. Many of the houses were built in the early 1850s, partly to provide accommodation for railway workers. St. Frideswide's church was founded in 1870, and the place discovered by Kate in Joannna Trollope's *The Men and the Girls* (1992) came into being:

> How, she asked herself, could she have lived in Oxford all her life and never known that just beyond the station lay this little water-girt place, these cottage streets of brick and painted stucco with their oddly, unmistakably foreign air, an island of distinct character protected from the surrounding schools and factories and newspaper offices by the quiet, olive-green barriers of river and canal? ... In South Street a child waved to her from an upstairs window; in East Street she met a man carrying a bird cage and a loaf of bread; and in Swan Street, a tiny cul-de-sac ending in a white bridge over the water, she met an exotic woman in a brocade hat leading a vast and fluffy white chow on a strip of purple leather.

Boars Hill: famous customers

The big houses on Boars Hill were so teeming with poets and famous people in the years after World War I that it would be difficult to give an entirely serious account of life there. Robert Graves, serving in the shop he and his wife Nancy Nicholson briefly ran on the hill, found himself "wearing a green-baize apron ... selling a packet of Bird's Eye tobacco to the Poet Laureate with one hand, and with the other weighing out half a pound of brown sugar for Sir Arthur Evans's gardener's wife" (*Goodbye to All That*).

Evans, excavator of Knossos and Keeper of the Ashmolean Museum, was among the earlier well-known residents. He built an enormous house, Youlbury, in the 1890s (replaced by a modern house in 1969). He also, partly in order to make work for the local unemployed, created Jarn Mound. Steps lead up an earthen mound, from Evans' wild garden, to a viewing platform; the view, now mainly of trees, used to include the "dreaming spires" Matthew Arnold had admired from Boars Hill. Graves' Poet Laureate customer, Robert Bridges, lived at Chilswell House from 1907 and was visited by Yeats and other poets. Bridges' successor as Laureate, John Masefield, was at Masefield House (or Hill Crest) from 1917, where he wrote in his hut and held poetry festivals in the garden. "We have very pure fresh air," his wife Constance reported, and "a jolly scent of gorse and bracken." And Gilbert Murray, Professor of Greek and apostle of the League of Nations, entertained generations of foreign visitors and earnest undergraduates at Yatscombe Hall, where he lived from 1919 until his death in 1957. (Yatscombe burnt down in 2003.) Graves found him "gentle voiced and with the spiritual look of the strict vegetarian."

Graves' and Nicholson's shop supplied such somewhat unworldly people with provisions; they were, according to *The Daily Mirror*, "Shop-Keeping on Parnassus." For a while sales were good, but the inexperienced couple bought too much stock from commercial travelers who "sweated up the hill with their heavy bags of samples" to "pitch a hard-luck tale." Other problems intervened, and they decided to sell, ending up only £300 in debt after help from Nicholson's family and from Graves' friend T. E. Lawrence. (Lawrence was in Oxford at this time, briefly and restlessly, as a fellow of All Souls.) Some found it safer to avoid Parnassus: "Keep clear of Boar's Hill," advises Charles Ryder's conventional Cousin Jasper in *Brideshead Revisited*. Nancy Nicholson's painted sign for the shop—the Wandering Scholar—can be seen at the Oxfordshire County Museum in Woodstock.

Sarcophagi and Burrows: imaginary expansion

The college grew, like most, gradually. "The buildings, which were grouped around three irregular quadrangles, dated from every period from the early Middle Ages to the mid-eighteenth century . . . and the final effect was one of jumbled and squalid grandeur." This, however, is not a real Oxford college, but the Jordan of Philip Pullman's *Northern Lights* (*The Golden Compass*): one of the many which, various though the real colleges are, writers have invented whether for creative, satirical, or libel-evading reasons. Scone College in Evelyn Waugh's *Decline and Fall* is loosely based on Hertford, and Shrewsbury College in Dorothy L. Sayers' *Gaudy Night* derives partly from Somerville. (With "monstrous impertinence," says the Author's Note, she has erected Shrewsbury on Balliol's real "spacious and sacred cricket-ground.") Inspector Morse is connected with Lonsdale, and in Veronica Stallwood's Oxford detective novels, there is a Leicester College. In *Jude the Obscure*, with more satirical intention, the names denote the stultifying, antiquated, and excluding nature of the university: Oldgate, Crozier, Rubric. The walls of Sarcophagus, "silent, black and windowless, threw their four centuries of gloom, bigotry and decay into the room [Sue] occupied, shutting out the moonlight by night and the sun by day."

Pullman's Jordan both resembles, and develops interestingly beyond, a traditional college. It not only has steep roofs for Lyra and her friend Roger to scale, but a library which "extended, burrow-like, for several floors beneath the ground." And there is not only a large and ancient wine-cellar, but crypts and catacombs with the coffins of former Masters and the skulls of scholars. But, much in the same way that different people may imagine or remember different but overlapping Oxfords, there is another Oxford—Will's rather than Lyra's—in the world of *The Subtle Knife*, the second book in Pullman's trilogy. Will's Oxford is more consistently like ours than Lyra's, which belongs in some respects to an earlier period: in Lyra's world there are no traffic-lights, chewing-gum, or cinema, for instance, and the scholars call their science "experimental theology." Lyra is as shocked as some trusting readers may be that here Jordan College simply does not exist. Will's town has such real places as what are evidently the Pitt Rivers Museum and Headington House—for many years the home, in Old Headington, of the historian of ideas Sir Isaiah Berlin but here, as "Limefield House," of the sinister Sir Charles Latrom. The hornbeam-lined Sunderland Avenue, at the top of Banbury Road, belongs to this Oxford; it became a popular place to visit in the wake of the immense popularity of Pullman's novels—and here, in *The Subtle Knife*, is a portal to a third world which apparently has no Oxford. Both Oxfords, we learn late in the third book, *The Amber Spyglass*, have a nearly identical Botanic Garden, but for a long time Lyra is deprived of such possible consolation. Jordan "simply wasn't there, and she wasn't Lyra of Jordan any more; she was a lost little girl in a strange world, belonging nowhere." Finding friendship and coming to terms with deception, loss, and different worlds are among the main themes of these large and complex books.

Architects and town planners, as well as novelists, have had many an imaginative plan for changing Oxford into another world. At intervals between the 1920s and 1970s an outrageous plan for driving a road through Christ Church Meadow was seriously discussed. In about 1712 Nicholas Hawksmoor produced a more elegant scheme for the town-center, to include a campanile; a classical, columned new University Church; and a piazza or "Forum Civitatis" at Carfax. Radcliffe Square achieves something of the ordered air of his proposed "Forum Universitatis," but most of the scheme remained unrealized. In 1720 the fellows of Magdalen considered demolishing the whole college apart from the tower. In the 1850s there was a plan for a Venetian-style bridge to link the Bodleian Upper Reading Room and the Radcliffe Camera; the books would have traveled along rails in trucks. And among the many architectural plans and fantasies examined by Sir Howard Colvin in *Unbuilt Oxford* (1983) is Charles Buckeridge's first design for the Anglican nuns of Holy Trinity Convent (now St. Antony's College) in 1864. Here, in an ambitious attempt to evoke the idea of the Trinity, Buckeridge "worked out a plan in the form of a spherical triangle ... with a trilobed chapel in the center, linked by staircases to circular rooms marking the three corners of the

THE URBAN MAP

building. Internal cloister walks provided access to the principal rooms, which were arranged on three floors." The nuns, in the end, settled for something less theologically appropriate but cheaper. A tapering, 260-foot, 25-story Department of Zoology tower was planned for the edge of the University Parks in 1962 but rejected overwhelmingly by Congregation. An even more extreme—not entirely serious—scheme for a 450-foot high pyramid in Christ Church Meadow was turned down by the City Council in 1975.

As an alternative to inventing a college or rebuilding one, you can send a fictional character to a real college. Nicholas Utechin, in the teeth of Holmesians whose detective work suggests a Cambridge provenance, argues ingeniously that Sherlock Holmes was at St. John's, Oxford (*Sherlock Holmes at Oxford*, 1977). Utechin investigates whether dogs were allowed in Oxford colleges—in "The Gloria Scott" Holmes says a fellow student's bull-terrier seized him by the ankle—and finds a man called Holmes (E. G. A. Holmes, admittedly) who matriculated at St. John's in 1869. Others have placed him confidently at University College or Christ Church. In the less explicable world of Will Self's *Great Apes* (1997), it is the apes who make such places their own: Simon Dykes finds, instead of the graceful city he remembers, a "tacky warren of aged buildings swarming with chimpanzees." "On top of the Randolph Hotel, swinging from the Martyrs' Memorial, scampering over the roofs of Balliol and St John's—everywhere . . . were chimp students, scrapping, mating and brachiating." (Such treatment of the Randolph, now Macdonald Randolph, is especially irreverent: William Wilkinson's grand neo-Gothic building of 1863–6, extended in 1923 and 1952, is the best known of Oxford hotels, a by-word for solidity and respectability.) Simon laughs to see that "contrary to what one expects of Oxford students," the simians are "all so lowbrow!"

3 | Landmarks
Buildings and Styles

"This Oxford I have no doubt is the finest City in the world," John Keats wrote when he stayed with his friend Benjamin Bailey of Magdalen Hall in September 1817, "it is full of old Gothic buildings—Spires—towers—Quadrangles—Cloisters Groves &c. and is surrounded by more clear streams than ever I saw together." Among the Gothic examples he had in mind, no doubt—though he spent much of his time boating on the "clear streams"—were New College and Magdalen. But already Oxford had a good range of buildings in other architectural styles. The Golden Cross Inn survived from the sixteenth and seventeenth centuries. Distinctively Jacobean work was to be seen at Wadham College or the Bodleian Library. James Wyatt's neoclassical Radcliffe Observatory (1773–9; now part of Green Templeton College) was inspired by the much smaller Tower of the Winds in Athens.

Later in the nineteenth century, styles continued to proliferate. What is now the Ashmolean Museum was influenced by the Temple of Bassae where the architect, C. R. Cockerell, had excavated. Keble College was resolutely neo-Gothic, and H. T. Hare's Town Hall of 1893–7 flamboyantly neo-Jacobean. Among twentieth-century experiments were the bulky, uncompromising library tower of Nuffield College (1955–8). More recent buildings by the Powell and Moya partnership—the New Building at Corpus Christi and Christ Church Picture Gallery, for example—have been "firm, solid, ponderous . . . as if they were carved out of the solid" as David Reed and Philip Opher put it in *New Architecture in Oxford* (1977). One of their most successful projects was Wolfson College (1969–72), a graduate college on a beautiful site by the Cherwell linked by bridge with meadows north of the University Parks: for Peter Heyworth in *The Oxford Guide to Oxford* (1981) it is a place of cool, long buildings with "no dramatic accents and no straining after novelty."

A pre-traffic view of Christ Church and St. Aldate's (Library of Congress, Washington DC)

Arup Associates, meanwhile, "have used their structural ingenuity to achieve a taut elegance" (Reed and Opher) at the Sir Thomas White Building at St. John's and the Departments of Engineering and Metallurgy (1971–6). Later observers have often been less sure about the enthusiastic use of concrete in some of these buildings. The Queen's College Florey Building in St. Clements by James Stirling (1971) has been the butt of public disapproval—it is habitually compared to a multi-story parking garage—and the delight of many of Stirling's fellow architects, who find it radical, dynamic, as if recently "on the move" (Bob Allies, *Architects' Journal*, 2010).

1980s developments include the Ice Rink (Nicholas Grimshaw and Partners) with its two steel masts, and the turreted shops, offices, and cafés of Gloucester Green (Kendrick Associates)—now familiar, but once received as either "vulgar monstrosity" or "wittily exuberant extravaganza" (Peter Snow). Among many interesting twenty-first century buildings one might single out the Saïd Business School (close to the railway station) with its green ziggurat and glassed front, allowing, after dark, the edifying view of other people working inside. Still to come, at the time of writing, are Zaha Hadid's Softbridge building for St. Antony's College and the massive glassy curves of the new Blavatnik School of Government in Walton Street.

Christ Church: "sumptuous, curious, and substantial"

Christ Church forces itself on the attention of visitors. It contains, unusually, both college and cathedral. Its Tom Tower is an Oxford landmark, its New Library with monumental white Corinthian columns is one of the most notable works of eighteenth century architecture, and a significant art collection is displayed in the Picture Gallery. The fellows are called Students. At one time a substantial proportion of the undergraduates were aristocrats, and the college has produced thirteen Prime Ministers, including Peel and Gladstone—more than any other. (Christ Church hall is heavy with portraits of college notables.) The founder, Cardinal Wolsey, himself a first minister, certainly intended to create a memorable place. He suppressed the Priory of St. Frideswide in order to appropriate its site;

31

work began on Cardinal College in 1525 and by 1528, according to Wolsey's right-hand man Thomas Cromwell, "Every man thinks the like was never seen for largeness, beauty, sumptuous, curious, and substantial building."

The Cardinal, however, fell from power in 1529 having failed to obtain a papal divorce for Henry VIII. The college buildings were unfinished. The projected cloister got as far only as the inner arches visible in the Great Quadrangle, and only the west end of the medieval cathedral—the priory church of St. Frideswide—was demolished. Henry VIII refounded the college as Christ Church, using what had been completed; in 1546 he established the church as both the college chapel and the cathedral of the recently created Oxford diocese. But it was not until the seventeenth century that an attempt was made to finish what Wolsey had begun. Dean John Fell was responsible for the building of the north range of the Great Quadrangle in the same style as the earlier ranges, and created the terrace and central basin. Fell also commissioned Christopher Wren's graceful completion, in 1681–2, of the stumpy gate-tower at the entrance to the college as a grand new belfry for Great Tom, the bell transferred from Osney Abbey to the cathedral in 1546 and recast in 1680. Wren's addition at once complements the Gothic base and provides something more modern: he told Fell that he chose the Gothic style "so as to agree with the founder's work" but that he had "not continued so busy as [Wolsey] began." Starting, as Kerry Downes points out in *Christopher Wren* (1971), "from the solid geometry suggested by Wolsey's massive bastions, he produced a bold simple shape, square at the base and rising to a buttressed regular octagon in the belfry stage." Tom Tower—the "elongated pumpkin" of Edmund Crispin's novel *The Moving Toyshop*—has become a familiar symbol of Oxford.

The cathedral, its chapter-house (now the gift shop), and its small cloister survive at least partly in their pre-Wolsey form. The cathedral was built mainly in the late twelfth century—whence its Norman arches. Its most spectacular feature is the star-patterned pendant-vaulting in the choir, the work in about 1500 of William Orchard, who also vaulted the Oxford Divinity School. There is some good glass, both medieval and Pre-Raphaelite. In St. Lucy's

Chapel, on the south side of the church, is a rare early fourteenth-century depiction of the martyrdom of St. Thomas Becket—rare because Henry VIII ordered the destruction of such images but in this case only the saint's face was obliterated. The four knights, grouped closely together like one deadly creature, stab and slash with their swords at the kneeling Becket while a cross-bearing monk tries, bravely but helplessly, to defend him. There are three more examples of fourteenth-century glass in the north wall of the Latin Chapel (so-called because services in Latin took place here until 1861) and, at its east end, Burne-Jones' scenes from the life of St. Frideswide. (For this window and the saint's restored shrine nearby, see p.143–44.) Later in his career Burne-Jones designed, and William Morris executed, three paler, perhaps more delicate windows for the cathedral. One commemorates Edith Liddell, daughter of Dean Liddell and sister of Lewis Carroll's Alice, and another Frederic Vyner, murdered by brigands in Greece in 1870. The third shows St. Cecilia, patron of music, with what Geoffrey Tyack calls "elegantly swaying angels holding musical instruments."

As you wander in the cathedral, you come upon a great range of memorial tablets, slabs, effigies, and busts. Above the fully armored figure probably of Sir John de Nowers (died 1386) is a wall-bust of Robert Burton, author of the compendious *Anatomy of Melancholy*. His staring eyes look earnest—or melancholy, or perhaps simply misjudged by the craftsman. The Latin inscription in memory of "Democritus Junior"—Democritus was the Greek philosopher who allegedly laughed at the vanities of the world while Heraclitus wept at them—does clearer justice to the mixed and paradoxical tones of *The Anatomy*, where Burton writes "of Melancholy by being busy to avoid Melancholy."

Christ Church: the Hall and Meadow Buildings

The hall and its hammerbeam roof date substantially from Wolsey's time, as does the great kitchen. The hall is a vast room, fortunately in view of the many thousands of visitors who pass through it each year. To John Ruskin, carefully educated at home and day-school until he came to Christ Church in 1837, the "change from our

Oxford

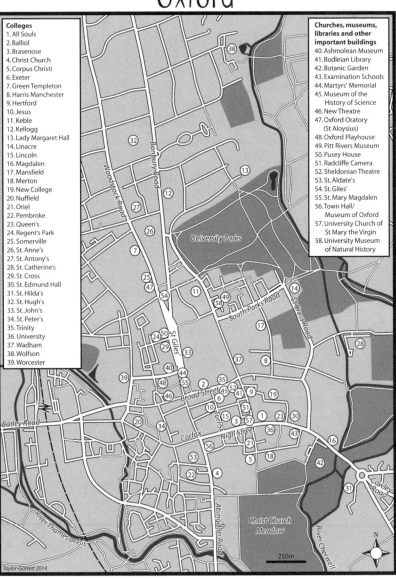

Colleges
1. All Souls
2. Balliol
3. Brasenose
4. Christ Church
5. Corpus Christi
6. Exeter
7. Green Templeton
8. Harris Manchester
9. Hertford
10. Jesus
11. Keble
12. Kellogg
13. Lady Margaret Hall
14. Linacre
15. Lincoln
16. Magdalen
17. Mansfield
18. Merton
19. New College
20. Nuffield
21. Oriel
22. Pembroke
23. Queen's
24. Regent's Park
25. Somerville
26. St. Anne's
27. St. Antony's
28. St. Catherine's
29. St. Cross
30. St. Edmund Hall
31. St. Hilda's
32. St. Hugh's
33. St. John's
34. St. Peter's
35. Trinity
36. University
37. Wadham
38. Wolfson
39. Worcester

Churches, museums, libraries and other important buildings
40. Ashmolean Museum
41. Bodleian Library
42. Botanic Garden
43. Examination Schools
44. Martyrs' Memorial
45. Museum of the History of Science
46. New Theatre
47. Oxford Oratory (St Aloysius)
48. Oxford Playhouse
49. Pitt Rivers Museum
50. Pusey House
51. Radcliffe Camera
52. Sheldonian Theatre
53. St. Aldate's
54. St. Giles'
55. St. Mary Magdalen
56. Town Hall/ Museum of Oxford
57. University Church of St Mary the Virgin
58. University Museum of Natural History

front parlor at Herne Hill . . . to a hall about as big as the nave of Canterbury Cathedral, with its extremity lost in mist, and its company, an innumerable, immeasurable vision in vanishing perspective" seemed "more appalling than appetizing." But his distaste resulted mainly from the use of the hall not, disappointingly, for "festivity and magnificence" but as "a majestic torture chamber." For here Dean Gaisford presided over the termly "Collections" or examinations: "scornful at once, and vindictive, thunderous always, more sullen and threatening as the day wore on, he stalked with baleful emanation of Gorgonian cold from dais to door, and door to dais" as the "doleful" examinees attempted to hide their cribs. (The curriculum at the time was so tedious, and its delivery so uninspired and inconsistent, that its victims can hardly be blamed for cheating.) Ruskin did not use a crib but claimed to believe that "the Dean would rather I had used fifty" than look so "puzzled and hopeless" by the afternoon. No doubt he exaggerates his ignorance—his "Latin writing" was very clearly not, as he claims, "the worst in the university"—but the Dean was obviously not an easy man to please. Nor could he and his fellow dons live up to the serious young Ruskin's expectations derived from "what Holbein or Durer had represented in Erasmus or Melanchthon" or Titian's Venetian "Magnificoes."

Sebastian Flyte in Evelyn Waugh's *Brideshead Revisited* is a Christ Church undergraduate rather less learned than John Ruskin. He lives "high in Meadow Buildings," where he lunches on plover's eggs and lobster in rooms eclectically furnished with "a harmonium in a gothic case, an elephant's-foot waste-paper basket, a dome of wax fruit, two disproportionately large Sèvres vases, framed drawings by Daumier." After the lunch—Charles Ryder's first full experience of Sebastian and his set—the strange, exotic Anthony Blanche steps onto the balcony overlooking Christ Church Meadow. With the aid of a megaphone he recites "in languishing tones" parts of *The Waste Land* to "the sweatered and muffled throng that was on its way to the river." "*I, Tiresias, have foresuffered all,*" Anthony "sobbed to them from the Venetian arches." Harold Acton, the source of some aspects of the character (and the real owner of the Victorian furnishings of Sebastian's room) had used the megaphone to declaim his own poems with a similar intention of shocking the "hearties." He had opted to live in the 1860s Meadow Buildings, whose neo-Venetian style was inspired by Ruskin's polemical writings. Acton's choice was, Humphrey Carpenter points out in *The Brideshead Generation*, "an aesthetic and a social statement, a rejection of the classical formality of the college's principal quadrangles . . . and a separation of himself from the Old Etonians who traditionally thronged Peckwater, leaving Meadow Buildings for 'dim' men from obscure schools." (Peckwater is the substantial classical quadrangle by the library, designed by Dean Henry Aldrich in 1707–14.)

Blanche's evident homosexuality is one of many things about him which does not endear him to the college hearties. They deposit him in "Mercury," the pool in Tom Quad with a statue of the god. He claims to have gone into the fountain himself—"it was really most refreshing"—having avoided violence by telling the "clodhoppers," calmly, that a knowledge of sexual psychology would teach them that "nothing could give me keener pleasure than to be man-handled by you meaty boys." If it will satisfy their libido to see him bathe, "come with me quietly, dear louts, to the fountain."

All Souls: Baroque Gothic

At Agincourt, in *Henry V*, the Herald is pleased to tell the King that "the number of the slaughter'd French" is some ten thousand while "the number of our English dead" is only four "of name" and "of all other men/But five and twenty." Clearly Shakespeare and his patriotic source are exaggerating somewhat, and quite enough Englishmen perished in the Anglo-French wars more generally for Henry Chichele, Archbishop of Canterbury, to make daily prayer for the souls of those warriors who had "drunk the bitter cup of death," an aim and requirement of the college he founded in 1438.

The Archbishop's outlay has been calculated at over £4000. Stone was brought from Headington and Taynton, oak mainly from Shotover Forest. Much of the front quadrangle and the hammer-beam roof of the chapel are from Chichele's day. Also maintained is Chichele's decision that the college would, distinctively, have fellows but no undergraduates. Among the "grey-green cloisters" of All Souls, Henry James "found it agreeable to reflect" that

> This delightful spot exists only for the satisfaction of a small society of Fellows who, having no dreary instruction to administer, no noisy hobbledehoys to govern, no obligations but toward their own culture, no care save for learning as learning and truth as truth, are presumably the happiest and most charming people in the world.

James' English idyll, originally aimed at American readers, continues as he describes the Codrington Library at All Souls, "a cool, grey hall, of very great length and height, with vast wall-spaces of very rich-looking book titles and statues of noble scholars set in the midst. Had the charming Fellows ever anything more disagreeable to do than to finger these precious volumes and then to stroll about together in the grassy courts, in learned comradeship, discussing their precious contents?" ("Two Excursions," in *English Hours*).

But the beauty of the library and the number of the books originated in a more practical world: Christopher Codrington, a successful sugar-planter in the Caribbean, bequeathed £6000 for a new library and £4000 for the books. The building and the rest of the North Quadrangle, including twin pinnacled towers like those at the entrance to some cathedrals, were designed by Nicholas Hawksmoor in 1715 and completed in 1734. He managed to make the library Gothic outside and classical inside, and more generally achieved a unique balance of styles, preserving a Gothic look in harmony with the older part of the college but turning it to Baroque effect. It is "Gothic used scenically and romantically," as Howard Colvin says in *All Souls* (1989), "but within the conventions of a classical tradition which insisted on symmetry and would not permit the kind of deliberately irregular grouping" later favored by nineteenth-century Gothic Revivalists. Colvin notes, however, that the symmetry of the quadrangle was destroyed when Christopher Wren's 1659 sundial was moved from its original position, high on the south front of the chapel, to the south front of the library: "a splendid and disproportionate anachronism."

The Bodleian Library

Before the main entrance to the Bodleian Library stands a commanding bronze statue of William Herbert, 3rd Earl of Pembroke, by Hubert Le Sueur. (The earl retains his armored aplomb even when irreverent pigeons settle on his head.) Pembroke was Chancellor of the University, joint-dedicatee of the Shakespeare First Folio, and, more significantly here, donor in 1629 of 250 Greek manuscripts. Only a generation before, such an important nobleman might perhaps have contributed books and manuscripts to an individual college, but probably not to the university, which had, effectively, no library. Duke Humfrey's Library, the core of the later Bodleian, had opened in 1488. It housed the invaluable manuscripts given by Humfrey, Duke of Gloucester (1390–1447), brother of Henry V, and other material kept until then in the fourteenth-century Old Library of St. Mary the Virgin. But the collection was dispersed during the Reformation—following a visitation in 1550 in search of objectionably popish material, most of the books were burned or, as Anthony Wood puts it, "sold away for Robin Hood's pennyworths, either to booksellers, or to glovers to press their gloves, or tailors to make measures, or to bookbinders to cover books . . . and some also kept by the Reformers for their own use." It was almost entirely due to the energy and foresight of Sir Thomas Bodley (1545–1613) that this situation was as far as possible reversed and patrons like Pembroke attracted.

Bodley, in his early years an undergraduate and fellow of Merton College, had traveled in Europe in order to study languages and on diplomatic missions for Elizabeth I. At the same time he gathered his own collection of books and manuscripts. When he came back to live in Oxford in the late 1590s, he decided to revive the library, feeling that "in my solitude, and surcease from Commonwealth affairs, I could not busy myself to better purpose, than by reducing that place (which then in every part lay ruined and waste) to the public use of students." The restored library, stocked from Bodley's and others' gifts, opened in 1602. He negotiated in 1610 an agreement with the Stationers' Company of London by which a copy of every book published in England should be deposited in the Bodleian. (At this stage the library did not actually want every book—only learned tomes, no such "trifles" as English plays and poems—but the agreement was the ancestor of the Bodleian's status as one of Britain's and Ireland's six copyright libraries.) Bodley also made, in 1610–12, the first additions to the medieval building: the Proscholium or entrance-hall and above it, for books, Arts End. And he planned and provided money for buildings completed after his death.

The Schools Quadrangle (1619–24) was designed to replace with more dignified chambers the "ruinous little rooms" hitherto used for lectures and examinations. The Latin names of some of the subjects pursued in the ground and first-floor rooms—Moral Philosophy, Music, and so on—are painted over the doors. All were later absorbed into the Bodleian. (Perhaps suggesting changed priorities, the door marked Schola Astronomiae et Rhetoricae now leads to the Bodleian gift-shop.) A third story, for much of its history a picture gallery, is now the Upper Reading Room. The quadrangle is essentially Gothic, with its pinnacles and battlements, in spite of its Renaissance display on the gate-tower of the Five Orders of Architecture: the traditional Doric, Ionic, and Corinthian columns with Tuscan below and Composite above. Between the Composite pairs the enthroned figure of James I presents one of his own books to a kneeling woman who represents the university. Finally, Selden End, reached through Duke Humfrey's Library, was built in 1634–7 and later named in honor of the lawyer John Selden, who in 1654 bequeathed eight thousand volumes of books and manuscripts including much Greek, Hebrew, and Oriental material. Beneath Selden End is Convocation House, once a meeting-room for the university parliament.

The Bodleian is a major research library, which does not lend books—famously, even Charles I was refused and, with somewhat uncharacteristic good sense, accepted the refusal. Today it is full of people, and its eleven million books are kept not only in the Bodleian itself but underground, across Broad Street in the New Bodleian (Sir Giles Gilbert Scott, 1937–40; currently being extensively refurbished), in other libraries including the Radcliffe Science Library and the Radcliffe Camera, or out at the depository in Nuneham Courtenay. Staff can offer expert help and are unlikely now to suffer the fate of the man "grown grey in the service" whom Jane Welsh Carlyle, visiting in 1837, "made as red as a lobster by asking him simple questions which he could nowise answer." (Her guide could respond only with "a broad stare" when she asked provocatively—in this then dusty and conservative place—why there was no portrait of Oliver Cromwell.)

Staff and readers are now legion and learned. The library may no longer keep on display such assorted objects—cataloged in 1846 by John Norris, "Janitor of the Bodleian Library"—as a papier-mâché Martyrs' Memorial or "A very curious MODEL of an INDIAN SUBTERRANEAN PALACE and RESERVOIR, in teak, carved by native Indians, and Presented by Sir J. W. Awdry, Chief Justice of Bombay in 1842." But the Bodleian remains full of wonderful distractions. You can, if consulting early books or manuscripts, enjoy a sheltered alcove of Duke Humfrey and admire the early seventeenth-century painted roof panels. (They show the arms of the university and of Bodley.) Beneath Duke Humfrey, and open to visitors, is the fifteenth-century Divinity School with its superb fan vault by William Orchard. From their desks, people can pause to watch or listen to others marching—confident, harassed, attractive, shoes creaking, heels clopping—the immense length of the Upper Reading Room. Or, looking upwards, they can seek inspiration from the painted frieze of 200 sixteenth-century and earlier worthies. (They were painted in 1618–20, were covered over in 1830, and re-emerged in 1949.) Readers can engage in research—or more vaguely "poke about in the Bodleian," as Peter Walsh in Virginia Woolf's *Mrs Dalloway* thinks he might in retirement. Or you might simply, with Harriet Vane in *Gaudy Night*, snooze "a good deal in the arms of" Duke Humfrey. She, it is true, is tired because of her night-time efforts to investigate misdeeds in the corridors of Shrewsbury College, and her "research" is only a cover for her presence in Oxford. The Bodleian encourages people on more purely scholarly missions with the Latin inscription over the main entrance beginning *Quod feliciter vortat*, "'may it turn out well,'" for this library put up by Sir Thomas for the "academicians of Oxford and for the Republic of the Learned."

The Radcliffe Camera

By the will of Dr. John Radcliffe, who died in 1714, £40,000 was available to build a new university library. What eventually went up, between 1737 and 1748, to the design of James Gibbs, aimed as much to proclaim the glory of the donor and the university as to provide a suitable place for keeping books. Its dome, in timber covered with lead and surmounted by a lantern and another small dome, has become an essential component of Oxford views. On a rusticated ground story (originally open) the exterior of the main reading room is ringed by paired Corinthian columns, between which niches and windows alternate. David Hinton points out in *Oxford Architecture* that an impression of excessive verticality is cleverly avoided because the columns do not rise directly from "the accentuated bays of the ground floor" and "the ribs of the dome rise from above the spaces between the columns."

The Camera's active use as a library began mainly after it was taken over by the Bodleian in 1860. The domed reading room, reached by an impressive stone staircase, is more like a Baroque church than a traditional library. In 1941 the story beneath it was converted from a store for books to another reading room. For many years English was downstairs—increasingly crowded, with a rather frantic, essay-crisis atmosphere in the evenings—and History in the calmer, perhaps more solemn, upper space. Some calm is still available outside, in Radcliffe Square, but it is now difficult to imagine the peaceful university vacation in which "the Camera slept like a cat in the sunshine, disturbed only by the occasional visit of a slow-footed don" (*Gaudy Night*, 1936).

Jesus College: "Cotswold manors on all sides"

Jesus is the only Oxford college which began during the reign of Elizabeth I. In 1571 she was the official founder, and her portrait hangs in the hall. The real founders were a group of lawyers and clergy, mostly Welsh—including Hugh Price, Treasurer of

St. David's Cathedral—and the Welsh connection has remained strong. Sir Leoline Jenkins (1625–85) is often regarded as the "second founder." As Principal between 1661 and 1673, he reorganized the college and himself provided £1440 for the new Fellows' Library (finished 1679) and the completion of the second quadrangle; at his death—after a successful career as judge and officer of state—he left Jesus substantial wealth and lands. Other college notables include Edward Lhuyd or Lloyd (c. 1660–1709), botanist, philological scholar, and Keeper of the Ashmolean Museum. Among many Welsh names on World War I memorial in the chapel are those of six Joneses, nearly ten percent of the total: three lieutenants, two second lieutenants, and a private. Today about fifteen percent of the students are Welsh and there are still a number of scholarships restricted to Welsh or Welsh-connected candidates. There is an annual Welsh-language service in the chapel on St. David's Day.

The buildings are unspectacular, well adapted to the needs of a residential community. Much survives from the sixteenth- and seventeenth-century First Quad and the later seventeenth-century Second Quad—"grassed squares," for John Betjeman, "surrounded by what look like Cotswold manors on all sides." The chapel is mainly 1620s–30s with Victorian additions. It has a copy of the St. Paul's Cathedral bust of the most famous of Jesus undergraduates (1907–10), T. E. Lawrence "of Arabia." In the early seventeenth-century hall, which gained an elaborate plaster ceiling in 1741, is a copy of Augustus John's portrait of Lawrence. (John was not connected with the college but in his autobiography imagines an Elizabethan Jesus "simply pullulating with my compatriots.")

The Queen's College: "magnificent vandalism"

Queen's, having demolished its fourteenth-century buildings in an act of "magnificent vandalism" (R. H. Hodgkin, *Six Centuries of an Oxford College*), became the first college in wholly classical style.

First came the new library (1693–6) in what later became Queen's Back Quadrangle. It was built over a loggia or "on a cloister of stately pillars" (John Ayliffe in his 1723 *The Ancient and Present State of the University of Oxford*), and is as bright and spacious inside as earlier college libraries had tended to be dark and constricted. There is a tradition that Sir Christopher Wren contributed to its planning; more certainly involved were Henry Aldrich, Dean of Christ Church, Provost Timothy Halton (who personally contributed £2000 towards the cost), and the master-mason John Townesend. Subsequent work, beginning in 1710 once more money had been raised, was the product of collaboration between later Provosts, George Clarke, Townesend's son William, and Nicholas Hawksmoor, originally Wren's assistant. Hawksmoor's designs—he was working also at Blenheim Palace—for a massive, palatial, and unaffordable Queen's were rejected, but he continued to influence Clarke and the others' plans.

In *Exploring Oxford* (1991), Michael De-la-Noy observes that the layout of the front quad is "imposing, self-assured, symmetrical." Not only were the old college buildings cleared away, but the houses which had separated them from the High Street were bought up and demolished. In their place came a formal gateway and blank screen (1733–6), topped by the cupola over Henry Cheere's statue of Queen Caroline, consort of George II. (The college takes its name from Queen Philippa, whose chaplain Robert Eglesfeld founded it in 1341. Caroline, however, was more immediately to be honored for her timely gift of £2000.) Opposite are the imposing, symmetrical hall and chapel block. The hall is high and barrel-vaulted. The chapel, unlike any other in Oxford, has the look and the atmosphere of a Baroque continental church. It incorporates windows from the earlier chapel, some from the 1630s by Abraham van Linge, the merits of which seem to have been clear even to zealous neoclassicists.

The University Museum of Natural History: "a station furnished with fossils"

For Clare Mayfield, in Penelope Lively's *The House in Norham Gardens* (1974), coming to the University Museum

> was like entering a Victorian station . . . but a station furnished with fossils and pickled jellyfish and whale skeletons hung absurdly from the glass roof. There should be trains shunting, steam oozing

around the gastropods and belemnites: instead there were flights of school-children dashing from case to case, and students on camp-stools, drawing vertebrae and rib-cages.

This extraordinary place aimed, according to a resolution of 1849 by the committee which wanted to build it, to gather "all the materials explanatory of the organic beings placed upon the globe." Henry Acland, Reader in Anatomy and later Regius Professor of Medicine, and the moving force of the committee, intended the museum to promote science in a university whose "intellect . . . was wholly given to ecclesiastical and theological questions." The design, by Benjamin Woodward of Dublin, was suitably bold: influenced both by John Ruskin's faith in the Gothic and by recent advances in technology, especially in the use of what Acland—Ruskin's close friend—called "those railway materials—iron and glass." The beautiful, the practical, and the instructive come together. Inside, the different mineral origin of the columns is clearly inscribed. "Serpentine, the Lizard, Cornwall" is shiny black from a distance, mottled with red and white when seen close up; "Porphyritic Granite, Lamorna, Cornwall" is gray flecked with white. The limestone capitals and the windows were carved with floral designs (inspired by specimens from the Botanic Garden) by the O'Shea brothers and their relative Edward Whelan. (Money ran out, unfortunately, before the work was finished.) On the spandrels between the arches are, in Acland's words, "large interwoven branches" in wrought-iron "with leaf and flower and fruit, of lime, sycamore, walnut, palm and other trees and shrubs." Leaves also decorate the iron capitals.

Scientific achievement—and, in Prince Albert's case, its encouragement—is celebrated in stone in the interior of the museum. The cloaked prince, in a memorial statue presented by the citizens of Oxford in 1864, looks out at the exhibits with energetic earnestness. The other figures usually look more modestly down, intent on scientific thoughts. Darwin ponders, and Harvey (who first accurately described the circulation of blood) holds a heart while experimentally pressing his own. Newton, finger crooked on chin and carrying some heavy tome, looks down at the apple which has fallen at his feet. ("He should have eaten it," a practical if perhaps unscientifically-minded grandmother tells a child.) Also present are Euclid, Leibniz, and a robed and ruffed Sir Francis Bacon. A few busts were added later, including one, at last, of a woman: the Oxford crystallographer Dorothy Hodgkin, Nobel laureate for Chemistry in 1964.

For all the grand names and cathedral proportions, the museum is home still to Lively's "flights" of children. They can hide behind the columns. They can be instructed or frightened by the human skeleton in the display on "The Rise of Modern Humans," or the rows of skeletal but bulky bison, rhinoceros, elk, and elephant. More approachable are the Shetland pony and the cheetah near the entrance. "Please touch," says a sign on the soft brown-haired Mandy the pony, late of Knaresborough Zoo. The cheetah also lived in a British zoo, we are told, and died "of natural causes," unlike some of the earlier specimens in the collection. Its legs are a bit rocky and its fur is wearing thin, felt by so many with so much love, curiosity, or trepidation. Also meant to be touched, and rather more difficult to wear away, are large samples of smooth orbicular granite, firm Lewisian gneiss, quartz crystals from the Polar Urals—sharp edges and smooth surfaces—and ten-million-year-old sparkling golden pyrite, metallic to the touch.

A natural history museum is usually full of dead things: skel-etons, fossils, rocks, Mandy, birds in cabinets, and other evidence of taxidermy. But here there is also an emphasis on life, as a model of the DNA double-helix reminds us. Upstairs is a specially designed beehive with viewing panel. Bees fly in and out, well placed for the Parks nearby. You can watch their active, gently heaving mass, where new patterns form as individuals move around—an art installation as much as a scientific demonstration. Swifts, without the museum having planned for them, nest in the tower—they have been studied here since 1948, and between May and August each year can be viewed by webcam at the museum or on www.oum.ox.ac.uk/swifts.htm. The dinosaurs may not be alive, but some have been fleshed out to make it more apparent that they once were. Next to the cast of a tyrannosaurus, for instance, is a model of its head, complete with evil, laughing, or rapacious eyes—part stage-villain, part mischievous spaniel, part Laughing Cavalier. And where everything might be bone-pale or gray, there is a determined effort to introduce color: a scarlet ibis, pictures of the highly-colored sea-life which has become the paler fossil Bryozoans, red sandstone, a booth to show fluorescent minerals—the intense green, red, and purple revealed by ultra-violet light.

Outside the museum a sculpture commemorates the British Association for the Advancement of Science meeting on 30 June 1860 in the room which was about to become the museum library. In the debate following a paper on Darwin, Samuel Wilberforce, Bishop of Oxford, dismissed evolution as "a theory founded upon fancy, instead of upon facts" and laughed at the idea of being descended from some "venerable ape." Thomas Henry Huxley, Darwin's friend and champion, is said to have riposted that "for myself I would rather be descended from an ape than from a divine who employs authority to stifle truth." For a time after the debate, William Tuckwell remembers in *Reminiscences of Oxford* (1900), "science was tolerated sceptically rather than cordially welcomed." But by the mid-1860s "science established itself in Oxford. The Museum buildings formed an object lesson which it was impossible to overlook."

The Pitt Rivers Museum

This museum is in an extension, built in 1885–8, to the University Museum and is reached through it. It is the interior which commands attention, showing innumerable ethnographic exhibits—complete with early handwritten and typewritten labels—which include and build on the major donation of General Augustus Henry Pitt Rivers in 1884. We are given some sense of the cluttered but discovery-filled world of a Victorian museum (or, for James Fenton, of the place "where myths/Go when they die"). Glass cases fill the main floor with eclectic displays on "The Human Form in Art," "Drums," "Treatment of the Dead" (the Pitt Rivers has always had a slightly ghoulish reputation for its shrunken heads and decorated skulls), "Coiled Baskets," and "Single and Double Reed Instruments." Bagpipes are present in their Spanish Galician, Bohemian, Greek, Syrian, and Algerian incarnations; the Transylvanian version, the labels point out, has "a carved goat's head on the chanter stock" and the Calabrian *zampogna* retains "the wide flared bell which is typical of shawms and medieval bagpipes." (Pitt Rivers was a disciple of Darwin; he collected objects by type in order to "trace out . . . the sequence of ideas by which mankind has advanced from the condition of lower animals.") There is a range of highly colored textiles and Hawaiian feather cloaks. "Objects Made from Ivory, Bone, and Horn" include a Maori club of sperm whale bone, a Buckinghamshire lace bobbin, and a killer whale in bone and haliotic inlay from a Haida medicine-man's apron. There are model houses, spirit boats, and a more worldly Canadian birch-bark canoe, and whistling arrows from Asia and South America. In China such arrows were used to warn of the Emperor's approach.

Since 1901 a Haida totem-pole (purchased then for $36) has towered over everything else. There are four levels, with watchmen at the top, a bear eating a frog, another bear holding a person, and a raven whose great projecting beak looms over "Model Boats and Rafts."

The Sheldonian: passing "the fourteen-fold sneer of the Caesars"

Oxford university careers traditionally begin and end with gowned processions to, and Latin pronouncements in, the D-shaped Sheldonian Theatre—the first major work, in 1664–9, of Sir Christopher Wren. Inspired by the Roman Theatre of Marcellus, it was one of the first important neoclassical structures in Oxford. It might have been even more strikingly classical: according to Wren's son, "he was obliged to put a stop to the bolder strokes of his pencil, and confine the expense within the limits of a private purse"—that of Gilbert Sheldon, Archbishop of Canterbury, former Warden of All Souls and Chancellor of the university in 1667–9. As it was, the project cost a substantial £12,000.

The Sheldonian is also used for concerts, sounds from which float out on summer nights across the much derided surrounding stone heads of emperors or sages—more correctly, herms. The originals of 1669 were replaced in 1868 by new versions which rapidly decayed until they looked, as John Betjeman puts it, like "illustrations in a medical textbook on skin diseases." They were once more replaced in 1970–2 with heads by Michael Black in better quality Clipsham stone. Generations of late-night revelers have paid their tribute to the Emperors by crowning them with traffic cones. Only in fiction have the heads themselves responded to a passerby: "sweat started from [their] brows" in anticipation of the disastrous effect the beauty of Max Beerbohm's Zuleika Dobson will have on the young men of Oxford. They continue, grave but powerless, to watch and sigh over developments in the novel and to look out for "their" Katie, the landlady's daughter across Broad Street who loves the Duke and scorns "that Miss Dobson." They look on too in Dorothy L. Sayers' *Gaudy Night*. After young Reggie Pomfret's hopeless (and to her, preposterous) marriage proposal, he and Harriet Vane walk "in resentful silence . . . past the fourteen-fold sneer of the Caesars." And in Edmund Crispin's *The Moving Toyshop* (1946) they stand "severe and admonitory as the totems of some primitive tribe."

The interior has a painted ceiling by Robert Streeter, showing a red cloth furled to reveal the sky and a wealth of Baroque allegorical figures enacting "The Triumph of Truth." But what was "most admirable therein" for contemporaries like John Ayliffe (1723) was "the contrivance of supporting [the roof] without the help of any beam; it being entirely kept up with braces and screws." The ceiling hid Wren's trussed roof, covering a span of seventy feet.

Before the Sheldonian, participants in university ceremonies had crammed into St. Mary the Virgin. The theater was a more spacious and dignified setting in which to confer degrees, honor eminent visitors, and hear successful students recite the winning entries for the Newdigate poetry prize. (They included Ruskin's and Wilde's pieces on the prescribed topics "Salsette and Elephanta" and "Ravenna.") But the audience responded, often, far from respectfully. "The interior of this edifice," notes Henry James in *English Hours*, "is the scene of the classic hooting, stamping, and cat-calling by which the undergraduates confer the last consecration upon the distinguished gentlemen who come up for the honorary degree of

D.C.L. [Doctor of Civil Law]." The racket contrasted curiously with the monumental building with its "double tier of galleries, with sculptured pulpits protruding from them: there are full-length portraits of kings and worthies; there is a general air of antiquity and dignity, which ... was enhanced by the presence of certain ancient scholars seated in crimson robes in high-backed chairs." Jarring or doubly funny in this setting must have been such cries as the one which greeted Matthew Arnold's Creweian Oration in 1864: "Cut it short! Give him beer!"

The Museum of the History of Science

The sober Old Ashmolean building, "less learned, but more of a piece" (Pevsner) than the Sheldonian next door, was put up in 1679–83 to house Elias Ashmole's collection of "curiosities." Much expanded, most of the collection would move into the new Ashmolean Museum in Beaumont Street two centuries later. A selection of the curiosities still to be seen in the old museum includes the snout of a sawfish, a turtle's head, and a powder horn made from antler. The Museum of the History of Science opened only in 1925, but in earlier centuries the basement had been used as a chemistry laboratory and the ground floor for "natural philosophy" lectures. Excavations in 1999 unearthed not only retorts, crucibles, and flasks but human and animal bones, suggesting anatomical dissection or display. (It was customary to use for these purposes bodies fresh from the gallows.)

Today the museum shows packed cases of early telescopes, microscopes, octants, and sextants (two belonging to Isambard Kingdom Brunel, c. 1830), sliderules, astrolabes, portable sundials, and the like. One of the less practical-looking exhibits is a superb silver microscope made by George Adams for George III with decorative figures, columns, and urns, and a ring of eight objective lenses. Bronze rather than silver dominates many of the cases on the ground and upper floors. The basement, however, is full of glass: nineteenth-century retorts, gas-jars, and vacuum flasks, the sort of equipment fiendish cinematic Dr. Frankensteins delight in setting up. Here too is material on the history of telegraphic and wireless transmission, early photographic equipment, and Einstein's blackboard, preserved after an Oxford lecture on relativity in May 1931. "The first three lines," the label explains, "establish an equation for D, the measure of expansion in the universe. The lower four lines provide numerical values for the expansion, density, radius and age of the universe." Suddenly the building seems small.

Brasenose College: "the immortal nose . . . still resplendent over the portals of its cognominal college"

Brasenose takes its name, very probably, from its knocker. This metal leopard's head was removed from the original Brasenose Hall (an academic hall founded probably in the 1240s) to Stamford by students wanting to study there in the 1330s. When it was finally recovered in 1890 it was given pride of place above the high table. In the early sixteenth century, in the meantime, a substitute brass knocker was attached to the college gate. Two more nasally extravagant heads feature in the seventeenth-century stained glass of the north bay window of the hall. The college nose became the stuff of legend—sometimes mingling with other legends, like the talking head of brass supposedly made by the thirteenth-century Oxford scientist and philosopher Friar Roger Bacon. In Thomas Love Peacock's *Crotchet Castle*, Rev. Dr. Folliott laments that "This was a seat of learning in the days of Friar Bacon. But the friar is gone, and his learning with him. Nothing of him is left, but the immortal nose, which when his brazen head had tumbled to pieces . . . was the only palpable fragment . . . and which is still resplendent over the portals of its cognominal college."

Beyond the outer knocker lies Old Quad, built a few years after Brasenose Hall was refounded as Brasenose College by William Smyth, Bishop of Lincoln, and Sir Richard Sutton, in 1504. (A third story was added in the early seventeenth century.) The painted sundial of 1719 has instructions for use on a brass plate by the hall steps. In Chapel Quad are the chapel and library of 1656–66. The chapel contains a hammerbeam roof which was transferred here from the college property at Frewin Hall in New Inn Hall Street and then covered by a fan vault in plaster. The college website points out that the main motive for re-using the roof was simply to save money and quotes the insistence of a 1970s editor of *The Brazen Nose* that "anything as strange and curious as Arts and Craft aestheticism [the ceiling was painted by Charles Kempe in the 1890s] overlaid on seventeenth-century fake Gothic, which in turn disguises a genuine fifteenth-century hammer-beam roof, is certainly worth keeping—if only for the sheer zaniness of it all." The college expanded to Sir Thomas Jackson's New Quad, begun in the 1880s, and Powell and Moya's Platnauer Building of 1960.

Brasenose has had a reputation, since the nineteenth century, for sport and heartiness; it was an improbable place to find Walter Pater (1839–94), the apostle of Aestheticism. Pater's rooms (now Old Lodge 2 and 3), as remembered by Edward Manson in the *Oxford Magazine* for 1906,

> were on the first floor, overlooking Radcliffe Square and St. Mary's. The Aesthetic Movement was then [1869] just beginning, and Pater's rooms embodied its highest aspirations. They were panelled in a pale green tint, the floor was matted, the furniture was oak and severe in style, there were a few choice prints on the walls, choice books on the shelves, and a dwarf orange-tree, with real oranges on it, adorned the table.

Other witnesses report that the rooms were "draped in a delicate harmony of blue and yellow," and that there were classical sculptures, engravings from Correggio and Michelangelo, and lilies of the valley. Even in these surroundings, according to an anonymous memorial in *The Bookman* in September 1894, Pater talked only occasionally of the subjects which really interested him. Usually he was polite and tried to set undergraduates at their ease, but remained rather diffident, "a man who had lost touch with the world early in life, and was always striving to regain that contact."

Pater struck many observers as enigmatic or paradoxical. His heavy mustache gave him a military more than an aesthetic air. And, says *The Bookman*, while "Oxford is noted for its laxity in the matter of dress," he

> possessed the most spotless and best brushed hat in the city. Precise in everything, he was in dress neatness itself ... Nearly every day, about five in the afternoon or a little later, he might be seen walking out of Brasenose College always in top hat and Chesterfield overcoat without stain or wrinkle. With heavy and laboured tread he would proceed down the High Street, at times looking into the picture shops, and turning eventually into the Union Library. His eyes were always on the path in front of him.

He ignored everyone he passed, "the tired pilgrim, wending towards a serious goal and not to be disturbed by the thoughts of anything else." Even within Brasenose, "there were few who could truly say that they knew him well, that they had penetrated beneath the surface." (His probable homosexuality, which hampered and might easily have ended his Oxford career, dictated some caution in personal relationships.) For Henry James, writing to Edmund Gosse, "faint, pale, embarrassed, exquisite Pater" was "the mask without the face."

Pater's memorial is in the ante-chapel at Brasenose: his bust, in a central medallion—mustached as ever, gazing afar or within—is surrounded by smaller medallions of his inspirations Michelangelo, Dante, Leonardo, and Plato.

St. Catherine's College: "geometric precision"

St. Catherine's College, the work (1960–4) of the Danish architect Arne Jacobsen, is difficult to ignore. Its long, symmetrically arranged blocks in brick and plate-glass can seem cold, rigid, an idea worked out to its logical conclusion. For Nikolaus Pevsner, "Here is a perfect piece of architecture. It has a consistent plan, and every detail is meticulously worked out. Self-discipline is the message, expressed in terms of a geometry pervading the whole and the parts and felt wherever one moves or stops." Austere lines are modified in places, however, by the growth of acers, magnolias, and acacias.

Visitors less attuned to such starkness have not held back from expressing their opinions. "Flimsy metal struts project from the outside walls; the 'campanile' is contemptible and the whole air is one of meagerness and futility," groans James Lees-Milne in his diary for 8 December 1975. Jan Morris thinks the "bare portentous hall" is "like an assembly plant in a munitions factory, or a trolls' gymnasium." The brick is "a bilious yellow." Yet the college provokes one of her characteristic flights of fancy:

> seen through the willows across the damp water-meadow . . . this hulking, crouching, alien structure has a truly exciting grandeur—not so calm or sublime as its predecessors, but possibly a little evil, like a younger son returned unannounced from foreign places, and waiting to poison the heir.

Oxford Castle as prison (Tejvan Pettinger/Wikimedia Commons)

4 | Rulers and Ruled
Town and Gown Politics

The Normans dominated Oxford from a strong castle, on whose site prisoners were held until 1996. Henry I built Beaumont Palace roughly where Beaumont Street is now, and his grandsons Richard I and John were born there. But local power and lands belonged mainly to monks and friars—for their abbeys and churches see Chapter 9—and then, beginning in the thirteenth century, to the university and colleges. They still wield considerable influence.

Oxford Castle

"Oxford is a city very securely protected, inaccessible because of the very deep water that washes it all round, most carefully encircled by the palisade of an outwork on one side, and on another finely and very strongly fortified by an impregnable castle and tower of great height" (*Gesta Stephani*, c. 1160, as translated by Edmund King in his *King Stephen*, 2010). Here the Norman baron Robert d'Oilly established his headquarters in the early 1070s. The main early survivals are the substantial mound on which the keep once stood, St. George's Tower—probably Anglo-Saxon work, incorporated by the Normans—and the crypt beneath it. For much of its later history the castle served as a prison. New buildings were added for this purpose in the eighteenth and nineteenth centuries; today plaques identify the debtors' tower of 1790 and the Governor's house of 1848. Much of the prison has been adapted since its closure in 1996 for use as offices, restaurants, and the Malmaison Hotel: "going to the slammer in style," as the hotel website puts it. A chandelier glitters through glass in the otherwise forbidding main entrance, cell-style doors lead to rooms with soft furnishings, the brasserie has a metal staircase.

The siege of 1142 is the only event in the castle's history likely to make a good film—it does feature in medieval chronicles, children's illustrated history-books of yesteryear, and modern historical novels. The antagonists were Henry I's daughter Matilda and her more successful rival for the throne, her cousin King Stephen. As civil war continued, Matilda arrived in seemingly impregnable Oxford, where her father, in more stable times, had built his Beaumont Palace. But Stephen took the town by surprise: he and his men swam intrepidly across the Thames and burned and pillaged at will. Matilda and her followers, within the castle walls, were cut off from their allies. Stephen settled down for a long siege. His avowed aim was to capture the woman who to him was a troublesome princess and to her supporters the uncrowned queen, "Lady of the English" or, from her first marriage, Empress.

Three months later the garrison must have been near to surrender or starvation. It was December, and the branch of the river which had been diverted to form the castle moat was frozen solid. (Later it silted up, full of the castle and town rubbish of centuries.) But Matilda turned the situation to her own advantage: she escaped across the ice. One account has her lowered from the ramparts on a rope. More likely she and a few followers slipped out by way of a postern. The chronicler Henry of Huntingdon claims that "wrapped in a white cloak, [she] deceived the eyes of the besiegers, dazzled by the reflection of the snow" (Thomas Forester's translation). The escapees struggled through to Abingdon on foot, where they obtained horses and rode on to the safety of Wallingford Castle. The Oxford garrison at once surrendered, but Stephen had lost his prey. After further invasions, withdrawals, and negotiations he would, eleven years later, name as his heir Matilda's son Henry, Duke of Normandy—the future Henry II. (Stephen and Henry held court jointly at Oxford in 1154: "a magnificent assembly," says Henry of Huntingdon.) By then the antagonists must have been fairly exhausted. They had, according to Sellar and Yeatman's *1066 and All That*, "spent the reign escaping from each other over the snow in night-gowns."

Oxford was again besieged during the Civil War. Having captured the city, Parliamentarian forces refortified the castle, destroying some earlier structures. According to Anthony Wood, they removed four towers and replaced them with "bulwarks on the mounts." But in 1652 these were in turn "in four days' space in a whimsy quite pulled down and demolished" and the garrison moved to New College. The keep was eventually knocked down in the eighteenth century.

The university as ruler

Tension between "Town and Gown" was at its most violent in the Middle Ages. The university gradually acquired rights and privileges concerning regulation of markets, food standards, rent, and justice. (Increasingly scholars who committed crimes were answerable to their Chancellor, not the courts.) When the town took the law into its own hands in 1209, the resulting dispute nearly destroyed the university. A student murdered a woman and fled; when the civic authorities hanged his two student house-mates, most of the teachers and pupils who constituted the university left Oxford in protest. (Some of them went to Cambridge and founded a new university there.) Eventually the papal legate worked out a settlement in 1214. Among its almost exclusively pro-university clauses, the town was to pay 52 shillings a year for poor scholars and provide dinner for one hundred of them on the anniversary of the students' hanging. Most of the scholars came back; the town regained its income from them, but subject to much restriction.

Town was subordinated even further to Gown following the St. Scholastica's Day riots of February 1355. At the Swindlestock tavern by Carfax two "clerks," according to the civic authorities, threw their wine in the landlord's face and knocked him about with the quart pot they had emptied. Three days of fighting followed, with much desperate ringing of the city bells of St. Martin's and the university bells of St. Mary's. Angry townspeople are supposed to have shouted "havock, havock ... smite fast, give good knocks!" They ransacked halls and killed some of the inmates. There were deaths on the other side too. Rival deputations sought out King Edward III in Woodstock. His judgement, then and after calm had been restored, was firmly in favor of the university. Its privileges were once more increased—it retained a controlling hand in local government until the nineteenth century. (Between 1604 and 1950 the university was represented by its own two MPs, as against the city's one.) And every St. Scholastica's Day the Mayor, other officials, and 63 citizens—the number of scholars said to have been slain—were required to participate in a memorial mass at St. Mary's and to pay a penny each in reparation. In one form or another, this public penance continued until 1825.

The university often felt obliged to reassert its rule: it "will not endure," according to its charter of 1636, "to be subordinate to mechanicall persons." Convicted felons' goods would henceforth be forfeit not to the city but to the university. In the late seventeenth and early eighteenth centuries, there were attempts to prescribe, on pain of rather vague "Due Punishment," prices and times for stagecoaches and wagons carrying students, their parcels, and letters from Oxford to London. But nothing could stop periodical brawling. (5 November was a particularly popular day for street scuffles.) In 1867, for example, according to *The Daily Telegraph*, there were clashes in Jericho between "rough bargees and railway labourers glad to 'lick a lord'" and hot-blooded young students who thought it "an equal luxury to thrash a cad."

Oxford dons

Within the colleges dons (from *dominus*) exercised authority *in loco parentis*. Some would be remembered as dull or quaint Oxford figures while others would have some influence on the wider world through their students. W. A. Spooner, Warden of New College, apparently a kind and admirable man, was doomed to be remembered for his "spoonerisms." Many another "Oxford eccentric" has had his or her sayings, etiolated or otherwise idiosyncratic voice, or gown-hitching mannerisms imitated wherever former pupils are gathered. Others have been brilliant teachers, brilliant scholars, or both. And some tutors have belonged simply, like two Balliol specimens described by Mark Pattison, Rector of Lincoln College, to "the genus 'dry stick.'" "Their wit and themselves had been kept too long," felt Louis MacNeice; "the squibs were damp, the cigars were dust, the champagne was flat" (*The Strings Are False*, 1965). MacNeice, who came to Merton in 1926, admits, grudgingly, that there were exceptions. But on the whole, "When I think of Oxford dons I see a Walpurgisnacht, a zoo—scraggy baldheads in gown and hood looking like maribou storks, giant turtles reaching for a glass of port with infinitely weary flippers, and chimpanzees, cod-fish, washing blown out on a line."

Only after the university reforms of the mid-nineteenth century did most dons—dry, wet, or engagingly fluid—take much interest in teaching. "Mr Southey, you won't learn anything from my lectures, sir," the poet was told by his tutor at Balliol, Thomas How, in 1793; "so if you have any studies of your own, you had better pursue them." Little had changed since the "idle and unprofitable" fourteen months Edward Gibbon spent at Magdalen in 1752–3. As a well-read fifteen-year-old he "fondly expected that some questions of literature would be the amusing and instructive topics of [the fellows'] discourse" but instead, "Their conversation stagnated in a round of college business, Tory politics, personal anecdotes, and private scandal." Their own hard drinking excused their juniors' "brisk intemperance." Gibbon's first tutor was mildly encouraging but accepted without demur his excuses for non-attendance. (The requirement to go to lectures was often relaxed for the benefit of wealthy gentlemen-commoners like Gibbon: "a pert and pampered race" of "privileged prodigals" spat *The Gentleman's Magazine* in 1798.) His second tutor simply failed to teach him. No one set him any work, no one stopped him from going off on "costly and dangerous frolics" to London and elsewhere. He was soon "betrayed . . . into some improprieties of conduct, ill-chosen company, late hours, and inconsiderate expense." Gibbon laments the lack of guidance from his elders and the uninviting cur-riculum—mainly plodding classical translation—which in his case they failed to enforce. It was the legacy of foundation "in a dark age of false and barbarous science"—the Christian age which, for the au-thor of *The History of the Decline and Fall of the Roman Empire*, had replaced civilization in the early Middle Ages. His interest in books revived, he says, as soon as he left Oxford. (His conversion to Roman

Catholicism in June 1753 was the main reason his father removed him; he soon reconverted.)

By the time the historian H. A. L. Fisher arrived at New College in 1884 the tutors had been forced to adopt a less cavalier attitude to teaching, but the past lived on in the person of the "venerable" Dr. Sewell, Spooner's predecessor as Warden. Sewell had, in an earlier, unreformed Oxford, been "elected to the comfortable emoluments of a Life Fellowship" on the basis of translation of a chapter of classical history and exposition of a single proposition by Euclid. Himself unlearned, "he gave it as his opinion," Fisher records in his memoirs, "that most of the trouble in the world came from the writing of books . . . He did not teach, he did not lecture, he did not publish, he rarely admonished." He did work hard in the interests of the college, and delighted or amused the young with his "charming old-fashioned courtesy." Sewell's favorite duty, Fisher discovered when he had become a fellow himself, was his annual inspection of the college estates over several weeks of July. On these occasions

> the Oxfordshire rustic might behold a little old clerical gentleman with a tall silk hat and white bands driving in a carriage and pair . . . his eyes shaded by an antique pair of spectacles bought at the time of the first railway train, and in his hand a little black bag from which he would extract a looking-glass and a comb in order that his grey locks, of which he was careful, might be at their best when confronted with the feminine charms of the farmhouse. He knew the farmers, their wives and families, asked after the fruit-trees and flowers, and was ready with shrewd comment on the crops.

But the little old gentleman was not all smiling benevolence. He was a stickler for full payment of rent, and when a farmer's wife asked for financial aid with disinfecting the house "after two cases of typhoid in her family, my venerable friend replied sternly, and to the lady's obvious amusement, 'It is you, madam, who should compensate the College for allowing its premises to get into such an insanitary condition.'" Gown could still, apparently, dominate country as well as town.

Trinity College: Kettell and Bathurst

Trinity College owes its foundation, in 1555, to both the religious faith and the secular opportunism of Sir Thomas Pope. He was a good friend of Sir Thomas More but was content to make a fortune as Treasurer of Henry VIII's Court of Augmentations, the body which valued and disposed of dissolved monasteries and their lands. ("He is such a money man . . . as I can do nothing with him," a correspondent told Sir William Cecil.) Probably Pope felt that establishing a college for the training of Catholic clergy, with the approval of Mary I, made sufficient amends for his earlier work. He was no doubt pleased to be able to install Trinity in the empty buildings of Durham College, which until the Dissolution had been a house for Benedictine monks from Durham Cathedral. The death of the Queen in 1558 put an enforced end to Trinity's Catholic orientation, but the college remained grateful to Pope and, after his death in 1559, to his widow Elizabeth, who continued to take an active part in college affairs until her own death in 1593.

Sir Thomas' portrait hangs above the dais in the college hall, with the demure but forceful looking Lady Pope beneath him. Their tomb (and that of Sir Thomas' first wife) is by the altar in the chapel. It was the only element to survive the 1690s demolition of the fifteenth-century chapel of the Durham monks. Sixteenth-century Trinity students made do with the monastic buildings; their extension and eventual replacement fell mainly to two seventeenth-century Presidents, Ralph Kettell and his step-grandson Ralph Bathurst. (The Old Library in Durham quad is almost all that is left of the monks' college now.)

Kettell is fated to be remembered by John Aubrey's vivid account of his eccentricities. He came to Trinity to study in 1579 and remained there for the rest of his life, becoming President from 1599 to his death in 1643. John Aubrey knew Kettell when he was nearly eighty and Aubrey was a sixteen-year-old student. He was fascinated by the older man's mixture of strengths and foibles—his irascibility and traditionalism made him something of a figure of fun—and loved collecting stories about him. The President was a "very tall well grown man. His gown and surplice and hood being on, he had a terrible gigantic aspect with his sharp grey eyes." (The hall has a copy of a portrait by his stepson, George Bathurst: austere, rather sad, small white beard, black cap, ruffed to the ears.) Every Tuesday in chapel he would "expound on the Thirty-Nine Articles of the Church of England" and reprove the faulty; it was a mistake to wear a white cap, for Kettell shrewdly suspected it was the sign of a hangover. At other times his "fashion was to go up and down the college, and peep in at the keyholes to see whether the boys did follow their books or no." If he thought someone's hair was too long, he cut it at once with scissors or a bread-knife. He had a choice vocabulary for scolding idlers: "he used these names, viz Turds, Tarrarags ... Rascal Jacks, Blindcinques, Scobberlotchers." But some of his oddities were more amiable: he decided, says Aubrey, that the best way to prevent drunkenness was to make sure that Trinity had the best beer: no one would be tempted to go off drinking in town. He was also "a person of great charity": for instance he would "put money in" at the windows of students who were diligent but poor. It is hard to know which of these stories are true, but Kettell seems to have been ideally suited for inclusion in Aubrey's musing, quizzical, fragmentary *Brief Lives*. "One of the fellows ... was wont to say, that Dr Kettell's brain was like a hasty pudding, where there was memory, judgement and fancy all stirred together. He had all these faculties in great measure, but they were all just so jumbled together." If you took him for a fool you would be surprised by his "subtlety and reach." If you took him for a wise man he might strike you as a fool.

Kettell worked hard for Trinity. He added new attic rooms to the Durham ranges, he built a new hall—after the old one collapsed into its new cellar—and at his own expense put up Kettell Hall (used in his time for college accommodation, later sold off but finally bought back in 1898). He was also an accomplished fundraiser. This was a quality he shared with Ralph Bathurst, who was elected to a fellowship at Trinity in 1640 and became President 1664–1704. Bathurst succeeded, by patient persuasion and personal contributions, in collecting the large sums of money needed to carry through his scheme of transforming the college into a modern, indeed a fashionably "superior" institution. His friend Christopher Wren designed a free-standing building (1665–8) with up-to-the-minute mansard roof. (The building was later adapted, with the loss of the roof, as part of Garden Quadrangle.) Wren also made some suggestions about the plans for the chapel of 1691–4, but the main architect is unknown; some favor Henry Aldrich, Dean of Christ Church. Celia Fiennes pronounced it, soon after its completion, "a fine neat chapel, new made, finely painted." Lime, pear, oak, juniper, and walnut were used for the paneling, reredos, and decoration. The delicate marquetry altarpiece glows slightly orange. The frame of carved flowers and fruits is almost certainly by Grinling Gibbons. The painting of the Ascension—full of dramatic but assured Baroque gestures—on the paneled and highly decorated plaster ceiling is by Pierre Berchet. Carved angels seem just to have alighted on reredos and screen.

The chapel catered satisfyingly to both spiritual and aesthetic needs, but Bathurst's modern college provided also for more immediate wants: the archives, Clare Hopkins points out in her history of Trinity, record the erection of "a new lavatory or 'bog house' . . . in stone and slate."

The present college was completed by the incorporation of Kettell Hall and several seventeenth-century houses in Broad Street, and by the addition of Sir Thomas Jackson's 1880s Front Quadrangle buildings, Library Quadrangle (1928 and later alterations), and the Cumberbatch Building (1966). But the garden, as laid out in the mid-nineteenth century, is much better known than the buildings. Once it was a wooded "grove"—Kettell's "Scobberlotchers" were, says Aubrey, such youth as "did no hurt . . . but went idling about the grove, with their hands in their pockets, and telling [i.e. counting] the number of trees there, or so." Then, in the early eighteenth century, it was transformed into a formal garden with topiary pyramid, pillars, and spheres; potential Scobberlotchers on its broad, straight paths must surely have walked elegantly, hands nowhere near their pockets. Next to this garden were two avenues of elms and lime-trees. Now there are spacious lawns and borders and beside them a freer "wilderness." Here is a polite sign which ought to have some wider metaphorical meaning: "Please could you keep to the grass paths when walking through wilderness."

Laud and St. John's College: "a ceremonial space"

William Laud (1573–1645), President of St. John's, Chancellor of the university, and Archbishop of Canterbury, easily wins his place in a chapter about rulers—except that he saw himself only as enforcing the higher rule of Charles I and of God. Laud was, as he said, "bred up" at St. John's, the college founded in 1557 by Sir Thomas White and incorporating some earlier buildings from St. Bernard's College. (The main survival is the 1470s gateway surmounted by a statue of St. Bernard; the figures on either side are White and the founder of St. Bernard's, Archbishop Chichele.)

Laud arrived as an undergraduate in 1589 and rose to become President in 1611–21. But his greatest influence on Oxford, as on the Church, came after the accession of Charles I in 1625. The two men shared a passion for order. They feared the spread of disorder from Puritans in the Church and the university, from unruly undergraduates, and from over-mighty college heads and fellows. The university was, Laud reported in 1628, "extremely sunk from all discipline, and fallen into all licentiousness." As Chancellor, from 1630, he took the opportunity to address the problem. He was responsible for the new statutes of 1636, which increased the Chancellor's power and tightened discipline, including the wearing of correct academic dress. (There were bans on long hair, "that absurd and assuming practice of walking publicly in boots," hunting, and frequenting inns, taverns, and houses of ill repute.) He worked to ensure religious conformity and to install his nominees for college headships and other important positions. In the college chapels, he and his allies enforced such "high church" practices as bowing at the name of Jesus and to the altar, erected altar-rails, and installed fine paving and carpets. He also founded a lectureship in Arabic and donated many manuscripts to the Bodleian.

Laud lavished particular attention, and large amounts of his own money, on beautifying his old college. Canterbury quad at St.

John's, built between 1631 and 1636, was to be, as Howard Colvin says in his book about it, "a permanent memorial to his high standing in Church and State." It mixes Gothic and Renaissance classical elements—fan-vaulting for the roofs of the passageways leading in and out of the quadrangle, for instance, but Renaissance-style arcades—to form "a ceremonial space of great subtlety and sophistication" (Geoffrey Tyack's history of St. John's, 2000). The effect is enhanced by the quality and color of the stone: walls in Headington and Burford limestone, columns originally in so-called "marble" from Bletchingdon (with later repairs and replacements in Portland and Clipsham stone). The quadrangle is decorated at east and west with bronze statues of Charles I and Queen Henrietta Maria by the court sculptor Hubert Le Sueur and, above eastern and western arcades, with busts of the seven personified Liberal Arts and Learning and of the seven Virtues and Religion. (They are identifiable by the symbols which flank them—Temperance, for instance, by water poured into wine, Justice by sword and scales, Religion by bibles and churches.) These were probably the work of John Jackson, the mason whose best-known work is the porch of the University Church (1637). The whole project cost £5553.

In August 1636 Laud welcomed King Charles and Queen Henrietta Maria to Oxford, showed them his new quadrangle, and feasted them and the court. The most important guests, including the royal couple and Charles' nephews the Elector Palatine and Prince Rupert (of subsequent Civil War fame), ate in the new part of the library. (This had been added by Laud to the existing 1590s building and was later called the Laudian Library.) Anthony Wood records that "The Chancellor conducted the king and queen up the Library stairs, where, as soon as they began to ascend, certain musicians above entertained them with a short song fitted and timed to the ascending the stairs." As they reached the top they were greeted in verse by a "young scholar as in a rapture, amazed by what had seemed to be angels singing the royal names wherein all music dwells." It was one more of the graceful welcomes offered whenever sixteenth- and seventeenth-century grandees arrived at banquets, cities, or country houses. They proceeded to their extraordinarily lavish feast of beef, lamb, venison, partridge, pheasant, fish; it cost, including presents and entertainments, over £2000. Even the "baked meats" conformed to the hierarchical predilections of King and Chancellor: they were shaped or "contrived," according to the diary of Thomas Crosfield, fellow of Queen's, in the form first "of Archbishops, then Bishops, Doctors etc. seen in order, wherein the King and courtiers took much content." Everything went according to plan. It was one of those moments in the 1630s where hindsight is inescapable: preening host and dignified guest cannot have expected to die by the axe—Laud on Tower Hill in 1645, by then an almost forgotten figure amid the troubles of civil war, and Charles more famously at Whitehall in 1649.

Laud's body was reburied in a vault at St. John's chapel, near Sir Thomas White, after the Restoration. The chapel was largely remodeled in the nineteenth century, but some earlier memorials including the recumbent figure of President Richard Baylie (d.1667) are in the Baylie Chapel left of the altar. Here too, in striking contrast to the cool stone decorum of much of the chapel, is an icon of St. John the Baptist painted for the chapel by Sister Sawsan of the monastery of St. Bishoy at Wadi Natroun in Egypt. Christ is immersed in the blue Jordan except for his haloed head. St. John clasps his staff on one jagged bank, the dove of the Holy Spirit descends above, and on the other bank are two angels. One carries a red veil standing (a notice explains) for sin and crucifixion, the other a white one for redemption and resurrection. There is also a tree with seven fruits for the Seven Sacraments.

Beyond Canterbury Quadrangle are the gardens. H. J. Wilmot-Buxton describes or imagines a May scene here in his novel *The Mysteries of Isis; or, the College Life of Paul Romaine* (1866):

> Under the sweet-scented chestnut blooms . . . the nursemaids sat and gossiped and giggled . . . Under the same trees (though apart, of course, from the sirens), a few university men, who were too lazy to row, or cricket, or walk, basked at their ease, and read Tennyson or Dickens, or dreamed that they were through the Schools [final examinations] . . . Here and there a somnolent Don strolled

leisurely up and down the paths, and looked in contemplative manner at the flowers, or stopped before a garden seat and eyed it in a sternly argumentative manner, as though it were the audience in St Mary's, assembled to hear his forthcoming Bampton lecture. The gardeners mowed the lawn in a sleepy way, and seemed to have visions of rest and beer . . . All things in fact, animate and inanimate, basked in the warm May sunshine.

Females fortunately may now bask with the "university men" or lecture garden seats with the don rather than functioning only as nursemaids or sirens. Women were first admitted to the college as undergraduates in 1979.

There are still smooth lawns with views back to the long garden front of Canterbury Quadrangle. There are generous borders, trees, shrubs—rhododendron, camellia, bamboo, heathers, quiet walks on bark near the back wall, glimpses of Garden Quadrangle (1994). The most noticeable addition to the garden since Buxton's day is the rockery. An inscription tells us about Henry Jardine Bidder (1847–1925), "Fellow, Tutor, Bursar, Vicar of St. Giles, Keeper of the Groves. This rock garden which he made and loved is his monument."

There is a country-house feel in the gardens; urban foxes are common enough but it seemed strangely apt when I came across one walking quietly among trees next to the lawn as snow fell one recent January afternoon. Some St. John's students call the foxes who live here "Giles"—generically—in honor of St. Giles' Street.

"Vigorous pokes of the fire": Jowett and Balliol

Benjamin Jowett (1817–93) was elected as a fellow of Balliol in 1838, became Regius Professor of Greek in 1855, and was Master of Balliol between 1870 and 1893. He was shy, somewhat given to sulking, not one to suffer fools gladly, and was regarded with suspicion by the orthodox for his liberal churchmanship. (He contributed an essay on the rational interpretation of scripture to the controversial *Essays and Reviews* of 1860.) But he exercised immense influence on Balliol students, impressing on them an ethos of hard work—"the sense of power which comes from steady working"—and helping to launch many of them on highly successful careers. They became politicians, diplomats, judges, academics, bishops, and colonial administrators (including three successive Viceroys of India). He was a ruler and a producer of rulers; he wanted to "inoculate England with Balliol men."

The college had already established itself, under Richard Jenkyns (Master 1819–54), as the most academically distinguished in Oxford. The Royal Commission of Inquiry into the university (1852) attributed this success to the college's freedom "from all restrictions which might prevent the election of the best candidates to its Headship, Fellowships [and] Scholarships." John Betjeman professed to think that the reason was, rather, Balliol's traditional Scottish connection. Dervorguilla of Galloway had been the main founder of the college, whose statutes she drew up in 1282; it had started, under the auspices of her late husband John de Balliol, as a house in what is now Broad Street in the 1260s. It was mainly in the nineteenth and early twentieth century, however, that there were large numbers of Scots at Balliol. It was these hard workers who made it "the place of brain boxes," in spite, Betjeman whimsically suggests in *An Oxford University Chest*, of all efforts to discourage them. Even the architecture fits an image of formidable academic influence: "Like a great battleship," says Betjeman, "the Gothic buildings by Alfred Waterhouse sail along Broad Street." Oscar Wilde allegedly suggested, less flatteringly, that the college could be mistaken for a railway-station. On the other hand the central area, the rectangular Garden Quadrangle, has a relaxed atmosphere in which, as the name suggests, garden and quadrangle meet. There are some large horse-chestnuts and beeches, unmown areas for long grass and spring flowers, and smooth lawns for croquet or sitting. At one end a silver ball (2009), commemorating the thirtieth anniversary of the arrival of the first Balliol women, reflects the scene. At the other end, the attractive surroundings mute what would otherwise be the severity of the hall up its steep staircase.

A distinctive element contributed by Jowett was his personal involvement with every undergraduate who came into his care. As Master he made sure he knew them all and took a fierce interest in their future, pushing the workers on, reproving any who had the temerity to be idle. In general he was a progressive influence. Although he courted the interest of the rich and well-connected, he also worked to help poorer students. He abolished compulsory chapel on weekdays, established a chemistry laboratory in the same building as Waterhouse's new Hall in the 1870s, and encouraged sport and drama (ignored or frowned on by most of his predecessors and contemporaries) as contributing to the college sense of community. An ambitious production of Aeschylus' *Agamemnon* in Greek took place in the Hall, with Jowett's encouragement, in June 1880.

Much of Jowett's influence on young men was exerted over breakfast, in the quadrangle, on local walks or vacation reading-parties in Scotland, or by letter—continuing often into their later distinguished careers. He was, also, however, a keen exponent of tutorial teaching. His pupil W. L. Newman remembered his methods:

> Moments of musing and abstraction were allied in him with a singular alertness and rapidity of mind . . . [H]e used commonly to seat himself in a chair placed immediately in front of the fire and close to it, and to intersperse his abrupt, decided and pithy comments on one's work with vigorous pokes of the fire. Occasionally he would lapse into silence, and say nothing whatever perhaps for two or three minutes; but, if one rose to go, one often found that his best remarks still remained to be uttered. The silent interval had been a time of busy thought.

Jowett is not now generally well known. His memorial in the chapel seems sadly small, with miniature effigy, columns, and urns. But few dons have wielded their metaphorical poker with more effect.

The "universally curious Dr Wilkins" and Wadham College

The first strong figure in the history of Wadham was Dorothy Wadham, who between 1610 and 1618, in her late seventies and early eighties, showed remarkable energy and decisiveness in establishing the college. She never saw it, but firmly directed—from her home in Somerset—the purchase of the site of a former Augustinian friary, the new buildings, the statutes, and the appointment of Warden and fellows. Funds were left for the purpose by her late husband Nicholas "to found," as the widow declared, "a certain perpetual college of poor and needy scholars . . . to the praise, glory and honor of Almighty God, the increase of sound letters, and the common utility of this kingdom." The Wadhams' statues (restored), with James I's, figure in the "frontispiece" of the symmetrical first quadrangle of 1610–13. The chapel was also built at this time; a noteworthy survival is the painted east window (1622) by Bernard van Linge, with upper scenes from the New Testament and lower, prefiguring them, from the Old. The unusually large dining hall retains its screen and hammerbeam roof of about 1612.

Wadham enjoyed its first bout of fame in the 1650s. In 1648 the parliamentary Visitors removed Warden Pitt for "high contempt and denial of the authority of Parliament"—royalism, in other words—and told the college to receive in his stead, "as they will answer to the contrary at their peril," John Wilkins. In spite of this element of compulsion, Wilkins won approval from people of differing political persuasions; he married Oliver Cromwell's sister, Robina, in 1656 yet would become Bishop of Chester under the restored monarchy. He was remembered not as a sectarian but as a founding father of the Royal Society, a promoter of religious and political moderation and scientific enquiry. At Wadham he was at the center of a group who came together at first, according to Thomas Sprat's history of the Royal Society, only for "the satisfaction of breathing a freer air, and of conversing in quiet with one another, without being engaged in the passions, and madness of that dismal age."

Anthony Wood calls Wilkins "A noted theologist and preacher, a curious critic in several matters, an excellent mathematician and experimentalist, and one as well seen in mechanisms and new philosophy as any of his time." He was also interested in cryptography, the possibility of travel to the moon, and the nature of language and communication. When John Evelyn dined, in July 1654, "at that most obliging, and universally curious Dr Wilkins's, at Wadham," he showed him his newly designed beehives and much else:

> the Transparent Apiaries, which he had built like castles and palaces and so ordered them one upon another, as to take the honey without destroying the bees . . . He had also contrived an hollow statue which gave a voice, and uttered words, by a long and concealed pipe which went to its mouth, whilst one spoke through it, at a good distance, and which at first was very surprising. He had above in his gallery and lodgings variety of shadows, dials, perspectives . . . and many other artificial, mathematical, magical curiosities: a way-wiser [or milometer], a monstrous magnet, conic and other sections, a balance on a demi circle, most of them of his own and that prodigious young scholar, Mr. Chr. Wren.

Wren, until recently an undergraduate at Wadham, was now a fellow of All Souls and would go on to become Savilean Professor of Astronomy before achieving fame as an architect. Other members of Wilkins' "Philosophical Club" at Wadham included Robert Boyle, whom the Warden was responsible for bringing to Oxford, and Boyle's assistant Robert Hooke, who tried out some kind of flying-machine in the garden. (In the High Street a plaque on the wall of University College commemorates Boyle, who lived in a house on the site between 1655 and 1668; "Here he discovered Boyle's Law and made experiments with an air pump designed by . . . Hooke, Inventor, Scientist and Architect, who made a microscope and thereby first identified the living cell.") At the Royal Society after 1660 these enquirers would continue to challenge received certainties about the world. Empiricism, not the works of Aristotle, was their yardstick.

Slaughtering sacred cows: Bowra and Wadham

Another famous Warden would have approved of Wilkins' desire to stimulate thought, but not his scientific interests. Maurice Bowra, fellow of Wadham from 1922, Warden 1938–70, knighted 1951, was perhaps the most dominating, witty, literate, outrageously biased, and famous of Oxford dons. The bias was against not only scientists but politicians, bores, people he felt to be disloyal to him or the college, and anyone who did not take easily to his colorful and allusive conversation, wide literary knowledge, and classical scholarship. (His work is no longer much read, with the possible exception of his popular *The Greek Experience*, 1957.) His superb wit is usually seen as counterbalancing his more difficult side, and an essential lack of self-confidence is sometimes diagnosed to explain it; but it is also worth noting that he was a dedicated teacher, himself tirelessly loyal to Wadham and its undergraduates—like Jowett he tried to know each of them personally. He transformed a relatively obscure college into a center of academic excellence and was an ambassador for the university more generally. "He had the extraordinary gift," remembered Noel Annan in *The Dons* (1999) "of making people feel that life was more exciting, more full of possibility, adventure, depth, comedy and poignancy than they had dreamt possible." To spend an hour with him "was like being given a blood transfusion." As Leslie Mitchell points out in his 2009 biography of Bowra, he sought to challenge and stimulate students, encouraging generations who had been taught the virtues of repression and denial instead "to laugh with Aristophanes, who enjoyed 'mocking the great,' most of whom he found cranks and crooks." They should live with the intensity of the Greeks and other poets, not just learn about them. At his dinner parties, undergraduates were introduced to good food and good conversation and, "as sacred cows were slaughtered evening by evening . . . learned that life could be about what was possible, rather than what was allowed" (Mitchell).

Particularly remarkable were Bowra's rapid speech and booming voice. According to his friend Sir Isaiah Berlin (quoted in his biography by Michael Ignatieff), "the words came in short, sharp bursts of precisely-aimed, concentrated fire as image, pun, metaphor, parody, seemed spontaneously to generate one another, in a succession of marvellously imaginative patterns, sometimes rising to high, wildly comical fantasy." The voice climbed, fell, swooped, exploded as he uttered "his scandalous, reckless comments" (Annan), flavored sometimes with World War I slang. His witticisms, real or attributed—"I am a man more dined against than dining" is the best known—were treasured, repeated, and imitated like Wilde's. He was widely renowned, had many connections in Europe, and "was often," as Mitchell puts it, "mistaken for Oxford" itself.

Bowra is commemorated in Wadham gardens by John Doubleday's 1977 statue: "monumental but emergent in rather ectoplasmic style," feels David Piper, "from the back of an armchair." Gardens have always been a notable feature of the college, from the formal garden, replacing the orchard of Dorothy Wadham's day, where Wilkins and his circle experimented with their bees and speaking-tubes, to the lawns and trees of 1796 onwards. (What has mainly varied since is the arrangement of boundaries between Warden's, Fellows', and more general gardens.) The modern garden is rich in gingko, ferns, bamboo. As befits its intimacy, there is, in one corner, a recess with three seats, ideal for trysting, debating, or revising.

Querulous and quarrelsome?: Mark Pattison and Lincoln College

Richard Fleming, Bishop of Lincoln, founded his college in 1427 with the declared aim of overcoming (in Vivian Green's translation from the Latin) "those who with their swinish snouts imperil the pearls of true theology." (This may be the zeal of the convert: earlier in his career he had himself been suspected of holding heretical Lollard beliefs.) The first quadrangle was completed in several stages by the 1470s; work on Chapel Quadrangle began in 1608 and the chapel itself was built in 1639–41. Its cedar fittings and painted glass survive. The glass, mainly or wholly by Abraham van Linge, provides "typological" prefiguring of the New Testament by the Old, with twelve prophets in the north windows and the twelve apostles in the south, and more detailed links in the east window. Especially noticeable here is Jonah, who has just been belched up by the serried-toothed, tail-swirling whale—one baleful eye is visible— and, above, Christ who has burst, resurrected, from the tomb. (The parallel originates from Matthew 12:40.)

"Lincoln retains the comfortable sense of corporate security which characterized all the smaller late medieval colleges, echoing the inward-looking protective character of contemporary gentlemen's country houses," observes Geoffrey Tyack. Mark Pattison (1813–84), as one of the mid-nineteenth-century proponents of university reform, certainly found Lincoln "inward-looking" when he was elected to a fellowship in 1839. "The corporeal stature of the fellows is large, their intellectual small," he muttered to his sister in a letter; the older ones are "of the Port and Prejudice school." As a tutor at the college between 1843 and 1855, Pattison developed a reputation as a dedicated teacher. He was expected to become Rector (head) of Lincoln in 1851, but was kept out by the machinations of those opposed to his progressive views. Maneuvers included a meeting of "the opponents of college reform," unknown to Pattison, at the Mitre Inn, and a fellow being "knocked . . . up at 3 a.m." for negotiations (Pattison's *Memoirs*, 1885). True, as the candidate was aware, his social defects had not helped his campaign: working hard, he had failed to cultivate, as he saw it, "the life of easy sociability to which tutors of colleges were then accustomed." Dinner began at 5PM; leaving, even at 8PM, to give individual tutorials to his students, gave offense and his "lassitude and depletion of spirits" from overwork caused him to be "generally set down as unsociable, ungenial, and morose." When he missed the Rectorship, "My Satan had triumphed, and had turned my little Paradise into a howling wilderness."

After further vicissitudes Pattison was, ten years later, elected Rector. His manner had not improved, and he now seemed at least as interested in his own scholarship as in the welfare of the college. "For many people," Jo Manton notes in her introduction to the *Memoirs*, he "represented that archetypal British folk-figure, the querulous, quarrelsome, Victorian don." He was frequently sarcastic or silent with undergraduates and fellows alike. His marriage—permissible at the time for heads of colleges as not for other dons—to a woman 27 years his junior was, perhaps predictably, unhappy. One tradition claims him as the original of Mr. Casaubon in George Eliot's *Middlemarch*, the cold, selfish pursuer of outmoded learning and exhausting husband of the young Dorothea Brooke. In fact his scholarship was rather more up-to-date than Casaubon's, and he seems to have remained on friendly terms with George Eliot. Nevertheless, the difficult, somewhat sour Pattison may have contributed elements of the even more difficult Edward Casaubon. In 1875, several years after *Middlemarch* came out, he published a book about the real Renaissance scholar, Isaac Casaubon.

Oscar Wilde in 1882, four years after leaving Oxford: photograph by
Napoleon Sarony (Library of Congress, Washington DC)

5 | The Written Word
Oxford in Literature

Oxford has produced, consumed, and featured in literature since the days of Chaucer's Clerk of Oxenford. Oxford-connected poets include Donne, Shelley, Matthew Arnold, W. H. Auden, Elizabeth Jennings, Philip Larkin; among the novelists are Tolkien, Evelyn Waugh, Dorothy L. Sayers, Iris Murdoch, Penelope Lively, Vikram Seth, Philip Pullman. Since the late eighteenth century writers have often subscribed to versions of the "Oxford myth"—beauty, youthful joy, timelessness, privileged peace, perhaps intellectual or moral superiority, perhaps superiority to such concerns. "O ye spires of Oxford! domes and towers!/Gardens and groves! your presence overpowers/The soberness of reason," proclaims Wordsworth in a sonnet of 1820. (Reason is so overthrown that he is prepared, for a moment at least, to prefer Oxford even to Cambridge—to "slight my own beloved Cam.") Others question or contest the myth, rejecting the "static city preserved in syrup" (Javier Marías, *All Souls*, 1989).

A frequent starting-point for both devotees and critics is Arnold's hymn to the university, as its Professor of Poetry, in *Essays in Criticism*:

> Steeped in sentiment as she lies, spreading her gardens to the moonlight, and whispering from her towers the last enchantment of the Middle Age, who will deny that Oxford, by her ineffable charm, keeps ever calling us nearer to the true goal of all of us, to the ideal, to perfection,—to beauty in a word, which is only truth seen from another side? . . . Adorable dreamer, whose heart has been so romantic! who hast given thyself so prodigally, given thyself to sides and heroes not mine, only never to the Philistines! home of lost causes, and forsaken beliefs, and unpopular names, and impossible loyalties!

For Arnold the "lost causes" are mainly political and religious, for instance royalism during the Civil War, and religious belief doomed to decline in the nineteenth century. Later the loss is often more personal—the golden, decadent Oxford of Sebastian Flyte in *Brideshead Revisited* which can neither bring true fulfillment nor cease to inhabit Charles Ryder's dreams. And already, not long after Arnold created his Oxford, its "ineffable charm" lures the protagonist of Thomas Hardy's *Jude the Obscure* (1895) to his destruction. When after years of longing he arrives in "Christminster" and wanders enraptured, in the moonlight, from college to college, the danger signs are there. The stonework is decayed, the chambers "decrepit and superseded." And a policeman, suspicious of loiterers, moves Jude on after he has spent some time rapt in imaginary conversation with the great men of the university. As a stonemason he will later be able to do something about the external fabric of the old buildings, but nothing to make them less exclusive to someone from the wrong social background. He "daily mounted to the parapets and copings of the colleges he could never enter, and renewed the crumbling freestones of mullioned windows he would never look from." Jude's cause is lost from the beginning. Even within the academic community, and many years after *Jude the Obscure*, there are possible exclusions: "All that tawny stone, the enclosed gardens, the spires, the gates, everywhere gates!" is the first impression of Oxford for the heroine of Marilyn French's *The Bleeding Heart* (1980), a visiting scholar who feels shut out both as a woman and as an American.

Oxford has also provided an environment in which poets can develop their own myth, experiment with different versions of themselves as well as different forms of verse. Stephen Spender, himself searching for poetic and personal identity at the time, gives an impression of his friend W. H. Auden's mixture of self-certainty and youthful affectation in *World Within World* (1951). As a nineteen-year-old at Christ Church in 1927, Auden received selected fellow students "in a darkened room with the curtains closed" and cross-examined them about their tastes in poetry. Visitors might be dismissed at any moment, or treated to lectures "by one young writer to another" of the sort Auden once gave Spender when they were picnicking on a hillside—lectures "with their mixture of sense and nonsense, fun and portentousness, malice and generosity." The poet, he told him, is an everyman-figure with short hair, pin-stripe suit, and bowler (a sartorial choice which must surely derive from T. S. Eliot). He is no Keats or Shelley. The "most beautiful walk in Oxford," similarly, "was that along the canal, past the gasworks." But in other moods Auden was faddish about food, "sometimes carried a cane and even wore a monocle." Another friend of Auden, Louis MacNeice, trod the streets being even more conspicuously poetic. As recalled by John Hilton in the appendix to MacNeice's *The Strings Are False*,

> He was certainly a romantic figure . . . with his . . . large, dark eyes flashing and crackling with raging rhetoric, opening to enormous size in mimed astonishment at some banality or narrowing to slits to put him at an infinite distance of sardonic scrutiny . . . About this time he acquired a large knobbed ash walking-stick which was sometimes a danger to passers-by . . . "I Hate the world?" he would chant (with full value for the vowels and the "r") walking along one of Oxford's narrow lanes and swinging at the world's imaginary head; "don't you hate the world?"

Chaucer's Clerks of Oxenford

The Clerk or student of Oxenford is introduced in the General Prologue to *The Canterbury Tales* as sober, thin, and completely dedicated to his studies. He would rather have twenty books of Aristotle by his bed than fine clothing, fiddle, or "gay sautrie" (a psaltery—an instrument like a harp). What little money he can obtain is spent "On bookes and on lernynge." He speaks only when necessary, and then his words are always full of "hy sentence" and in line with "moral vertu." Later, accordingly, he will tell his fellow pilgrims the Tale of Grisilde, proverbially patient and obedient through the extraordinary sufferings her husband chooses to impose on her.

The pilgrim tellers move in and out of focus at different points in their Prologues and Tales. It is difficult, however, not to imagine a somewhat horrified or embarrassed pilgrim Clerk when the drunken Miller launches into his bawdy Tale of an Oxford student who cuckolds and tricks the carpenter he lodges with. Nicholas is apparently as keen on astrology as the Clerk is on his Aristotle, and the carpenter is somewhat in awe of him and his seeming ability to foretell the future. But Nicholas is much more interested in the carpenter's young and remarkably sexy wife, Alysoun; the Miller and Chaucer produce a tour-de-force of a description, part glowing and part gloating, of this "wylde and yong" creature, this "popelote." While the carpenter is off at Osney (perhaps doing some work for the abbey there), the student makes advances to the wife and she soon starts responding. Nicholas has a wheeze to get his landlord out of the way for longer than usual. He keeps looking upwards, which persuades the carpenter his studying has sent him mad. When questioned, the young man explains that he has discovered, through astrology, that the world is to be drowned in a flood the following Monday. But there is hope for some: Alysoun, her husband, and Nicholas will use flour-kneading troughs or tubs as miniature Noah's Arks, tethered at the top of the house. Cutting the cords, they will smash through the roof with axes and, as the water rises, float away. No one else, of course, must know. Naturally the carpenter falls asleep in his tub while the lovers climb back down and head "withouten wordes mo[re] . . . to bedde."

Alysoun has another admirer likely to embarrass the pious bookworm Clerk: Absolon, who is the parish clerk but also something of a dandy—curled golden hair like a fan, elegant clothes—and a womanizer. He even knows "twenty ways to trip and daunce" in the Oxford style. Alysoun, however, is not interested. With the cruelty allowable in farce and fabliau, she and Nicholas trick him, in the dark, into kissing not her expected lovely lips but her "ers." Absolon's revenge involves singeing Nicholas' backside—stuck out of the window to fart over him—with a heated plough-coulter. Finally, Nicholas' scream of "Water!" has the carpenter (temporarily forgotten by the listener or reader) cutting his rope, crashing down, and being passed off by the tricksters as a lunatic obsessed with Noah's Flood. It is, after all, a fabliau—a vulgar or corrective counter-balance to tales of Patient Griselda and the like.

Most of the pilgrim audience laughs at the Miller's Tale. The exception is Oswald the Reeve, at whom it was partly aimed. The Miller suggested he was a cuckold, and he used to be a carpenter. In revenge for the Miller's story of an Oxford student tricking a carpenter and having sex with his wife, the Reeve tells one in which two Cambridge students do much the same for a miller. The rivalry between the two universities seems to have been already, in about the late 1380s, well established. Both have claimed Chaucer for their own, but no one knows for certain whether he had any connection with either.

"What Ills the Scholar's Life assail": Samuel Johnson and Pembroke College

> I have heard from some of his contemporaries that he was generally seen lounging at the College gate, with a circle of young students round him, whom he was entertaining with wit, and keeping from their studies, if not spiriting them up to rebellion against the College discipline, which in his maturer years he so much extolled.

How much truth there is in this picture is unclear—"contemporaries" reported it to Bishop Thomas Percy, who told James Boswell. The depressive but determined Johnson throughout his life alternated bouts of hard work with periods of idleness. True, when he first arrived at Pembroke in 1728 thanks to a small family legacy, he casually failed to go to lectures—unaware, it is assumed, that attendance was expected. Years later Johnson recalled for Boswell the tutor's polite enquiry about his whereabouts over the last few days. "I answered I had been sliding in Christ-Church meadow. And this I said with as much *nonchalance* as I am now talking to you. I had no notion that I was wrong or irreverent to my tutor. BOSWELL: 'That, Sir, was great fortitude of mind.' JOHNSON: 'No, Sir; stark insensibility.'"

Much of the time, however, Johnson clearly did apply himself to learning. He had brought with him one hundred books from the stock of his father, a kindly bookseller in Lichfield. He read most "solidly," he said, in Greek, especially Homer and Euripides. At his tutor's suggestion he translated Alexander Pope's poem *Messiah* into Latin verse "as a Christmas exercise." (He spent Christmas in college, lacking the funds to go home.) "He performed it with un-common rapidity," says Boswell, "and in so masterly a manner, that he obtained great applause." But it did not, as he must have hoped it would, attract any kind of financial reward or the attention of a patron.

Johnson clearly knew more, and would have gone on learning more, than most of his contemporaries at Oxford. But he ran out of money. He stopped going across the road to Christ Church, where he was reading a friend's notes from a lecturer more inspiring than those available at Pembroke, when the Christ Church men started noticing that his feet were showing through his shoes. Someone tried to help by leaving an anonymous gift of shoes outside his room, but he "threw them away with indignation." Boswell says that Johnson left without a degree after "little more than three years"; in fact it was little more than one year.

Eventually Johnson succeeded in the world nevertheless, becoming known as an essayist, editor, biographer, poet, and author of the moral fable *Rasselas*. He was delighted to receive the degree of Master of Arts from Oxford University in 1755, in time for him to use it after his name on the title page of his great Dictionary. In 1775 Oxford conferred on him the more prestigious degree of Doctor of Civil Law, whence the authoritative "Dr Johnson." And he often visited Oxford between the 1750s and his death in 1784. His reading during his brief time at Pembroke laid some of the foundations of his learning. But leaving so soon, and in such poverty, must have been a bruising experience, and had been fol-lowed by much further struggle before success was achieved. In *The Vanity of Human Wishes* he remembers the optimistic enthusiasm of the beginning student, who burns with fever for renown and imagines "O'er Bodley's Dome [the Bodleian Library, 'dome' as in *domus*, house] his future Labours spread." But in reality life will not be easy, even if the "illustrious Youth" can win through to "the Throne of Truth" undistracted by false praise, difficulty, "tempting Novelty," sloth, beautiful women, disease, or depression. He should "pause awhile from Letters to be wise;/There mark what Ills the Scholar's Life assail,/Toil, Envy, Want, the Garret and the Jail." He later altered "the Garret" to "the Patron"—demanding or unreliable even if you could get one.

Against such adversity Johnson deployed prayer, friendship, and immense quantities of tea. His capacious teapot is preserved at Pembroke. There his "apartment . . . was that upon the second floor, over the gateway. The enthusiast of learning will ever contemplate it with veneration," says Boswell. Equally conducive to contemplation is the pale golden stone of the Front Quadrangle. John Betjeman, as an undergraduate wandering from Magdalen, admired clipped ivy and pink geraniums, "creeper-hung walls, intimate quads." In the spacious second quad he liked the "rich chapel decorated by Kempe" in 1884–5. Charles Kempe, one of Betjeman's heroes, provided highly colored stained glass, statuettes, and ceiling in red and gold. The original decoration, completed in 1732, had been notably plainer, perhaps more in keeping with the "polite and shy" Pembroke praised in Betjeman's *Summoned By Bells*.

"The late violent tyrannical proceedings of Oxford": Shelley and University College

Percy Bysshe Shelley, like Johnson, did not complete his degree. The circumstances of Shelley's leaving were, however, rather more dramatic. He came up to his father's old college (usually called "Univ") in 1810. His family were wealthy Sussex gentry, and he was expected to follow a career as landowner, liberal but respectable Whig member of parliament, and eventual patriarch. But he had already broken the mold, reading very widely in literature and philosophy— he must have been immensely more educated than most of the senior members of his college, let alone the junior—and publishing a Gothic novel, *Zastrozzi*. At Eton he refused to conform and was called "Mad Shelley." In Oxford he was soon known as a radical and eccentric. He was also passionately interested in scientific investigation; Thomas Jefferson Hogg, his only close friend at the time, remembered his rooms in the front quadrangle as equipped with "an electrical machine, an air-pump, the galvanic trough, a solar microscope, and large glass jars and receivers."

Shelley engaged in more dangerous intellectual investigation, writing his pamphlet *The Necessity of Atheism*. The eighteen-year-old author argues, with remarkable clarity, that proof is needed for any proposition and that hearsay is insufficient as proof. Most of his contemporaries, at least in public, regarded this as an outrageous and pernicious position—partly, no doubt, because it is difficult to answer. But the essay provides readers with food for thought whatever their religious beliefs. Throughout his brief, intense career Shelley insisted on examining and re-examining the deepest questions of existence: it was, it has often been suggested, an essentially religious response. He did go so far as to qualify his atheism when he revised *The Necessity* as one of the many notes to his long poem *Queen Mab*: the denial of God "must be understood solely to affect a creative Deity. The hypothesis of a pervading Spirit coeternal with the universe, remains unshaken."

Perhaps Shelley had turned a questioning eye on the Old Testament tales in the stained glass of the college chapel (by the Dutch artist Abraham van Linge, 1641). Adam and a curiously male-looking Eve are surrounded in Eden by happy animals, including a dromedary and a unicorn; temptingly luminous apples grow on the serpent-wreathed Tree of Life. In the background the couple are chased vigorously from the Garden by the Archangel, prompting thoughts of the coming expulsion of the pair of impious undergraduates. More to Shelley's taste might have been the memorial in the ante-chapel to Sir William Jones, the poet, oriental linguist, and judge who died in India in 1794. Jones writes calmly and intently, in Flaxman's sculpture, beneath a banana tree, as he gathers information from Indian scholars.

Summoned before the college authorities, Shelley refused to deny authorship of the pamphlet and was therefore sent down. Hogg, also loyally refusing to identify the author, suffered the same fate.

Shelley claimed in a letter to his horrified father that "I am perfectly indifferent to the late violent tyrannical proceedings of Oxford." He began an immensely complicated but poetically productive life in London, Wales, Ireland, Scotland, Switzerland, Marlow, and eventually Italy, where he drowned in 1822, just short of his thirtieth birthday. Once, in early September 1815, he came back to Oxford during a rowing trip up the Thames from Windsor with his friend Thomas Love Peacock, his future second wife Mary Wollstonecraft Godwin, and her stepbrother Charles Clairmont. He showed them, with a mixture of pride and irreverence, the sights; in one version of Mary Shelley's novel, Frankenstein visits Oxford and is puzzled, to satirical effect, by the "devotion to established rules" in a place where "some of the gentlemen wore light coloured pantaloons when it was the use of the college to wear dark." They were therefore "on the point of being expelled."

Oxford eventually found itself prepared to honor the former reprobate. The university was less keen, eighty years after Shelley's expulsion, on controlling undergraduates' religious beliefs or their choice of pantaloons. Mary Shelley and then her daughter-in-law, Jane, Lady Shelley, had worked hard to improve the poet's reputation—they emphasized his love of humanity and made him not a dangerous radical but a visionary, an idealist, a lyricist. In 1893 Lady Shelley donated important Shelley papers to the Bodleian Library, including his precious, interlined notebooks full of draft and finished poems and essays, canceled lines, jottings, and the rapid sketches of boats, domes, cubes, faces, and trees which he produced, his friend Leigh Hunt says, "in the intervals of thinking." Lady Shelley also commissioned, for a domed purpose-built chapel or shrine at University College, a sculpture of the drowned poet by Onslow Ford. Naked, he lies beneath a painted blue sky with stars and quotations from his *Adonais*, originally an elegy for John Keats. The Shelley Memorial has been much mocked for the seriousness with which it takes itself. Francis Haskell, in the *Oxford Art Journal* (1978), sees it more interestingly as drawing on "that slight ambiguity between death and sexual lassitude which had been so much exploited during the Baroque period in the portrayal of young martyrs."

Lewis Carroll

> She looked at the Queen, who seemed to have suddenly wrapped herself up in wool. Alice rubbed her eyes, and looked again. She couldn't make out what had happened at all. Was she in a shop? And was that really—was it really a *sheep* that was sitting on the other side of the counter? Rub as she would, she could make nothing more of it: she was in a little dark shop, leaning with her elbows on the counter, and opposite to her was an old Sheep, sitting in an arm-chair, knitting, and every now and then leaving off to look at her through a great pair of spectacles.

Such is the experience of Alice in the dream-world of *Through the Looking-Glass, and What Alice Found There*. Soon she will find herself in a boat, rowing the old sheep, and then back in the shop where an attempt to buy an egg effects her introduction to Humpty-Dumpty. The shop, however, has taken on a more fixed reality at 83 St. Aldate's, which John Tenniel drew to illustrate the scene—reversed, in looking-glass manner—and which is now active as Alice's Shop. Here you can buy not eggs but puzzles, earrings, pictures, cups, spoons, cut-outs, games, and books involving Alice, the Mad Hatter, Tweedle-Dum and Tweedle-Dee, and so on. The Disappearing Cheshire Cat Mug leaves only a smile when hot liquid is poured in.

Rev. Charles Lutwidge Dodgson (1832–98) arrived at Christ Church, on the other side of St. Aldate's, in 1850; obtained a Studentship or fellowship in 1854; lectured in mathematics; and continued to reside in rooms in college until his death. He lived at one time in Peckwater Quad, and later in a suite in the northwest corner of Tom Quad, with a roof-top studio for his photography. One of his former "child-friends," Ethel Arnold (Matthew Arnold's niece) reported in *Harper's New Monthly Magazine* in 1890 that the rooms of "Lewis Carroll" were "at one time a veritable children's paradise." The cupboards contained "endless stores of fascinating things" including "Musical boxes, mechanical performing bears, picture-books innumerable, toys of every description." He filled his albums with photographs—Arnold says of "boys and girls," but mainly girls—and let the wide-eyed children watch as he poured the strong-smelling collodion onto the negatives to develop them. The Museum of the History of Science has Carroll's box of photographic chemicals for use in this process.

Dodgson, who liked to keep his everyday and Carrollian identities separate, was rather displeased about Arnold's article. But entertaining and photographing children were clearly among his great enthusiasms in life. This preoccupation may now make us feel uncomfortable, and many a book and article has probed Dodgson's psychology—and that of Victorian society more generally—in search of closet pedophilia. It is difficult to completely accept the traditional idea that he was simply a shy bachelor who only fully relaxed in the company of children, although there is certainly some truth in it. One of his more hostile adult contemporaries, Rev. William Tuckwell, saw him as impossibly stiff: "austere, shy, precise . . . watchfully tenacious of his dignity," utterly conservative, "his life mapped out in squares like Alice's landscape," and generally a damper on college life. Several modern biographers have concluded that he was seeking an escape from the complexity of his relationships with adult women. Morton Cohen (in his biography of 1995) suggests that "suppressed and diverted sexual energies" were in fact the source of his creativity.

Dodgson first met Alice Liddell, her two sisters, and her brother soon after they came to Christ Church. They were the children of the new Dean, the distinguished Rev. Dr. Henry Liddell—former Headmaster of Westminster School, university reformer, and co-author of the authoritative Greek Lexicon. Dodgson understandably found the great man rather intimidating, but quickly developed a bond with the children, and especially Alice. He and a friend, Rev. Robinson Duckworth (the "Duck" in Alice's Pool of Tears), later took the girls on summer rowing trips on the Thames, usually downriver to Nuneham and occasionally upriver to Godstow. Dodgson told stories as he rowed, "yet," he remembered in 1887, "none of these many tales got written down: they lived and died, like summer midges, each in its own golden afternoon until there came a day when, as it chanced, one of my listeners petitioned that the tale might be written out for her." A note which Dodgson added to his diary entry for 4 July 1862 suggests that it was then, when the group picnicked at Godstow, that "I told them the fairy-tale of *Alice's Adventures under Ground*"—the first version of *Alice's Adventures in Wonderland*. He remembered a "golden afternoon," and the adult Alice Liddell Hargreaves talked about "a blazing summer afternoon with the heat haze shimmering over the meadows." Keen scholars have seized upon the less summery weather reports for 4 July to suggest that in fact their memories were at fault—it probably was not that day, and they may have gone to Nuneham not Godstow. But whether or not the details are accurate, an attractive myth of the creation of the Alice books had been born.

Since the publication of *Alice's Adventures in Wonderland* in 1865 and *Through the Looking-Glass* in 1872, readers have delighted in spotting Oxford references and visiting Alice-connected sites from Godstow to the Sheep Shop. The "old conger-eel" who is the Mock-Turtle's "Drawling Master" has been seen as John Ruskin, who taught the girls drawing at the Deanery. Tenniel's Alice with stretched neck may be inspired by the brass "fire-dogs" in Christ Church hall. Mark J. Davies (*Alice in Waterland: Lewis Carroll and the River Thames in Oxford*) proposes Alderman Thomas Randall, hatter of 22 High Street, as an original for the Mad Hatter to rival the traditional candidate, the top-hat-wearing Theophilus Carter, upholsterer at 49 High Street. Oxford adds yet another layer to the books—with Victorian politics, chess, class, parodied proverbs and poems and novels, natural history, mathematical patterns and jokes, and unsuspected Freudian psychology.

Alice's Day, each July, stages Alice-related events all over Oxford. It is coordinated by the Story Museum, whose premises in Pembroke Street are planned to open fully following refurbishment in 2015.

"The infamous St Oscar of Oxford": Magdalen College

My big sitting room looks north and from it I see nothing, not even a gable or spire, to remind me that I am in a town. I look down on a stretch of level grass which passes into a grove of immemorial forest trees . . . Over this stray the deer. They are erratic in their habits. Some mornings . . . there will be half a dozen chewing the cud just underneath me, and on others there will be none in sight— or one little stag (not much bigger than a calf and looking too slender for the weight of its own antlers) standing still and send-ing through the fog that queer little bark or hoot which is these beasts' "moo" . . . On my right as I look from these windows is "his [Joseph Addison's] favourite walk." My smaller sitting room and bedroom look out southward across a broad lawn to the main buildings of Magdalen with the tower beyond it.

C.S. Lewis, writing to his father in October 1925, gives an impres-sion of the size, rurality, and variety of the college where he taught for thirty years. The "eight-spired tower, delicately fluted and embossed . . . - the perfect prose of Gothic" of Henry James' tale "A Passionate Pilgrim" rises "in temperate beauty" above the traffic on Magdalen Bridge on one side and the peaceful walks of Magdalen on the other. Different worlds and times also seem to meet when, on May Morning each year, the choir climb the tower to sing their seventeenth-century hymn at 6AM with modern Oxford celebrating noisily below. Within the walls are the fifteenth-century chapel, the huge, cloister-like Great Quadrangle, and, up a staircase from it, the hall with linenfold paneling and portraits of college notables since the founder (in 1458), William of Waynflete, Bishop of Winchester. There has been a herd of fallow deer in the Grove, as described by Lewis, since 1700.

Lewis also mentions Addison's Walk. (By a bridge across a branch of the Cherwell, between the Walk and the Grove, is a round stone plaque inscribed, in Lewis' memory, with his poem "What the Bird Said Early in the Year.") Addison, the essayist, was a fel-low of the college between 1698 and 1711. His Walk, among trees, circles an extensive water meadow dotted in spring with purple and white snake's-head fritillaries. Lewis' view was from his rooms on Staircase III of the spacious New Building—new by comparison with much of the college—of 1733-4.

In the 1870s this seclusion was inhabited, or infiltrated, by an author very different from Addison or Lewis. Oscar Wilde moved from Trinity College, Dublin, to Magdalen in 1874. Stories and sayings, real and apocryphal, soon began to be attached to him; it was here that he first really worked at his flamboyant and paradoxical persona. His rooms were full of fine furniture, lilies, expensive china, ruby champagne glasses, and friends drinking from bowls of gin and whisky-punch. His remark that "I find it harder and harder every day to live up to my blue china" caused much, probably intended, public outrage against aesthetes. His scout, according to the 1929 memoirs of a fellow undergraduate, had to glide about in felt slippers. In Magdalen Chapel Wilde claimed, later, to have been reproved for such "levity at the lectern" as attempting to read from the sensuous Song of Solomon instead of the dry Deuteronomy.

While evolving or crafting his public character, Wilde also worked hard, on the whole, at his Greats (Classics) degree, although he got into trouble for failing to return for the beginning of term in April 1877 from a tour to Greece and Italy with his former Dublin tutor J. P. Mahaffy. "I found myself now in Corfu," Wilde wrote blithely to the Dean of Magdalen, expecting to persuade him of the educational merits of the trip. The college, unimpressed, fined him £47 and 10 shillings, and rusticated him until October. More creditably, he won the Newdigate Prize with his poem "Ravenna" in 1878 and eventually took the top first-class degree in his year. After this the college returned him the money he had been fined for his Greek escapade. He nearly—though it is difficult to imagine this phase lasting long—became an academic, failing only through a dearth of available fellowships. He also spent some time in anguished religious debate, became a Freemason, and flirted, sometimes quite seriously, with the idea of becoming a Roman Catholic.

Wilde was aware of his own contradictions. As his biographer Richard Ellmann explains,

> gradually while at Oxford he came to see [them] as a source of strength rather than of volatility . . . His paradoxes would be an insistent reminder of what lay behind the accepted or conventional . . .

> He would be neither a Catholic nor a Freemason; aesthetic one
> moment, he would be anaesthetic the next. This conclusion jibed
> with what was perhaps involuntary, his oscillation between the love
> of women and of men. As a result, Wilde writes his works out of a
> debate between doctrines rather than out of doctrine.

The Picture of Dorian Gray, for example, at once celebrates and warns
against the kind of life that may result from too much attention to
blue china or blue eyes. More humorously, Wilde described himself
at the end of his life as "the infamous St Oscar of Oxford, Poet and
Martyr."

"Centuries of youth": Hertford College and Evelyn Waugh

> Hertford was a respectable but rather dreary little college . . . The
> buildings are nondescript . . . The front on Cat [now Catte] Street,
> it has often been remarked, looks like a bank. But those who ad-
> venture beyond the lodge find a medley of odd constructions.
> There are ancient but unremarkable buildings in the front quad
> and a chapel and hall in Jackson's French renaissance manner. Its
> peculiarity is the "Bridge of Sighs" leading over New College Lane
> to the new buildings. There are no gardens.

Evelyn Waugh's account of his college in *A Little Learning* (1964) is
not very flattering. The "ancient but unremarkable" elements survive
from the medieval Hart Hall, which became a college in 1740 and
was re-founded in 1874. Most people think more highly than Waugh
of T. G. Jackson's contributions, including the grand hall staircase
inspired by the sixteenth-century spiral at Blois. Tourists traditionally photograph the Bridge of Sighs, whose popular name—which
must surely have started as a joke—salutes the Venetian version it
vaguely resembles.

Whatever his feelings about the architecture, Waugh admits
that in general his Hertford was a relaxed and tolerant place—not
the sort of college which, like Scone in his first novel *Decline and*

Fall, would have expelled an innocent young man whose trousers had been removed by his less scholarly colleagues (see p.133–34). Waugh himself lived peacefully in rooms overlooking New College Lane, above a pantry which left him with memories "of the rattle of dishcovers on foggy afternoons and the smell of anchovy-toast and honey-buns as the scouts filled their trays." But he felt that he had not yet found the "quintessential Oxford." This lay, for him, outside Hertford in his friendships with rich and outrageous undergraduates from Christ Church, Magdalen, and Balliol: in parties and clubs and in "the deep impulse to frivolity—maybe a delayed reaction to the austerities of wartime—that moved so many of [his] contemporaries" (Humphrey Carpenter, *The Brideshead Generation: Evelyn Waugh and his Friends*). He was keen to enter into this spirit, whether as an enthusiastic drinker and club member or a speaker at the Union so (deliberately) reactionary that he was admired as a comic turn.

In *Brideshead Revisited* (1945) Waugh made one of the most significant contributions to the myth of an Oxford which is all about champagne, lolling about on summer days, and eccentric young men with teddy bears. (Sebastian's bear Aloysius was inspired by John Betjeman's Archie.) Near the beginning of the novel, Charles looks back nostalgically to a time when "Oxford was still a city of aquatint" with "spacious and quiet streets . . . her autumnal mists, her grey springtime, and the rare glory of her summer days . . . when the chestnut was in flower and the bells rang out high and clear over her gables and cupolas, exhaled the soft airs of centuries of youth." Waugh later said that the rich language, food, and drink of the novel were a reaction to the "bleak period of present privation and threatening disaster" during which, in 1944, he wrote it. Hence the exaggerations and in part, as he rightly feared, readers' reluctance to see *Brideshead* primarily as a religious novel concerned with "the operation of divine grace on a group of diverse but closely connected characters." Sebastian's example might warn against a life of excess, but Charles is haunted by their Oxford days and mythologizes them as a glimpse of paradise. As Waugh was aware, he had subscribed to the Oxford myth even before he arrived at Hertford, long before he made his own contribution to it: he had "read all the Oxford novels that came into his hands." The 1981 television version and 2008 film of *Brideshead* cemented the glorious image.

Academic work featured as minimally in Waugh's and his friends' Oxford as in that of Charles and Sebastian. (One of their main activities was the consumption of large quantities of beer at the Hypocrites' Club.) Mr. Samgrass, the don in *Brideshead*, is merely mocked for his time-serving and vanity. Worse was reserved for Waugh's hated history tutor and Dean at Hertford, C. R. M. F. Cruttwell, an admittedly difficult man who had the temerity to re-prove Waugh for drunkenness and for not working. Waugh and a friend spread the rumor that Cruttwell engaged in bestiality. They put a stuffed dog in the quad and barked and sang for the Dean's benefit. Waugh persistently wrote stupid or objectionable characters called Cruttwell into his novels and stories. In "Edward of Unique Achievement" the history tutor is called Mr. Curtis but is obviously aimed at Cruttwell. Edward murders him. A dim nobleman gets the blame but the deferential authorities merely fine him thirteen shillings.

Beer and elves: the Inklings

One day in 1930, J. R. R. Tolkien, marking at his house in Northmoor Road, found that an exam candidate "had mercifully left one of the pages with no writing on it." So he wrote on it himself: "'*In a hole in the ground there lived a hobbit.*' Names always generate a story in my mind. Eventually I thought I'd better find out what hobbits were like." But without the equally memorably named Inklings the long gestation of Tolkien's best known books might have been even longer.

The group was, according to Tolkien, "an undetermined and un-elected circle of friends who gathered around" C. S. Lewis. The name was adopted, in about 1933, from an earlier literary club which Lewis and Tolkien sometimes went to at University College. "Inklings" was ideally suited to the new group: it suggests not only "inkling" as in "to have an inkling" but, humorously, a small person covered in or making much use of ink. It also sounds Saxon, Germanic, fitting with the philological and literary interests of several members. Tolkien was Rawlinson and Bosworth Professor of Anglo-Saxon from 1925 (later, in 1945, he became Merton Professor of English Language and Literature); Lewis, a fellow of Magdalen also from 1925, was his ally in the successful campaign to increase the early and philological content of the English course. Their friendship was, especially before World War II, at the center of the circle.

Lewis was effectively "at home" to the Inklings, on Monday or Tuesday late mornings, in the wood-paneled back parlor of a pub in St. Giles', the Eagle and Child, or "Bird and Baby." (Occasionally they met elsewhere, for instance across the road at the larger Lamb and Flag.) Beer and pubs appealed to their faith in robust Englishness and masculinity, their conservativeness, and their interest in northern legends where, again, there is little place for women or fine wine. But it was in the slightly more formal surroundings of Lewis' substantial sitting room at Magdalen, on Thursday evenings, that the Inklings put their own writing to the test. The poet and novelist John Wain remembered in *Sprightly Running* (1962)

> the electric fire pumping heat into the dank air, the faded screen that broke some of the keener draughts, the enamel beerjug on the table, the well-worn sofa and armchairs, and the men drifting in, ... leaving overcoats and hats in any corner and coming over to warm their hands before finding a chair.

With tea poured and pipes "well alight," Lewis, says his brother Warnie (Major Warren Lewis), would ask those assembled "Well, has nobody got anything to read us?" They read from work in progress as diverse as *The Lord of the Rings*, Warnie Lewis' book on the times of Louis XIV, C. S. Lewis' *The Problem of Pain*, and a nativity-play by Charles Williams (author of what T. S. Eliot diagnoses as "supernatural thrillers," an Inkling between 1939 and his death in 1945). They would settle down to "real unbiased judgment," according to Warnie, "often brutally frank." ("Oh no! Not another f-ing elf!" the Inkling Hugo Dyson is said to have groaned as Tolkien read yet more of his great work.)

Talk ranged, in fact, away from elves, lions, witches, and wardrobes to whether dogs have souls, the work of Conan Doyle, religion—most Inklings were believers—and "the nature of women." This last was not one of their more obvious areas of expertise. Lewis' relationship with and sadly brief marriage to Joy Davidman (1915–60) seems to have been one factor in the eventual cooling of his friendship with Tolkien in the 1950s. But even before Lewis met Davidman, Charles Williams seems to some extent to have taken Tolkien's place in his affections. Inevitably the old ties began to loosen. Lewis was appointed to a chair in Cambridge in 1954, though even in term-time he managed to spend long weekends at home in Oxford (see p.20), meeting some surviving Inklings at the pub on Tuesday mornings before he caught his weekly train. (He was helped by the existence of a direct rail link between the two cities, abolished in 1967.)

Although his *Narnia* books and his Christian apologetics were bestsellers, Lewis suffered less from the consequences of fame than the more sensitive and longer-lived Tolkien. His pipe-smoking, family-man normality, his very love of privacy, became aspects of a myth which appealed to some people as much as his writing. Sightseers began to bother him and his wife, by phone or in person, at 76 Sandfield Road in Headington—the otherwise peaceful street where they lived from 1953. They fled to Bournemouth in 1968. Tolkien returned to Oxford in 1972, after his wife's death, and himself died in 1973. His grave at Wolvercote Cemetery has become another place of pilgrimage. Among the visitors are people attending the annual "Oxonmoot" of the Tolkien Association on the weekend closest to 22 September, the birthday of both Bilbo and Frodo Baggins.

"The dance had entered a new phase": Iris Murdoch's *The Book and the Brotherhood*

Iris Murdoch (1919–99) had strong Oxford connections: she was an undergraduate at Somerville and Philosophy fellow and tutor at

St. Anne's between 1948 and 1962, and she lived much of her life either in Oxford or fourteen miles away in the village of Steeple Aston. She died at the Vale Nursing Home in Botley Road, a few years after she began to suffer from Alzheimer's—the subject of her husband John Bayley's *Iris*.

As a student, Murdoch was Chairman of the Oxford University Labour Club and a member of the Communist Party. But like many in her generation, she then moved further right while retaining keen liberal and humanitarian views. Her late novel *The Book and the Brotherhood* (1987) involves a group of former Oxford students who are now, similarly, distant from the Marxist ideals they once espoused. Since their radical youth they have been financing David Crimond to write a major book on politics. His radicalism is still untamed; he confronts, and on occasion physically assaults, members of the group; he challenges both their beliefs and their relationships.

Loss emerges early as a theme, with the characters' reunion at the summer ball of their old college, which is evidently Magdalen. There are the usual scenes of youth enjoying the night:

> Time passed, supper was over, and the dance had entered a new phase, the big expanse of grass between the glowing stripy marquees was covered with beautiful people, the handsome boys in their frilly shirts, now somewhat undone at the neck, the girls in their shimmering dresses, sleek and flouncy, now considerably less tidy, where here and there an errant shoulder strap, snapped when dancing the Gay Gordons, was being exploited by a laughing partner, and elaborately woven mounds of hair . . . had come undone or been demolished by eager male fingers and streamed down backs and over shoulders. Some couples in darker corners were passionately kissing each other or locked in wordless embraces, the longed-for climax of the longed-for evening. Some dresses carried tell-tale stains of grass . . . The dancing in the various tents was slightly less dense but wilder.

But the bliss at least temporarily available to the "beautiful people" cannot do much for their elders, who have lost both their looks and their ideals. "All those clear smooth transparent unspoilt unworked faces!" comments one character. "Not like ours," says Jenkin, "scrawled over with passion and resentment and drink!"

First-century CE Roman tragic mask, Ashmolean Museum
(Carole Raddato/Wikimedia Commons)

6 | Sound and Image
Oxford Film, Art, Drama, and Music

Film and Television

Film in Oxford started in the 1890s with a "cinematograph exhibition" at St. Giles' Fair and rapidly developed after 1910, when the Oxford Electric Theatre in Castle Street opened. Next came the Picture Palace in Jeune Street (1911) and four more cinemas by the end of 1913. One of them, the North Oxford Kinema in Walton Street, has had an unusually long life; it became the Scala in 1920 and the Phoenix in 1977 (now part of the Picturehouse chain).

The Picture Palace survived ten years or less but the building was reopened as the Penultimate Picture Palace in 1976. Distinguished by the large fiberglass hands of Al Jolson as sculpted by John Buckley—he based door-handles on Mae West's lips—it was one of a colorful range of enterprises involving the BBC Radio Oxford presenter Bill Heine. (The cinema closed again in 1994 but reopened as the Ultimate Picture Palace in 1997.) Heine also took over the Moulin Rouge (built as the New Cinema in 1923) in New High Street, Headington, and renamed it Not the Moulin Rouge. Here Buckley provided an appropriate pair of dancing-girl legs, transferred to a cinema in Brighton when this venue, too, closed in the 1990s. (In 1961, when the cinema opened as the Moulin Rouge, actual dancers greeted the Mayor with a can-can.) There were larger cinemas on the same site as the current George Street and Magdalen Street Odeons. The vast Majestic in Botley Road, which could hold over 5,000, had been built as an ice-rink in 1930 and was also used for dances and boxing-matches before going over to films only in 1934. It was commandeered as an evacuation center in 1940, and became the Frank Cooper marmalade factory between 1947 and 1967.

Film *of* Oxford is usually "dreaming spires" in emphasis. The splendor of Oxford in panorama underlines the poignancy of C. S. Lewis' late, brief relationship with Joy Davidman in Richard Attenborough's *Shadowlands* (1993). The locations for Hogwarts in the Harry Potter films include Christ Church hall and the Divinity School. The "Bridge of Sighs," Sheldonian, and other Oxford buildings are substituted for Harvard in the historical epic *Heaven's Gate*. The city stands for the idea of Englishness in *A Yank at Oxford* (1938) and its Laurel and Hardy parody *A Chump at Oxford* (1940).

Oxford scenes were made familiar to a wide television audience by Charles Sturridge's *Brideshead Revisited* and, often in more kaleidoscopic form, in *Inspector Morse* (1987–2000) and its successor *Lewis* (2006–14). Sometimes we linger as Morse, Lewis, or Sergeant Hathaway considers the murkiness of life over beer at the Trout Inn, or interview some arrogant don or shifty student in a quadrangle. Stretches of the Thames towpath are recognizable. A *Lewis* episode has a Tolkien convention at what is clearly the Lamb and Flag in St. Giles'. (Delegates wear elf-ears and the "sword of truth" is removed to be used as a murder weapon.) Often, however, the dome of the Sheldonian flashes past as the detectives race to a crime scene or drive up Headington Hill only to emerge—as far as Oxford viewers are concerned—somewhere completely unconnected. The more serious effect of the settings, in *Lewis* especially, is to pit violence and intrigue against idyllic quads, punts, and willows. *Morse* strayed rather more often into less idyllic streets, shops, and parking lots, sometimes but not always filmed in Oxford. But between them these very long running, rather slow, and ruminative programs have constructed a clear, identifiable—if mythical—Oxford: a police artist's impression of the criminal.

Oxford students themselves exploited the Brideshead image in *Privileged* (1982), advertised by a poster with Hugh Grant and the words "In the city of dreams . . . in a class of their own." Grant made his first appearance on screen as Lord Adrian (something of an "upper-class twit," as he himself was aware) in this low-budget (£30,000) piece directed by Michael Hoffman, an American Rhodes Scholar. Hoffman persuaded John Schlesinger, whose films included *Sunday, Bloody Sunday* (1971), to work with him as consultant director. Schlesinger helped secure finance and coached the student actors in Oriel gardens. The film, involving a complicated plot *about* student actors (they play in *The Duchess of Malfi*), was generally regarded as rather embarrassing, but it successfully drew attention to participants, including Grant, Hoffman, Imogen Stubbs, and Charlie Mole.

"These theatricals": drama in Oxford

"I've lost an awful lot of time over these theatricals," says Lord Fancourt Babberley ("Babbs") of St. Olde's College, Oxford, in Brandon Thomas' farce *Charley's Aunt* (1892). "But next term I mean to work." He does not yet know that, having tried on women's clothes for play-acting, he will be forced, with comic and complicated results, to impersonate a fellow-student's aunt, an old lady who has lived for many years in Brazil "where the nuts come from," for the rest of the play. Other Oxford undergraduates have for generations shared Babbs' thespian passion—usually meaning to work next term, but rarely co-opted as college aunts. They perform Aristophanes and Beckett, Pirandello and Ayckbourn—and Brandon Thomas. Students, and a great variety of non-student groups, act at the Playhouse, the Old Fire Station in George Street, the Pegasus in East Oxford (used mainly for children's and youth theater), the North Wall Arts Centre in Summertown, pubs, churches, halls, schools, and gardens. Also within reach of Oxford are the Mystery Plays at the church in Long Crendon (near Thame), with actors drawn from the local community and to be seen not only on stage but as devils and apostles driving vans on their way to act. Knights who guarded the tomb of Christ refresh themselves, swords piled outside the pub.

"Trimming up a stage": college drama

Considerable industry went into the plays and shows with which colleges entertained themselves in the sixteenth and seventeenth centuries. Most productions were in the halls of the larger colleges such as Christ Church, St. John's, and Magdalen, with a stage close to one end across which two "houses" faced each other. Carpenters constructed scaffolds for the more important spectators—the rest may have stood like the "groundlings" in public theaters. A list of "Recknings about the Playes" survives in the archives of St. John's College, where expenses in 1617 included two shillings for a joiner to fix a "Cornish" or cornice on the screen, twelvepence for "sending to Wolvercote, for arras, and for horse-hire," and over forty shillings for the carpenter's main work of "setting up the stage and scaffold." Various sums were dispensed for "New College Gentlemen, which sang both nights," for mending canopies, for candles, for a quire of paper on which to write out two copies of the tragedy. Much of the expenditure relates to costume: two shillings for two pairs of black gloves; eighteenpence "for making the two Judges' hats"; sixpence worth of pins; payments to Boswell and Chillingworth the mercers, Jennings the tailor, and the maid who delivered some "apparel"; eighteen shillings for vizards or masks "lost, and broken and the loan of other." The list also includes payment of some ten pounds, six shillings, and sixpence for wine, nearly a pound for "buttered beer etc.," and sixpence for "sugar candy."

It seems to have been generally felt that such costs—even the drink and the candy, perhaps—were justified by the educational value of the plays. They were often in Latin, often by college playwrights; in 1584 the Earl of Leicester called them "commendable and great futherances of learning." At the same time, as Chancellor of the University, Leicester reinforced earlier regulations banning professional players from performing there. (He was thus able to please the university on the one hand and his Puritan political allies on the other.) The city, not the university, was left to finance such more popular fare as the 1610 production of *Othello* by Shakespeare's company, the King's Men. Probably they acted in the yard of the King's Arms, probably with Richard Burbage in the title role, perhaps with Shakespeare also present.

Even within the university, of course, there were those who had distinct reservations about stage-playing in general. John Rainolds, President of Corpus Christi College between 1598 and 1607 and author of *Th'overthrowe of Stage-Plays* (1599), thought it no "good work or service unto Christ, to spend thirty pound in trimming up a stage and borrowing robes out of the revels" (the office of the royal Master of the Revels).

Playing your part: Elizabeth I in Oxford

Royal visits were a golden opportunity to show off loyalty, learning, and dramatic ability—and thus perhaps to gain worldly advancement. When Elizabeth I came in 1566, the plays she watched at Christ Church were only part of the larger performance. Leicester and "three doctors in scarlet gowns and hoods" had met her at Wolvercote and staffs of office had been ceremonially presented and returned. A welcoming speech was given here and another, by the Mayor, a mile further on. Gracefully no doubt, he gave the Queen not only words but "in the name of the whole city a cup of silver double gilt in value ten pounds, in the which cup was about forty pounds in old gold." At last she reached the North Gate and, having paused to hear more learned speeches, processed along Cornmarket to Carfax and on to Christ Church. The streets were lined with scholars in order of precedence. As she passed in her litter they knelt and shouted "Vivat Regina!" and she gave thanks. There were yet more orations at the gate of Christ Church.

The Queen impressed the spectators, as usual, with her wisdom and apparent spontaneity. She apologized for her little learning and satisfyingly contradicted the apology by answering a Greek speech in Greek. But decorum seems to have broken down when it came to the presentation of Richard Edwards' play *Palamon and Arcite* (derived from Chaucer's *The Knight's Tale*) in Christ Church hall. The occasion started unfortunately when "the press of the multitude who thrust down a piece of the side wall of the stair" killed a student, a cook at Corpus, and a brewer, and injured five others. The Queen sent her surgeons to do what they could, and after some delay the performance went forward, with her soon laughing "full heartily . . . at some of the players." Perhaps her laughter after the deaths was a little insensitive by modern standards. But she was not, in any case, supposed to be laughing at most of the actors. Like the superior on-stage spectators in *A Midsummer-Night's Dream* a generation later, she joked about the dramatic situation or acting abilities of the student playing the lover Palamon: "I warrant him he dallieth not in love when [i.e. 'if'] he was in love in deed." Miles Windsor, a fellow of Corpus who acted in the play and gives this account of it, could apparently hear everything she said. (His narrative, and a wealth of other material, is given in *Records of Early English Drama: Oxford*, edited by John R. Elliott and others.) Perhaps Windsor was on stage or in one of the stage "houses," open-mouthed, weak with laughter or with worry about what Elizabeth might say next. She went on to admire—sarcastically?—Palamon's rival Arcite as "a right martial knight who had indeed a swarse [swarthy] and manly countenance." A certain John Dalaper, not surprisingly, was "out of his part" and missed his cue. He swore either by the mass or by God's blood and started whistling a hornpipe; both the Queen and Master Secretary Cecil called him a knave. They may have been enjoying themselves, now, after listening to so many speeches by pompous characters in gowns.

Windsor tells us that Elizabeth did admire the acting of the lovers, including whichever young man sang and gathered flowers as Emily. She was tactful enough, at least, to tell them so, and to give out some rewards, one of them to Queen Hippolyta—or John Rainolds, the future voluble Puritan critic of cross-dressing and other such ungodly behavior. And she said it was Edwards' best play (no text survives), even better than his *Damon and Pythias*. But the audience interaction had not ended with the Queen's earlier comments. A spectator became agitated when the characters were throwing jewels and other "tokens" into Arcite's funeral pyre, and grabbed an actor by the arm. The nobility often provided actors with discarded garments, and in this case it was known that Elizabeth had given a cloak belonging to her brother, the late King Edward VI. "God's wounds!" said this "stander by," "what mean ye? Will ye burn the King Edward cloak in the fire?" A near brawl developed, with the playwright himself, who was probably also one of the players, calling the man a fool and the Queen intervening to ask him to let go of the actor, who only "playeth his part." It seems unlikely that the cloak was really going to be burnt; the disruptive bystander seems to have had a defective grasp of the principles of dramatic illusion. Perhaps he was over-excited by the presence of the real royal spectator.

Student drama: from *The Floating Island* to OUDS

Other dramatic entertainments were put on for visiting royals. Elizabeth came back in 1592 James I came in 1605 (allegedly falling asleep during one lengthy Latin play). But some of the most interesting records concern two productions at Christ Church for Charles I in 1636: William Strode's *The Floating Island* and William Cartwright's *The Royal Slave*. What excited particular interest was their innovative staging by Inigo Jones. He had designed simpler perspective sets for Oxford in 1605, but this time the technology and the effects were more spectacular. Flats and grooved shutters delivered what Brian Twyne, the university archivist, described as "A goodly stage . . . after the new fashion." In *The Royal Slave* there were scenes of "a curious temple and the sun shining on it . . . and curious prospects of forests and the like . . . with villages and men visibly appearing . . . going up and down here and there, about their business etc." Most of the audience, used only to minimalist Renaissance staging conventions, had seen nothing like it. Christ Church spent, for the two plays, £300 on costumes, £260 on the scenes, and £122 on music. The student actors had been coached by Joseph Taylor of the King's Men, and music was supplied by the court composers William and Henry Lawes.

Historians of drama and theater have found relatively little to say about Oxford between the late 1630s and the 1790s. The university, banning students from acting and even paying professionals to go elsewhere, now took a view of drama not unlike Rainolds' and his fellow Calvinists. (Students and some of their elders often contrived, nevertheless, to get to plays in Abingdon, Woodstock, and other nearby towns and villages with theaters, inns, or halls.) The Licensing Act of 1737 further hampered free performance. And even in much later times there was a common—sometimes justifiable—concern that involvement in drama was detrimental to students' work. "Dons . . . most dons anyway," Irwin warns a 1980s

Oxbridge candidate in Alan Bennett's *The History Boys* (2004), "think the theatre is a waste of time. In their view any undergraduate keen on acting forfeits all hope of a good degree." Nevertheless, in the 1840s students—sometimes with the help of the odd don—started forming acting clubs and performing burlesques in private rooms or away from Oxford. There were many reversals—all student acting was banned again for a time after 1869. But eventually, successful dramatic societies were formed: the Philothespians in 1879 and then, in 1884, the longer-lived Oxford University Dramatic Society, or OUDS.

The Victoria and New Theatres

Victorian students had the opportunity, unlike many of their predecessors, to watch some professional theater. Visiting companies played sometimes in the Town Hall. The Victoria or Theatre Royal in George Street opened in 1836, originally showing plays out of term-time and music-hall when the students were in residence. It had a poor reputation. The actor-manager Sir Frank Benson claimed that during and just after his Oxford student days the pit

> had to take umbrellas to shield themselves from being pelted and spat on by the gods in the gallery. The umbrella was not only a shield but a weapon of offence when the pit rushed upstairs to retaliate. The front row of the stalls spent most of its time in destroying the instruments of the orchestra . . . The dress-circle would rush on to the stage, via the boxes, dance with those prima donnas who were pretty, engage in pugilistic encounters with the officials and actors, or attempt to give impromptu performances of their own, until driven back to their places by volleys of stones, sticks, bricks, eggs, oranges, teacups and potatoes from pit and gallery.

If there was a raid by the Proctors and Bulldogs—university disciplinary officials—the undergraduates fled in all directions, breaking windows and drainpipes and stage ventilators. No doubt Benson is exaggerating somewhat, but reports of riotously non-educational events at the Victoria were one factor in encouraging

Benjamin Jowett, as Vice-Chancellor, to decline to renew the theater's license for 1884–5. Instead, next door, the New Theatre was built, opening in 1886 with an OUDS production of *Twelfth Night*. At first the society was allowed to perform only Shakespeare and Greek drama; Jowett had been heartened about the prospects for student drama by the production of Aeschylus' *Agamemnon*, in which Benson played Clytemnestra, at Balliol in 1880. It was a grand and, in some accounts, impossibly tedious experience.

There were some notable performances at the New Theatre, including several directed by John Gielgud. But it proved too big for student productions, especially after its rebuilding in 1934 in what Humphrey Carpenter calls "brash Art Deco"; the last OUDS production here was in 1938. The building—renamed the Apollo between 1977 and 2003, now again New—is well suited to big theater including touring opera and musicals. At the operas, before surtitles and electronic devices, an intimate atmosphere remained possible when, high in the Balcony, people used to consult synopses with the aid of juddering bicycle-lights.

The Playhouse

Between 1923 and 1937 the original Oxford Playhouse functioned at 12 Woodstock Road, a building put up in 1906 which had been used as a garage and a big-game museum "where the mouldy heads of disconsolate tigers and buffaloes looked down from distempered walls" (*Picture Post*, 5 November 1938). Apparently "the hall was cold, and shook whenever a bus went by," and for a time in 1930 it closed down and became a miniature golf-course. Audiences, too, were often small. But the company struggled on until 1937 when, with the new Playhouse in Beaumont Street under construction, the old hall—often called "the Red Barn"—was bought by the city. Later it was used for gas-mask distribution. It is now a language center.

The new Playhouse, which cost £24,000, contributed partly by the London theater-owner Eric Dance, was opened by the MP and comic writer A. P. Herbert in 1938. The first production was *And So To Bed*, a play about Samuel Pepys by the old Playhouse's first director, J. B. Fagan. Since then running the theater has rarely been easy. There has been a long history of uneasy relations between university and theater, and between aesthetic and commercial considerations. Between 1961 and 1987 it was owned by the university. There were productions by OUDS, by visitors, and by the resident company—first the Oxford Repertory Players, then from 1956 Frank Hauser's Meadow Players, then Anvil Productions (1974–87) which became the Oxford Stage Company. But it was always difficult to fill the theater, and government spending-cuts eventually caused it to close between 1987 and 1991. It was then taken over by the Oxford Playhouse Trust, set up by the university. Don Chapman, in his history of the Oxford Playhouse (2008), concluded that "a new, more understanding and mutually beneficial relationship" between theater and university had been worked out. Modernization of the theater was made possible by an award of £2.5 million from the National Lottery in 1995.

All sorts of drama have been produced here: Stephen Spender's version of the *Oedipus* plays, farces, protest plays, romantic comedies, Shakespeare, musicals, Gilbert and Sullivan, operas, Chekhov, annual pantomimes, and *Spot's Birthday Party*. Many actors and performers well known either at the time or later have played here, among them Sean Connery (a now improbable Pentheus in Euripides' *Bacchae* in 1959), Judi Dench, Ian McKellen, Leonard Rossiter, Hugh Quarshie, Rowan Atkinson, Imogen Stubbs, Antony Sher. Oxford's later Pythons Terry Jones and Michael Palin appeared in 1964 in the circus-like, anti-capital-punishment production *Hang Down Your Head and Die* (written by David Wright, directed by Braham Murray for the ETC, the Experimental Theatre Company founded by Nevill Coghill in 1936). At the end Jones, a clown, went screaming to the gallows while the rest of the cast took their bows.

Burton-Taylor: *Dr. Faustus* at the Playhouse

Richard Burton was involved, in 1966, in the production which attracted more attention than any other. He had first acted in Oxford in 1944 when, as an eighteen-year-old RAF officer cadet on a six-month course at Exeter College, he played Angelo in a production of *Measure for Measure* in Christ Church cloisters. The director had been his English tutor at Exeter, Nevill Coghill. Burton told him he would like to come back and act for him again. In the meantime, in 1956, by then very well-known, he provided £2000 to help Frank Hauser establish the Meadow Players. Finally in 1966 he agreed to appear in the title role of *Dr. Faustus* in Coghill's production at the Playhouse. Students played lesser parts but Elizabeth Taylor, Burton's wife and one of the most talked-about film stars of the day, was Helen of Troy—a silent apparition in the play, but one who elicits "Was this the face that launched a thousand ships, and burnt the topless towers of Ilium?" Don Chapman, in *The Oxford Mail*, thought that

> The appearance of the one woman whose beauty can stand comparison with Marlowe's rolling words inevitably lifts the atmosphere of the evening. Her reappearance somewhat after the fashion of a marine Venus raises it to fever pitch and Burton's quiet, soulful delivery of "Was this . . . ?" provides the perfect springboard for the tempestuous magnificence with which he encompasses the torment of Faustus' end.

The popular view that Burton, the classical actor, had sold his soul in a Faustian pact for Taylor, money, and Hollywood added piquancy to the choice of play. "Everybody is offered a choice," he said of Faustus at the press conference. Many reviewers felt he had underplayed the part—perhaps not wanting to out-gun his student partners too obviously. He seems to have rehearsed for only ten days. He was not word-perfect, and got his breathing wrong.

The film version of the production failed at the box office, but Burton and Taylor were still able to provide badly needed financial help for the Playhouse. After many delays a studio theater, offices, and workshops were built at the back of the theater, opening in 1976 as the Burton-Taylor Building. Burton had dreamed of doing *King Lear* in Oxford and, even, of coming back as an Oxford don. A miner's son taken up and adopted by his schoolteacher and allowed to glimpse university life in 1944, he was a persistent reader with a special passion for poetry. In 1968 he was approached by Francis Warner—poet, playwright, and tutor at St. Peter's College—with the idea that he should stand in for him for a term. Burton was excited, planning, in his diary, to teach either medieval or Metaphysical poetry; he "will lecture them until iambic pentameter comes out of their nostrils." Finally—work and alcohol having intervened—he did do some teaching at St. Peter's in 1973. "All accounts agree that he was a quirky but inspiring teacher," says Melvyn Bragg in *Rich: the Life of Richard Burton.*

Worcester College: "a shower of golden stars over the dark garden"

The first recorded OUDS piece to be done outside was in the gardens at Worcester: a version, in 1895, of *Alice in Wonderland.* Humphrey Carpenter in his book on OUDS notes that, when the Vice-Chancellor ruled that admission fees could not be taken, the company found the aptly Carrollian solution of charging "a fee for *going out.*" The elegant gardens and lake, laid out in the early nineteenth century, complement the buildings, almost all of which are eighteenth-century. Other periods contributed the fifteenth-century "camerae"—the houses of the monastic Gloucester College which was replaced by the secular Gloucester Hall which in turn became, in 1714, Worcester College—and the dramatic Victorian decoration of the chapel by William Burges. The 1983 Sainsbury Building by MacCormac, Jamieson, and Pritchard "rises romantically from the edge of the lake in a picturesque arrangement of cubes and pitched roofs, with much external wood and rubble stone" (Geoffrey Tyack).

Worcester gardens hosted the most famous production as well as the first. In 1949 Nevill Coghill, English don at Exeter College, renderer of Chaucer into modern verse and popular amateur director, put on *The Tempest.* The cast included Nigel Davenport as Gonzalo and John Schlesinger as Trinculo. But the production was remembered more for visual effects than for acting. The goddesses for the masque in Act Four materialized from the dark lake in a disguised punt, and just before the end a large, lighted galleon appeared—again a structure supported by several concealed punts. Next, Carpenter quotes the Ariel, Charles Hodgson, as remembering, "Prospero set Ariel free, and bade farewell to Caliban who dropped back into the water whence he had ... crawled" at the beginning of the evening—in fact he went back into his lake's edge "galvanized iron tub." The boat moved off with Prospero and the others bound for Italy. And then, thanks to a runway of duckboards just beneath the water and a ramp in the garden, Ariel astonished the audience by running across the lake and back and up into the trees. Coghill's former student, the art historian Sir Michael Levey, describes (in the 1966 retirement volume *To Nevill Coghill from Friends*) how Ariel "ran out across the water in farewell and escape, abruptly metamorphosed into a firework that soared and then broke in a shower of golden stars over the dark garden." As the flare exploded, says Hodgson, every other light went out "as though dowsed by the magic of Ariel himself."

The lake continued useful. In the 1970s, for instance, two empty-headed marquis in Molière's *Le Misanthrope* arrived rowing a boat, and Petruchio in *The Taming of the Shrew* threw Kate—amid audience gasps of "Surely he won't?"—into the water. On dry land, also at Worcester, the now familiar facial and verbal contortions of Rowan Atkinson, then a graduate student at Queen's, convulsed spectators when he played Touchstone in *As You Like It*.

Oxford Art

The city and landscape are popular subjects for painters. J. M. W. Turner visited often from his teens, in the late 1780s and early 1790s, onwards. For commercial as well as artistic reasons he made frequent watercolor studies of Christ Church and Magdalen. He provided topographical drawings for the *Oxford Almanack* between 1798 and 1804, setting off grand Gothic buildings with rustic or homely figures in the foreground. Working in oil, he painted, in 1808, cows beneath a broad, empty sky at Dorchester Mead, the confluence of the rivers Thame and Thames; and in 1810, the High Street with picturesque figures in caps and gowns and the spires of St. Mary the Virgin and All Saints (now in the Ashmolean Museum). In later years, and styles, Turner continued to use Oxford subjects. A watercolor of the High Street from the 1830s dissolves it in hazy light in the manner of his Venice. A view of Christ Church of the same period shows its bright, imposing bastions and Tom Tower dwarfing the everyday efforts of the building workers across St. Aldate's Street. (They are demolishing old almshouses to make room for a new entrance to Pembroke College.)

William Turner of Oxford (1789–1862), so called to distinguish him from his more famous namesake, grew up in Oxfordshire and frequently returned to it for his subject matter: topographical views of Oxford (he lived at 16 St. John Street from 1833), landscapes around Woodstock and on Otmoor, water-lilies and eel-traps on the Cherwell. It is a sometimes nostalgic vision of an older, freer world: Otmoor before it was enclosed, a scene in Wychwood Forest (1809)—horses and flourishing trees—"where a pleasure fair was formerly held" before the Duke of Marlborough began to restrict it. On a different note, satirical artists had much Oxford fun: Thomas Rowlandson, for instance, treats us to some rotund, lecherous, and greedy "Bacon Faced Fellows of Brasen Nose, Broke Loose" (1811).

Oxford is itself full of art. There are exhibitions of recent and contemporary work at Modern Art Oxford (an imaginatively converted brewery in Pembroke Street). Hundreds of local artists exhibit around Oxfordshire each May in the Artweeks festival. Summer degree shows at the Ruskin School of Drawing and Fine Art are also open to the public. (The university Department of Fine Art has been established here, at 74 High Street, since 1978. The Drawing School was founded, largely financed and provided with an art collection by John Ruskin as Slade Professor of Fine Art in 1871.) Innumerable portraits decorate the college halls and public buildings, and the Randolph Hotel has Osbert Lancaster's paintings illustrating Max Beerbohm's *Zuleika Dobson*. Aristide Maillol's nude *Flora* stands outside the Maison Française in Norham Road, Barbara Hepworth's *Achaean* at St. Catherine's College. *Another Time XI*, Antony Gormley's seven-foot man, bought by Exeter College, stands on the roof of Blackwell's Art and Poster Shop at the corner of Broad and Turl Streets; to the question "What is that naked iron bloke doing up there?" Gormley hopes "there will never be a single satisfactory answer" (*Oxford Times*, 29 January 2009). The cockerel at the top of John Piper's framed Nativity Window in Magdalen ante-chapel is more certain, proclaiming "Christus natus est!" He is sitting on the topmost shoot of a plant or tree on which other creatures pose and answer questions designed to suit their particular voice or call. "Ubi? ubi?"—"where?"—asks the hooting owl, for instance, and the sheep, at the bottom, beneath a shoot with luminous orange-red leaves or fruits, baas back "Bethlem! Bethlem!" Most of the creatures are pale, with the owl looking white at first but with a shade of green. The cockerel, however, irradiated by the divine message or the sunrise, is yellow, blue, red.

One of the most ambitious attempts at interior decoration was in 1857, when Rossetti, Burne-Jones, William Morris, Arthur Hughes, and other Pre-Raphaelite sympathizers painted with Arthurian scenes the upper walls of the new debating chamber of the Oxford Union. (Since 1878 it has been the library—now a comfortable room with leather armchairs, green-shaded brass table-lamps, and a good selection of books.) Unfortunately the young enthusiasts' lack of training in fresco meant that decay rapidly set in. After desperate attempts at restoration, fragments of the paintings remain: here and there faded faces, chain-mail, a shield, a bounding stag, a skull, and hourglass. Morris by 1869 had doubts about the "whole affair," which "was begun and carried out in too piecemeal and unorganized a fashion to be a real success." But he returned to paint the ceiling, to more lasting effect, in 1875.

Among early Oxford photographers Henry Taunt (1842–1922) produced sensitive, and very popular, studies of Oxford and Thames scenes, and Sarah Angelina Acland (1849–1930) was a pioneer of color photography. Acland, the daughter of Henry Wentworth Acland, the Professor of Medicine and main establisher of the University Museum, was also responsible for lucid character-portraits of her father and many of his contemporaries before the advent of color. Her best known portrait is of Acland and John Ruskin together in old age, and some of her most successful work in color shows the Botanic Garden and the garden of her house in Park Town in North Oxford. The Bodleian Library, owner of much of the original material, published Giles Hudson's finely illustrated and annotated catalog of her work in 2012.

Christ Church Picture Gallery

The Christ Church collection of Old Master drawings and paintings used to be kept in the college library. But in 1968 the architects Powell and Moya built the present "reserved and elegant" gallery, "an example of immaculate if rather sterile good taste" according to David Reed and Philip Opher in *New Architecture in Oxford* (1977).

The drawings, mainly from the eighteenth-century collection of John Guise, are shown in regular exhibitions. The permanent display includes notable paintings by Piero della Francesca (a Virgin of severe dignity) and Tintoretto (smoldering light from the grill on which St. Lawrence suffers, writhing but holding his hand up to heaven). There is a large, unusual canvas by Carracci, possibly a trade sign, of a butcher's shop with workers, hooks, cuts, and carcasses. Judith, as painted by Bernardo Strozzi (1581–1644) holds Holofernes' head in one hand and a bloodied, elaborate-hilted sword in the other. She wears a jeweled necklace and ribbons and jewels in her hair, her lips are red, and she seems partly relieved at, and partly exalted by, her deed. What renders the picture a little more enigmatic is the presence, between Judith and the head, of the "maid" from the biblical account. She is a gray-haired, ruddy-faced older woman, her lips compressed (Judith's are parted) with an expression perhaps to be read as "this had to be done, these were his deserts." Perhaps Judith's zeal and piety have achieved what her companion's age and experience could not.

The Ashmolean Museum: Elaboratory

John Tradescant and his son, also John, were seventeenth-century gardeners to the King and nobility. They went on foreign expeditions—the father as far as Muscovy and the son to Virginia—and collected not only bulbs and plants but what the seventeenth century called "curiosities." These formed the basis of their museum or "Ark" in Lambeth. John Tradescant the Younger left the collection to Elias

Oxford skyline (Photo by DAVID ILIFF. License: CC-BY-SA 3.)

The High Street, 1890s (Library of Congress, Washington DC)

William Turner of Oxford, *A View of Oxford*, c. 1850
(Yale Center for British Art/Wikimedia Commons)

St. Michael at the North Gate, built c. 1040
(Catriona Davidson)

Tom Tower, Christ Church, built by
Christopher Wren
(Andrew Gray/Wikimedia Commons)

Oxford Castle: the eleventh-century St. George's Tower and later additions
(Tejvan Pettinger/Wikimedia Commons)

View from Carfax tower (chensiyuan/Wikimedia Commons)

Christ Church Meadow, c. 1890 (Library of Congress, Washington DC)

Mob Quad, Merton College, thirteenth- and fourteenth-century
(DWR/Wikimedia Commons)

All Souls College (Ozeye/Wikimedia Commons)

The Second Quadrangle, Jesus College (Krzysztof Ilowiecki/Wikimedia Commons)

Corpus Christi College
(Godot13/Wikimedia Commons)

Magdalen College, Cloisters and New Building
(http://gagravarr.org/photos)

Keble College Chapel
(Diliff/Wikimedia Commons)

St. John's College, Canterbury Quadrangle
(Godot13/Wikimedia Commons)

The Bridge of Sighs, Hertford College   (Tom Murphy/Wikimedia Commons)

St. Catherine's College; Barbara Hepworth's *Achaean*   (Steve Cadman/Wikimedia Commons)

St. Frideswide, stained-glass window by Edward
Burne-Jones, Christ Church Cathedral
(Pruneau/Wikimedia Commons)

Martyrs' Memorial
(Catriona Davidson)

University Church of St. Mary the
Virgin, south porch (Catriona Davidson)

SS Mary and Nicholas, Littlemore,
founded by Cardinal Newman
(MaxKolbe/Wikimedia Commons)

The Bodleian Library; William,
3rd Earl of Pembroke, by Hubert Le Sueur
(Arnaud Malon/Wikimedia Commons)

The Sheldonian
Theatre and the Caesars
(Bernard Gagnon/
Wikimedia Commons)

The Oxford University
Museum of Natural
History
(Swevku/Wikimedia
Commons)

Inside the Pitt Rivers
Museum
(Einsamer Schütze/
Wikimedia Commons)

Port Meadow (courtesy *The Oxford Times*)

The Botanic Garden (Ozeye/Wikimedia Commons)

Addison's Walk, Magdalen College (CC-BY-SA-2.5.)

Blackwell's Bookshop,
Broad Street
(Catriona Davidson)

The Macdonald Randolph Hotel
(Catriona Davidson)

The Covered Market
(Catriona Davidson)

Elizabethan architecture and modern
finance, Cornmarket Street
(Catriona Davidson)

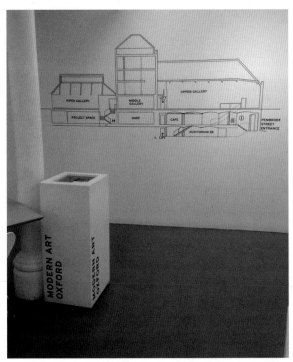

Antony Gormley's sculpture "Another Time" overlooking Broad Street (James Ferguson)

Detail from Paolo Uccello, *The Hunt in the Forest*, c. 1470, Ashmolean Museum
(The Yorck Project/Wikimedia Commons)

Minimalist Modern Art Oxford (Catriona Davidson)

The Clerk of Oxenford (third from left) in
William Blake's *Chaucer's Canterbury Pilgrims*
(Wikimedia Commons)

Matthew Arnold, the creator of
the Scholar-Gypsy, by George
Frederick Watts, 1880   (WikiArt)

The Shelley Memorial, University
College
(Godot13/Wikimedia Commons)

John Tenniel, "The Old Sheep Shop",
an illustration from Lewis Carroll's *Through the
Looking Glass*

"Bucks of the First Head", Thomas Rowlandson's satire on Oxford undergraduates (Google Art Project/Wikimedia Commons)

Academic dress, New College Lane (James/Wikimedia Commons)

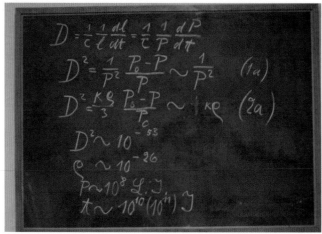

Einstein's blackboard, used at a 1931 lecture, at the Museum of the History of Science   (decltype/Wikimedia Commons)

The Oxford Canal and St. Barnabas Church, Jericho
(Kenneth Yarham/Wikimedia Commons)

College boathouses on the Isis (Diliff/Wikimedia Commons)

The 1869 Oxford and Cambridge
Boat Race in London
(Library of Congress, Washington DC)

Punting (Surreal Name Given/Wikimedia Commons)

Headington Hill Hall, once the home of Robert Maxwell, now part of Oxford Brookes
University (Oxford Brookes University)

Park Town, North Oxford (CC-BY-SA-3.0-MIGRATED)

Binsey (Catriona Davidson)

Bartlemas or St. Bartholomew's Chapel,
Cowley, fourteenth-century
(Wikimedia Commons)

Detail, St Mary the Virgin Church,
Iffley, c. 1170-80 (Catriona Davidson)

Cowley Road Carnival   (Damian Cugley/ Wikimedia Commons)

Dovecote, Minster Lovell (Philip Garrett)

Blenheim Palace (Magnus Manske)

Kelmscott Manor, home of William Morris

Ashmole, a founder member of the Royal Society with interests in astrology, alchemy, heraldry, manuscripts, and numismatics. Ashmole, whose enthusiasm for Oxford probably began when he spent a year there during the Civil War, added to the Ark and later gave its contents to the university "though I was tempted to part with them for a very considerable sum of money." To house them, the Old Ashmolean building in Broad Street—now the Museum of the History of Science—was built in 1679–83. The museum opened in 1683 and continued to let visitors in: it became, after the Ark, the first public museum in Britain.

The collection, still mainly of curiosities or "rarities"—the deerskin cloak which allegedly belonged to Powhatan, father of Pocahontas, is still on show—was called an "Elaboratory" by Anthony Wood. Others, more bluntly, thought it, Arthur MacGregor notes in his history of the Ashmolean, a "Knick-Knackatory." In later years antiquities, coins, manuscripts, and specimens of flora and fauna periodically swelled the collection and were often redeployed to other parts of the university. In the early nineteenth century the small building was crammed full of stuffed animals (including a giraffe) and skeletons which would later inhabit the University Museum. (Exhibits there now include the Tradescants' head of an "Alegator or Crocodile, from Aegypt" and a remarkably long "Sea Horses pissle.") But eventually, partly in association with the move to a much larger and more suitable building in Beaumont Street, the Ashmolean came to specialize in sculpture, antiquities, and painting.

Charles Robert Cockerell's long Greek Revival, Bath stone building of 1839–48, was intended to house both the University Galleries, which would become the new Ashmolean, and the Taylor Institution, endowed by Sir Robert Taylor for the teaching of modern languages. The Taylorian, as it is usually known, occupies the part of the building facing onto St. Giles'. (Its main library is a carpeted room with large central table, high windows, and gallery. There are marble busts of the benefactors Robert and Thomas Finch above the fireplace on either side of a portrait of the wigged Sir Robert, scroll in hand; it is a room as elegant yet relaxed as the library or drawing-room of some great house.) The Ashmolean has the central range and the pavilion opposite the Taylorian; together they form, says David Hinton, an "open quadrangle."

The Ashmolean collections

Although the modern collection is better ordered than any "Knick-Knackatory," it remains wonderfully eclectic: the Beazley collection of Greek vases, Rubens landscapes, a wardrobe by Philip Webb and Edward Burne-Jones (1857–8) illustrating Chaucer's *The Prioress' Tale* with rich Pre-Raphaelite poppies, angels, saints, and golden sky. As a graduate student working in the elegant chamber of the Taylorian described above, I would break off to visit the museum, strolling perhaps along the line of "Arundel Marbles"—the Hellenistic and Roman statues collected originally by the 2nd Earl of Arundel (1586–1646). A more interactive encounter with the ancient world was also possible: I knew exactly where to stand—so, apparently, did many other people—to make a golden Scythian necklace, with dangling acorns, dance as if its owner had just lifted her fingers to take it off. (The 22 slightly dented, shining acorns hang from rosettes, alternating with small gold beads. The necklace was found with the remains of a woman in a tumulus at the Greek colony of Nymphaion, between the Black Sea and the Sea of Azov.) Then I would go back and doodle ancient jewelry in the margins of my notes.

Since my minutes out in the museum, it has been radically remodeled. Fortunately for their conservation, the firm floor of Room 16 will not allow the Scythian acorns to vibrate. More importantly, the recent refurbishment by Rick Mather has delivered a light-filled, multi-leveled, new Ashmolean which seems bigger, bolder, and less provincial than the old. The way the paintings are displayed on the upper floors has changed relatively little, but on the lower levels there is a sense of opening vistas, new areas to explore. For instance you can stand looking at farming implements from Roman Oxfordshire while half-aware of the reflected profiles of the Greco-Roman physician Claudius Agathemerus and his more formidable wife, Myrtale, with her high, curled wig. Looking left, if you are not too distracted by a splendid picture reconstructing

Pompeii in the spring of 79 CE, compact beneath the towering volcano which will soon bury it, you can see into the cast gallery. This used to be a separate annex, used mainly for teaching, but has now been integrated into the museum proper. Larger-than-life figures from the arch of Trajan at Benevento lead on to casts including the writhing Laocoon and his sons, tormented by Poseidon's sea-serpents, from the Vatican Museum. (Sometimes, as in the "Human Image" gallery, periods are more daringly mixed.)

The Arundel Marbles, left of the entrance, still lead towards the Egyptian rooms dominated by the four-meter-square sandstone shrine to the gods built by the Nubian Pharaoh Taharqa in about 680 BCE. Standing before the shrine—once it guarded the entrance to the pillared hall of the temple at Kawa—is a robust gneiss ram of the god Amun. Between its folded front legs and under its chin is a small figure of the mighty Taharqa, ruler of Egypt as well as Nubia. (Connected with Amun also is the mummy-case of Meresamun, covered with the sweeping, colorful wings of painted protective deities. She was a musician of the god's cult.) The museum is rich in eastern art, too, including Chinese and Japanese ceramics and sculptures from ancient Gandhara—schist scenes of the birth and death of the Buddha—with their usual mix of Greek and Indian elements.

One of the most popular exhibits in the Ashmolean, old or new, has long been the so-called Alfred Jewel, 6.2 cm long, 3.1 cm across the middle, and of uncertain function. It shows, in cloisonné enamel on gold plate, a man in a green tunic who seems to be holding two flowers. Beneath is a gold unidentified beast, on the back trees or vines, and cut into the rim an inscription in Old English "Ælfred mec heht gewyrcan"—"Alfred ordered me to be made." Alfred is fairly certainly King Alfred (ruled 871–99); the man represented may be, according to various theories, him, St. Cuthbert, or some such figure as Sight. One theory about its use is that it is an *æstel*, a form of pointer for use with a manuscript. The probability of a connection with Alfred is increased by the fact that it was found near Athelney in Somerset, where in 878 the King took refuge from the Danes who had all but overrun Wessex, and from where he began the fight back. People like to imagine him carrying the jewel into battle—not a pointer but some proud fitting for a banner, spear, or crown, or an amulet to bring good fortune.

The other best-loved piece in the collection, given in 1850, is Paolo Uccello's *Hunt in the Forest* (c. 1470). Horsemen rush after deer among tall oaks and against a dark background—it seems to be night in this energetic but unrealistic hunt. The horsemen are mostly in scarlet and the light-colored hounds have scarlet collars. Hounds curve, people shout and point and gesticulate, a rider reins hard. The perspective, leading to a central vanishing-point, is carefully mapped out; Ruskin, following Giorgio Vasari, thought Uccello "went off his head with love of perspective." But, as Catherine Whistler suggests in the gallery book about the *Hunt*, "mathematics and rationality" are only one aspect of the painting. There is a "dramatic tension between the logical perspectival system ... and the sheer vitality, colour and rhythm of the hunt itself." Our eyes are drawn both to "the notionally distant vanishing point" and "back to the surface of the picture, thanks to the rhythms of pattern and colour across the lower half." So appealing is this combination that Uccello's hunters grace, in the Ashmolean gift-shop, postcards, jigsaw puzzles, high-class mugs, ties, and earrings.

The Hunt in the Forest is one in a range of notable, very different landscapes in the Ashmolean. Claude's *Landscape with Ascanius Shooting the Stag of Sylvia* depicts a scene from *The Aeneid* in characteristic silvery greens and blues. Piero di Cosimo's bizarre but fascinating *The Forest Fire* (c. 1505) is a "dream-intense" vision "with its panic rout of animals and birds (some lumbering ominously through the air as if heavy with bombs), all the more disquieting because some of the animals that turn to look at you have human faces" (David Piper, *The Treasures of Oxford*). The Impressionist display has Pissarro's *The Tuileries Gardens, rainy weather*—blotched figures with umbrellas, the spires of Notre Dame in the distance—and Monet's *A Mill Near Zaandam*, a windswept scene in browns, grays, and whites with choppy water and grass which looks only residually green, as if the color has been leeched out by the wind. (The more solid yellow and greens of Paul Sérusier's *Breton Women in a Hayfield* provide a strong contrast in the same room.) Manet's *Mademoiselle Claus*, recently saved for the nation after a campaign to raise £7.83 million, looks out, straight but enigmatic, from the opposite wall. There is also almost a whole roomful of Sickerts. It is not, ideally, a museum to be visited briefly or only once.

Music

Students have always been able to emit a variety of loud, sometimes musical noises, from the licentious songs banned by the statutes of University College in 1292 to the more organized sounds made by college choirs. New College choir has flourished since the late fourteenth century and Magdalen since the mid-fifteenth. The third great choral foundation, at Cardinal College and its successor Christ Church, followed in the reign of Henry VIII. These three colleges, and the choir schools associated with them, remain important centers for sacred music-making.

Secular music, including fanfares and accompaniments for official ceremonies and processions, was performed by the city waits. From the early 1630s there were also university waits, who promised to provide "loud music in the winter mornings to the several colleges and halls and to particular privileged persons of quality in the said university, and with very commendable low music to be always in readiness to wait upon all occasions of the university" (*Records of Early English Drama: Oxford*). John Gerrard, of the city and later the university waits, also kept a shop selling books and instruments (and an alehouse); the shop inventory made after his death in 1635 suggests, as the *Records* notes, the variety of instruments available in Oxford at the time. They include treble and tenor violins, bass viols, bandoras, lutes, a sackbut, citterns, recorders, and four different types of cornet. Many such instruments are on display, and can sometimes be heard, at the Bate Collection at the music faculty in St. Aldate's. Here is everything from a Javanese gamelan to a nineteenth-century morris dancer's tabor and beater, a comprehensive gathering of flutes, piccolos, fifes, and flageolets, and a selection of reed calls: crow, duck, quail.

One of the grandest of musical occasions in the following century was George Frederick Handel's visit, in 1733, for the "Act," the annual degree-giving ceremony and attendant celebrations. (Part of the Act survived as Encaenia, when honorary degrees are still conferred.) Handel, for unknown reasons, refused the offer of an honorary music doctorate. (He was too miserly to pay up, claimed Thomas Hearne.) But he supervised, for substantial and largely enthusiastic audiences at the Sheldonian Theatre, performances of his work including the Utrecht *Te Deum*, *Esther*, *Deborah*, and his new oratorio, *Athalia*. (*Acis and Galatea* was given in Christ Church Hall.) Hearne, who as a Jacobite seems to have disapproved on principle of the Hanover-connected composer, noted acidly the presence of "one Handel, a foreigner" and his "lousy crew, a great number of foreign fiddlers." Josef Haydn, who happily accepted his honorary doctorate in July 1791, was received more uniformly well. "I thank you!" he cried from the organ loft before performing in his doctoral robes, and the company replied, according to one witness, "You speak very good English." Again in the Sheldonian, he led a performance of his new Symphony number 92 in G, which became known as the "Oxford." "It was generally deemed one of the most striking compositions ever heard," *The Gentleman's Magazine* reported, "and the ingenious author was applauded very warmly."

Works by Handel, Haydn, and others were most often, however, performed in more intimate settings. The Holywell Music Room, which opened in 1748, is thought to be the oldest surviving purpose-built concert hall in Europe. In the late seventeenth century a music club had been formed to play regularly in taverns and college buildings. (An early member was Henry Purcell's brother, Daniel.) Needing a more ample and appropriate venue, the club launched a successful appeal for subscriptions in 1741, and bought land from Wadham College (which is now again the owner). The building, by Thomas Camplin, Vice Principal of St. Edmund Hall, is simple, elegant, and known for its good acoustics. The club, renamed the Musical Society, gave subscription concerts here, with resident Holywell Band and distinguished visitors, until the early nineteenth century.

Concert venues today include the Music Room, college halls, the Sheldonian, and the Town Hall. A more recent addition is the Jacqueline du Pré Building at St. Hilda's College (van Heyningen and Haward, 1996, with acoustics by Arup), whose main auditorium seats 200. (There is also an electro-acoustic studio.) Among the best-known Oxford-based choirs and orchestras are the Oxford Bach Choir (founded 1896, mixing town and university singers), the Oxford Symphony Orchestra (1902), Schola Cantorum of Oxford (1960), and Oxford Pro Musica (1965).

Meanwhile Oxford was emerging as a center for many different sorts of music. From the 1980s it was the home of several successful rock bands. Radiohead, most famously, debuted at the Jericho Tavern in 1987 as "On a Friday" and remained closely involved with the Oxford music scene. They were among the most important supporters of the establishment of the Zodiac at 190 Cowley Road—later the Carling Academy Oxford and since 2009 the O2 Academy Oxford.

THE OXFORD ELEVEN IN 1886.

A. H. J. COCHRANE.   H. T. HEWETT.   A. R. COBB.   H. T. ARNALL-THOMPSON.   K. J. KEY.

H. O. WHITBY.   H. V. PAGE (*Capt.*).   J. H. BRAIN.   L. D. HILDYARD.

W. RASHLEIGH.   E. H. BUCKLAND.

7

Leisure and Pleasure
Oxford Pastimes

"Dancing upon the rope and vaulting upon the saddle"

Things to be seen for money in the city. 1. Plays. 2. Dancing upon the rope and vaulting upon the saddle [a sport later popular in Westerns]. 3. Virginals and organs playing by themselves. 4. A Dutch wench all hairy and rough upon her body. 5. The history [performed by puppets] of some parts of the Bible, as of the creation of the world . . . Nineveh besieged and taken . . . 6. The dancing of the horses at the Star [Inn].

Thomas Crosfield made this list in his diary for 11 July 1631. There were other sports for other seasons—at Shrovetide 1633, for instance, Crosfield specifies "1. Frittering"—the equivalent of making pancakes—"2. Throwing at cocks. 3. Playing at stoolball in the city by women and football by men." In September came St. Giles' Fair, in icy winters there was skating, at all times of year street music and dancing.

Students in most periods have managed to join in the fun. Simon Forman claims that when he was at Magdalen in the 1570s his patrons, two well-off graduates, would take him on long hunting trips on Shotover "and they never studied nor gave themselves to their books, but to go to schools of defence, to the dancing schools, to steal deer and coneys [rabbits], and to hunt the hare, and to wooing of wenches." For Thomas Dibdin (1771–1841) at St. John's "Boating, hunting, shooting, fishing—these formed in days of yore the chief amusement of the Oxford Scholar." Sir Richard Burton says that he "began a 'reading man'"—later he remained enough of one to translate *The Arabian Nights*—but, failing to make progress, "threw up the classics, and returned to my old habits of fencing, boxing and single-stick ... and sketching facetiously, though not wisely, the reverend features and figures of certain half-reformed monks, calling themselves 'fellows.'" When the Afghan War broke out and he wanted to join in, he got himself rusticated (suspended) and left Oxford in a dog-cart with "a companion in misfortune too-tooing lustily through a 'yard of tin,' disturbing the dons at their bowls."

Some have engaged in more seriously athletic pleasures, most famously Sir Roger Bannister, a former student at Exeter who was later Master of Pembroke. Competing for the Amateur Athletic Association, he ran the first sub-four-minute mile at the Iffley Road track on 6 May 1954. (The refurbished track was renamed after Bannister in 2007.)

Rowing

> I set my teeth and tugged as I had never tugged before; the voices on the bank grew louder and more confused, our oars went slashing through the water, and our boat tossed like a cork in the wake of the boat before us.
>
> "Three strokes more, and you're into them," shouted Wingfield [the cox]. There was a loud roar on the bank, a slight shock through the boat, an "Easy all" from Wingfield, and all was over. We had made our bump, and were happy. I would not have exchanged places that minute with any man you like to name.
>
> Never before, and never since, have I felt anything like the calm triumphant happiness of rowing back to our barge with Oriel behind us, and the cheers of half the river ringing in our ears.

Thus the crew of a fictional college in *Boating Life at Oxford* (1868) catches and bumps Oriel in Torpids. The race was first run in 1838 and its name is thought to reflect the days when it involved only the college's second, slower boats. Torpids happens today in late February or early March, and the other, most important of college races, Eights, in May. Eights is also a bumping race and the course in both instances runs from Iffley Lock to Folly Bridge.

The Oxford City Bumping Races, in April, are organized by the Oxford City Rowing Club.

Spectators in the nineteenth and early twentieth centuries cheered teams on from the roofs of the college barges moored near Folly Bridge. Photographs show crowds of men in blazers and women with parasols. "The interiors of these barges," Alfred Rimmer tells us in *Pleasant Stops Near Oxford* (1878), "are beautifully fitted up with reading-rooms and dressing-rooms." Later they were replaced by boat-houses. (Beerbohm's Zuleika Dobson offends the Duke of Dorset by calling the Judas College barge a "houseboat.") The modern college boat-houses are practical constructions, far from picturesque. (The Oxford University Boat Club boathouse is downstream at Wallingford, twelve miles away.)

In 1815, when the first Oxford race for eight-oared boats is recorded, the pace must have been less furious than in 1868—much less so than now. Early rowers went out at first in "high hats," then in Tam o' Shanters, then in straw hats with various identifying ribbons. At the beginning of the nineteenth century they seem even to have retained their gowns and tasseled caps. (Women, when grudgingly allowed to row in the early twentieth century, had to contend with long skirts.) The boats were wider and heavier than modern ones; significant change began with the first use of outriggers in the Oxford and Cambridge Boat Race of 1846. (The first such race was at Henley in 1829, moving to London in 1836, and to the present course from Putney to Mortlake in 1845.) Oxford used keelless boats from the late 1850s, and sliding seats, making possible an immense increase in speed, from the 1870s.

Few real rowing enthusiasts have gone so far as the character in *Zuleika Dobson* who, in the process of drowning himself on the last night of Eights, comes up one last time to check whether the Judas College boat has bumped Magdalen. Indeed he makes it happen— the Magdalen cox, disconcerted to see his head bobbing up, lets slip the cords of the rudder, "whereupon the Magdalen man who rowed 'bow' missed his stroke" and they are soon bumped by Judas. The drowning man goes down smiling. This is comic fiction, but the sport has certainly provoked much serious passion. Some earnest commentators were keen on the idea that it taught men "pluck"—courage and endurance. The narrator of *Boating Life* says that he rows for the thrill of the chase, for team, and college spirit—and for the opportunity to impress the teammate's sister he later marries. Less fortunate in their love for Zuleika, Beerbohm's oarsmen and spectators hurl themselves into the river from the boats and the roofs of the college barges.

Osbert Lancaster, who illustrated *Zuleika Dobson*, was an "aesthete" rather than a "hearty" in the days when undergraduates thought of themselves as divided along those lines. Yet on arrival at Lincoln College in 1926, he improbably decided to try out his skills as an oarsman. "After a very few days on the river," he remembered in *With An Eye to the Future* (1967), "it became abundantly clear to me why rowing had in more rational societies been confined to the criminal classes and prisoners of war." After "a grim two weeks I cast in my lot with the aesthetes, laid down my oar and joined the O.U.D.S. [Oxford University Dramatic Society]." Alan Coren, who also "turned . . . to the stage" when at Wadham, claims to have been put off even more quickly on noticing how "in the chill fog, hundreds of young men paddled about in their underwear, their skin tripe-dimpled, their teeth leaving on the icy air the impression of a Flamenco eisteddfod" (*My Oxford*, 1977).

Punting

Before the days of university and tourist punting, flat-bottomed boats were used for fishing and for ferrying. Matthew Arnold mentions them in "The Scholar-Gipsy" as a means of "Crossing the stripling Thames at Bab-lock-hythe." The leisure punt became popular as traffic on the river declined with the growth of the railways; good for drifting, reading, picnicking, and love as well as for vigorous poling, it is associated especially with the quiet, grassy-banked, hawthorn-lined reaches of the Cherwell. (There is, however, a tradition of punt-racing on the Thames.) Punters' memories are often of stationary boats: Alan Coren has a surreal vision of the scene in the summer of 1958 when "in the various waterways around Oxford the punts coagulated sluggishly into log-jams as their polers hove to in order to read aloud to one another. Through the mists of spiralling gnat, snatches of Salinger and Scott Fitzgerald filtered from boat to boat."

Another tradition is that of falling into the river. Punters who choose to grip the pole firmly when it sticks in the Cherwell mud can find themselves poised in mid-air as the boat glides on with their friends. In theory you are less likely to fall in than at Cambridge—Oxford punts are poled from a sloping deck whereas both ends of the Cambridge boat are covered and so higher. But misfortune may still come upon pilot and passenger alike. In Barbara Pym's *Crampton Hodnet* (written in 1939–40, published 1985), for instance, Barbara Bird falls in with a splash and a cry while attempting to tie the boat to a branch. Her married tutor and would-be lover Francis Cleveland "dithered about, encumbered by the long, awkward pole" before finally floundering into the water after her. For a moment it seems that his "action had somehow turned a ridiculous mishap into a romantic episode," and Pym is too subtle simply to suggest that cold water has (literally) been poured on the relationship. But the liaison is clearly not going to work—neither of them really wants it to. "The poor bottle of wine" which Francis thought he ought to bring "lay abandoned among the cushions, still unopened." "Dull, virtuous, middle-aged" and rooted in staid North Oxford, he has in any case forgotten the corkscrew.

Parsons' Pleasure: "the forbidden bend"

A climactic scene occurs at this male naturist bathing place in the University Parks in Robert Robinson's *Landscape with Dead Dons* (1956). Inspector Autumn, the one clothed man amidst much unappealing nakedness, tracks down his murder suspect. Soon, at his entreaty, the bathers will rush, still naked, out of Parsons' Pleasure and all the way to Beaumont Street in pursuit of the murderer. But even before this there are scenes of confusion as a women's rowing crew comes "round the forbidden bend" in the Cherwell. (Tradition long dictated that "ladies" must take a detour on foot or simply close their eyes.)

Men who had been taking their ease—sprawled on their bellies or hugging their knees in the sun—started up like spring-loaded automata and ran for their lives. Flying figures cannoned into each other, hurled themselves into the hedges, dived six-deep into the bathing huts. One fat don started to climb a tree. The ground shook. Out in the river the water boiled as the bathers made grimly for the shore. One man crawled out and squeezed himself miserably beneath the spring-board, another crouched in the bulrushes, his bottom sinking deeper into the ooze. Another, despairing of concealment, opened his spectacle case and spread it hopefully before him.

Eventually Parsons' Pleasure closed, in a world where nudity had become a little less shocking or funny, in 1991. A female equivalent, Dames' Delight, existed nearby between 1934 and 1970.

Soccer: Oxford United

Thomas Crosfield's list of diversions available at Shrovetide 1633 includes "Playing at . . . football by men." Such enjoyments were not, however, in the forceful view of William Laud as Chancellor, suitable for the young men of the university. Soccer was banned in his statutes of 1636—with hunting, fighting, dice, and card-games—and thirty years later Anthony Wood records that four undergraduates were suspended from taking their degrees for a year because "they had been convicted of playing football."

Later soccer and any number of other sports would flourish at Oxford University. But the city's most important soccer club—there is another, part-time Oxford City—was founded as a village team at the Britannia Inn in Headington in 1893. They became known as "boys from up the hill" and were based in Headington until 2001. (The club was called Headington, then Headington United, before becoming Oxford United in 1960.) At first they played at Quarry Recreation Ground, on the frontier between the villages of Headington Quarry and Headington. Here the main hazard was losing the ball—youths from Quarry, resenting the incursion on their territory, simply "pinched" and went off with it, according to an article in *Jackson's Oxford Journal* in 1898, cited with much other interesting material in Martin Brodetsky's *Oxford United: the Complete Record* (2009). The club's income in 1896, Brodetsky tells us, was £12, 9 shillings; after expenditure on balls, strips, and fees a balance of £2, 18 shillings, and fivepence was left. In its early days the team played such opponents as the Oxford City Reserves, College Servants, and Clarendon Press. Home matches took place on various fields in Headington, including one by the Britannia—now part of Lime Walk—across the London Road from their more permanent home, from 1925, at the Manor Ground.

The club turned professional in 1949. In the long term their best-known player (1959–71) was Ron Atkinson, later manager of Manchester United. As captain he took Oxford United from non-League to Division Two soccer, with his brother the midfielder Graham Atkinson scoring many of the goals. But the club was eventually relegated to Division Three in 1976. Attendance went down and major financial difficulties began. Robert Maxwell stepped in as an immediate savior; the problems, as in most of his enterprises, came later. When Barclays Bank was about to foreclose, Maxwell bought a majority share in the club for £121,000 in December 1981, and became chairman the following month. (His son Kevin took over as chairman in 1987.) The 1980s were one of Oxford United's most successful periods, including its extraordinary progression from the Third Division to the Second to the First in successive years, and the crowning glory of its 3–0 victory over Queen's Park Rangers at Wembley in the Milk Cup final of April 1986.

Robert Maxwell, having tried to gain as much of the credit as possible for this success, moved on to other clubs and schemes, but remained the chief shareholder. Soon after his death in 1991 it became apparent that, given the illusory nature of his wealth, Oxford United was again in serious financial trouble. New buyers were found in 1992, but the club's fortunes remained mixed, and by 1998 it owed £10 million. Firoz Kassam bought it and became chairman in 1999. By this time the Manor Ground was in a state of near-collapse; the club had spent many years looking at alternative sites. After a long sequence of different plans, impassioned debate, and legal difficulties, the Kassam Stadium at Minchery Farm, between Littlemore and Blackbird Leys, opened in 2001.

"Some of the company fell a' laughing": pranks and hoaxes

Students may have a reputation for wild, usually alcohol-fueled behavior today, but some of their antics in Oxford in the first third of the last century were extreme even by modern standards. Before World War I it was the usually scholarly J. R. R. Tolkien of Exeter College who—no doubt indulging his hobbit side rather than his elfin—made off with a bus one evening in spite of determined opposition from police, university officials, and townsmen. He "drove it up to Cornmarket . . . " he says. "It was chockfull of undergrads before it reached the Carfax. There I addressed a few stirring words to a huge mob"; abandoning the bus, he went on to the Martyrs' Memorial "where I addressed the crowd again. There were no disciplinary consequences of all this!" While the proctors might have taken action against those involved in such capers, the police seem to have taken a rather lenient approach to the young "gentlemen." Roger Dataller, a Yorkshire miner who came to Oxford on a Miners' Welfare Scholarship in 1928, reflected on how differently the "high spirits" of young men abusing the police in Cornmarket amid 5 November fireworks, pranks, and skirmishes might be interpreted "in the setting of a northern coalfield." There the newspapers would report "Disgraceful Fracas in Mining Village. Police Defied" (*A Pitman Looks at Oxford*, 1933).

Somewhat milder was the old tradition of screwing up the outer doors or "oaks" of your colleagues' or tutors' rooms. More ambitious, and more amusing, were such student hoaxes as the "rag psychology lecture" given by "Dr. Emil Busch" in the early 1920s. Christopher Hollis, in whose rooms at Balliol the lecture was "concocted," tells the story in his memoir *Along the Road to Frome* (1958). Freud was all the rage; George Edinger of Balliol put in "bogus psychological jargon" and sentences which, while filled with references to "complex" and "compensation," were essentially meaningless. At the Town Hall Edinger appeared as Dr. Busch of Vienna—or Frankfurt, says one report—and completely took in his "thronging and distinguished audience." (Helpfully, it was not yet possible actually to study psychology at the university.) Himself of German origin, he knew how to speak exactly the right brand of "slightly broken English." The learned doctor was introduced, no doubt in contrastingly impeccable upper-class tones, by "Professor Heythrop," his suitably disguised fellow undergraduate James Scrymgeour Wedderburn, future Earl of Dundee. (It was Wedderburn too who had a habit, according to Evelyn Waugh, of substituting "gin for water in the carafes which stood on the Union table, from which speakers often refreshed themselves to punctuate their *bons mots*.")

Such 1920s high-jinx are usually seen as a reaction to the horrors of 1914–18. It was soon after the war, according to John Mabbott in his *Oxford Memories*, that what was at first thought to be an attempt to poison an unpopular Vice-Chancellor generated the headline "*Toothpowder Plot: Professor Hoaxed*. We understand on reliable authority that the Vice-Chancellor's chocolate filling was in fact toothpaste." All the same, Vice-Chancellor Farnell himself notes in his memoirs that the powder contained ground glass; he forgave the undergraduate culprit who confessed, but not the "elderly and idle clergyman" who had egged him on. Hoaxes, however, were nothing new. In September 1659, says Anthony Wood, one "Kinaston a Merchant of London with a long beard and hair over-grown was at the Mitre Inn and feigning himself a Patriarch" of the Greek Orthodox Church. Various royalists came to him, swooning at the prospect of being blessed "by a Patriarch instead of an Archbishop or Bishop," and the Professor of Greek "appeared very formally and made a Greek Harangue before him." At this point "some of the company who knew the design to be waggish," and had clearly been less well trained than Dr. Busch's team, "fell a' laughing and betrayed the matter." William Lloyd, whose idea it all was, was forced to leave his post as private tutor to an undergraduate at Wadham and run away. But after the Restoration—doubtless displaying all due patriarchal dignity—he went on to become Bishop in turn of St. Asaph, Lichfield, and Coventry.

Fairs and carnivals

The best known Oxford fair, St. Giles', fills the whole wide St. Giles Street every September. It grew from a small parish celebration starting perhaps in the seventeenth century, to a fair for children—still modest in scale—in the early nineteenth century, to a much bigger, noisier, and more various affair from the 1830s. At the Victorian fair you could buy "baskets, glass and china ornaments, cheap tools, sweets, gingerbreads, cakes etc . . . fruit . . . cocoa nuts, hedge nuts, cheap jewelery, photographs, ices, canaries and other cage birds, braces, gilding fluid, potato peelers, name stamps, and other things too numerous to mention" (*Jackson's Oxford Journal*, 10 September 1887). Bands, equestrian circuses, waxworks, peep-shows, and freak-shows came. Traveling menageries brought their gorillas, lions, and tigers. Rides, long driven by people or ponies, began to use steam-power in the 1860s and became ever faster, bigger, and more popular. At the end of the century moving pictures came, shown at first in simple wooden booths, later in structures with comfortable seats, stage curtains, and decorations.

Other delights, to the recurrent dismay of the authorities trying to police this vast gathering, included throwing rice and confetti, knocking off your fellow fair-goer's hat, blowing a kazoo-like instrument into his or her face, and daubing passersby with paint. There was also some more serious fighting (usually alcohol-connected). But attempts to end the fair were successfully resisted and it flourishes still. At the north end of the street and the fair, the spacious thirteenth-century church of St. Giles remains somehow calm amid both the usual busy traffic and the September festivities.

A more recent addition to the city's festivities (in July) is the Cowley Road Carnival, which was officially established in 2001. It was canceled in 2012 due to lack of funds but re-established in 2013. James Attlee, in *Isolarion: a Different Oxford Journey* (2007), describes the carnival in action:

> a chaotic collage of sounds and impressions: a troupe of bhangra drummers in purple and gold costumes spin like dervishes; African dancers in fake leopard-skin bikinis crouch low . . . ; a Chinese brass

band of serious-faced elderly men in black suits blast their long-stemmed trumpets in our faces, while an orange dragon writhes furiously at their feet.

There have also been men on stilts, a giant mermaid, reggae, steel bands, school bands, and samba bands; all the road's many restaurants are enthusiastically involved.

Clubs

Clubs and societies of Oxford University and its colleges meet for dinner, sport, music, prayer, debate, and foosball. There are an OU Buddhist Society, an OU Darts Society, a Magdalen Swing Band, and groups practicing origami, punting, and kendo. With Oxford Brookes, city, and other clubs there must be several hundred functioning societies.

The Archery Club at St. John's gathered for "lunch and rather inaccurate shooting," writes John Mabbott in *Oxford Memories*. The Three Hours for Lunch Club seems self-explanatory. Other groups took more exotic names. As an undergraduate at Exeter College, Tolkien founded the Apolausticks—"the ones devoted to self-indulgence"—although its debates sound serious enough. The Vanoxists, a breakfast-club which met at the Trout inn in Wolvercote, were inspired by a dream of one of Waugh's friends about "the unknown vice of 'vanoxism,'" possibly "connected with scourging raw beef with lilies" (*A Little Learning*). Waugh also patronized the Hypocrites, who gathered upstairs at 34 St. Aldate's and were so known because the club's motto, from Pindar, was "Water is best." The university closed the club down after a particularly uproarious fancy-dress party in 1924.

Waugh also knew about the Bullingdon, the most notorious of Oxford clubs. In his *Decline and Fall*, the mild and inoffensive main character, Paul Pennyfeather, has an unfortunate encounter with the men of the thinly disguised "Bollinger." A theology student at Scone College, he returns one evening from a meeting of the League of Nations Union and "a most interesting paper about plebiscites in Poland." He makes his way across the quad, intending to smoke a pipe and read some more of the *Forsyte Saga*. But it is not to be, for he blunders into the champagne-swilling, glass-smashing, roaring aftermath of the annual dinner of the Bollinger. "It was a lovely evening. They broke up Mr Austen's grand piano, and stamped Lord Rending's cigars into his carpet, and smashed his china" and threw Mr. Partridge's "Matisse into the water-jug." A Bollinger man does not like Paul's tie; his trousers are duly removed and he is rather casually sent down for "indecent behaviour"—running through the quad minus the trousers. The Bursar is happy extracting fines from the revelers which will pay for "five evenings of Founder's port" at High Table. As far as the college is concerned Paul is "someone of no importance"—unlike the Bollinger members, who are rich, titled, or the bearers of double or even triple-barrelled names like Sir Alistair Digby-Vane-Trumpington.

Decline and Fall is fiction (savagely comic fiction) but the Bullingdon has often come to public attention, not least in recent years because its Old Etonian members have included David Cameron and Boris Johnson. Laura Wade's play *Posh*, first performed in 2010 and updated in 2012, deals with the "Riot Club," as clearly inspired by the Bullingdon as is the Bollinger. Wade has a more evident and left-wing political agenda than Waugh. The privileged young men riot their way through a meal at a country pub, abusing and assaulting the staff and getting "châteaued beyond belief." The godfather of the club president, a handy Conservative MP, helps them avoid the consequences of their actions. (In 2013 Lone Scherfig directed a film based on the play.)

The Botanic Garden

The Botanic Garden is a good place to wander through, pausing perhaps to sit on one of the curved wooden seats by the pool and small fountain at the center of the old garden. At the entrance still stands the 1632 gateway in the form of a triumphal arch with later statues of Charles I, Charles II, and the founder, Henry Danvers, Earl of Danby. (The arch was built by Inigo Jones' master mason, Nicholas Stone, but apparently not designed by him. Jones dismissed it as the lame effort of "some mathematicians of Oxford.") The Cherwell borders the site and there are views of Magdalen Bridge and Tower. But the Physic Garden, as it was called from its foundation in 1621 until 1840, was from the beginning a center for serious medical and botanical study. The garden was put to particularly full experimental use by Charles Daubeny, Professor of Botany from 1834 and active also in medicine, chemistry, geology, and the campaign for scientific degrees at Oxford. He used part of the garden to investigate "the effects of soils, or of chemical agents, upon vegetation," built the Daubeny Laboratory on site, and in the 1860s attempted to order plants in the garden in an evolutionary sequence inspired by Darwin's work.

The glasshouses are laid out much as they have been since the 1890s. One of the most impressively plant-filled is the Lily House. Creepers hang down at the door, a jade vine stretches along one side. The big pool is almost completely covered with waterlilies, and at the edges are tall papyrus and several varieties of rice: *oryza sativa*, *barthii*, *longistaminata*, and *rufipogon* (Asian, wild, longstamen, red). The Palm House has huge-leaved, thick-stemmed plantain. In the Arid House are cactus, aloe, and a range of sharp, spreading agaves including the broader-leaved, barbed, and aptly named *Agave ferox*, and a tall *Nolina gracilis* with swelling, skirt-like base. In the corridor, near the Alpine House and Fernery, the trunk of a *Philodendron Bipinnatifidum* winds upwards like a great lozenged jungle snake.

The university also owns the much more extensive Harcourt Arboretum at Nuneham Courtenay, a "satellite" of the Botanic Garden. It is rich in rhododendra, camellias, and azaleas, native trees and wild flowers.

The University Parks

Miss Morrow loved the Parks, especially in fine weather when they were full of people. In the spring there was a faintly ridiculous air about them, like Mendelssohn's *Spring Song*, but, as in the song, there was also a prim and proper Victorian element which chastened the fantasy and made it into something quaint and formal, like a ballet. Dons striding along with walking sticks, wives in

> Fair Isle jumpers . . . and governesses with intelligent children ask-
> ing ceaseless questions in their clear, fluty voices. And then there
> were the clergymen, solitary bearded ones reading books, young
> earnest ones, like chickens just out of the egg, discussing problems
> which had nothing to do with the sunshine or the yellow-green
> leaves uncurling on the trees. There were undergraduates too, and
> young women with Sweet's *Anglo-Saxon Reader* or lecture note-
> books under their arms, and lovers, clasping each other's fingers
> and trying to find secluded paths where they might kiss.

Such, according to Barbara Pym's *Crampton Hodnet*, was the atmosphere of the University Parks in about 1939. They had been established in the 1850s–60s. For some people they are a place for more vigorous activity: hockey, cricket, rugby. But for most the Parks remain a huge grassy area for strolling in, for looking at the plants, trees, and steeply curved Rainbow Bridge (built by unemployed labor in 1923–4 and called officially High Bridge). Or they can watch other people's sporting efforts. (The cricket pavilion of 1881 is the work of Sir Thomas Jackson, architect of the Examination Schools.) In May and June students sprawl in the Parks as they attempt to revise for their exams and retain at least the memory of "a green thought in a green shade."

The Parks are not only themselves extensive, but lead on north through further meadows by the river to the Cherwell Boathouse, known since the late 1960s for its restaurant as well as its punts, Wolfson College, and the Victoria or "Vicky" Arms.

Food and drink: boar's head, mallard's blood, and "dirty toast"

A fourteenth-century undergraduate at Queen's College is said to have been walking in Shotover Forest. Usefully, he read Aristotle as he went: when a boar attacked him, he rammed the book down its throat and choked it. This improbable tale is commemorated by the Boar's Head Dinner, which has taken place in the college hall in December since 1395. The head, held high, processes in with the college choir singing their traditional "The Boar's head in hand bear I . . ." in a mixture of English and Latin.

Tradition has it that a more peaceable animal supplied an excuse for the Mallard Feast at All Souls, now held once every hundred years. According to one version of the story, the duck was found in a drain when the foundations of the college were being laid. By the seventeenth century the celebration involved much processing about with torches and bird. The Lord Mallard and his officers sang their ancient song and marched across the library roof. Eventually—according to the suitably eccentrically named antiquary Hannibal Baskerville—in the buttery the company filled their tumblers with "canary or other wine" and "he that bore the mallard chops off his head, dropping some of the blood into every tumbler." In 1901 the more animal-loving or squeamish fellows bore a stuffed duck, and in 2001 a wooden one on a pole. ("Oxford dons go quackers," quipped *The Guardian* that year.)

Even on less grand occasions, students have often eaten well. For much of the nineteenth century it was customary for under-graduates to breakfast with friends, at leisure, in their rooms. A contributor to *Cassell's Family Magazine* (1884) describes a fresh-man's "first breakfast party." In come "tea, coffee, cocoa, and a tower of dry toast" and then

> The feast commences with two enormous dishes of whiting and soles. After the edge of appetite has been blunted on these trifles, the serious business of the day begins. A couple of 'spread eagles', ie fowls squashed flat and embellished with mushrooms, face a mound of sausages enclosed in a rampart of mashed potatoes, and are supported on either hand by a regiment of boiled eggs and a solid square of beefsteak. These are backed up by a reserve of omelettes, sweet and savoury, anchovy toast, more graphically than elegantly known as "dirty Toast"—and "squish"—a synonym for marmalade.

The abundant leftovers find their way, the author is relieved to report, to the family of the scout or college servant. The only person who suffers, since he must pay the bill, is "poor paterfamilias."

Earlier, there had been coffee-houses. John Evelyn saw a Greek visitor drinking coffee at Balliol in the 1630s, "the first I ever saw drink" the substance. According to Anthony Wood the first coffee-house opened "at the Angel in the parish of S. Peter in the East" in 1650 "and there [coffee] was by some, who delighted in novelty, drank." In 1654 a rival establishment opened on the other side of the High Street, "in an house between Edmund Hall and Queen Coll. Corner," and in 1655 a royalist apothecary started selling coffee "in his house against All Souls Coll.." His customers—royalists and others who "esteemed themselves either virtuosi or wits"—included Christopher Wren. Wood, though himself not unknown in such establishments, maintains that "The decay of study, and consequently of learning, are coffee houses, to which most scholars retire and spend much of the day in hearing and speaking of news, in speaking vilely of their superiors." The Queen's Lane Coffee House flourishes on the site of the 1654 building, and across the road the much newer Grand Café lays claim to the 1650 site.

Many people preferred more intoxicating beverages, which were available, indeed, even at coffee-houses. Graham Midgley (*University Life in Eighteenth-Century Oxford*) gives a whole chapter to "Drinking and Riot." Samuel Johnson boasted that University College had witnessed his ability to drink "three bottles of port without being the worse for it"—unlike most of the carousers Midgley chronicles. Dr. Charlett, trying to get back to Magdalen after a drunken night out at New College, dismissed his servant-boy, who was drunk too, "for lighting him home with a silver tankard instead of a dark lantern." Wadham, it was claimed in 1704, was "no less famed for liquor than learning; here 'tis at your option to be a sot or a scholar." Students and their seniors consumed considerable quantities of port, wine, and ale; fought each other and the townsmen; fell downstairs; smashed doors and windows and furniture; and punctuated solemn ceremonies with their vomiting. The senior members in particular often had little else to fill their time and simply drank themselves to death.

More recently coffee-houses have been joined by an abundance of restaurants, gastropubs, cafés, bars, delicatessens, and farmers' markets. (One of the best is the East Oxford Farmers' and Community Market, on Saturday mornings at East Oxford Primary School.) Few eaters, however, have followed the adventurous example of the Oxford geologist William Buckland (1784–1856), at whose table could be sampled mouse toast, panther chops, crocodile, and even—he admitted he did not enjoy them—bluebottles.

Cranmer's burning, from Foxe's *Book of Martyrs* (Wikimedia Commons)

8 | Faith in the City
Oxford and Religion

> You know, I suppose, that they raise pa'sons there like radishes in a
> bed? And though it do take—how many years, Bob?—five years to
> turn a lirruping hobble-de-hoy chap into a solemn preaching man
> with no corrupt passions, they'll do it, if it can be done, and polish
> un off, like the workmen they be, and turn un out wi' a long face,
> and a long black coat and waist-coat, and a religious collar and
> hat, same as they used to wear in the Scriptures, so that his own
> mother wouldn't know un sometimes.

Such, a carter tells the impressionable young Jude Fawley, is
Christminster—Oxford in Thomas Hardy's *Jude the Obscure*. The
carter's knowledge, it turns out, comes only from hearsay, but for
much of the university's history its major aim was indeed to raise
parsons like radishes. They were still much in evidence in the 1920s
Oxford of *Brideshead Revisited*, where Sebastian Flyte and Charles
Ryder, motoring off to the country in a borrowed two-seater Morris
Cowley, narrowly avoid "collision with a clergyman, black-straw-
hatted, white-bearded, pedalling quietly down the wrong side of
the High Street." Visibly religious personnel, mostly engaged in less
dangerous activities, are still a commoner sight in Oxford than in
most towns—robes, wimples, clerical capes billowing in the wind.

Different creeds have flourished here, from the Oxford
Movement to the "Bible moths," a name given to the Wesleys and
their early adherents in the 1720s and 1730s, when John was a fellow of Lincoln and Charles an undergraduate at Christ Church.
(Later in the century the first Oxford Methodist preaching house
was at 32 and 34 New Inn Hall Street, near the Wesley Memorial
church, which was built in its present form in 1878.) Different traditions of Anglican worship survive at the evangelical St. Ebbe's
and St. Aldate's and the High Church or Anglo-Catholic Pusey
House, founded in 1884 by Henry Parry Liddon to provide "a home

of sacred learning and a rallying point of the Christian faith" and to guard against "those speculations which, with the caprice of ever-changeful fashion, occupy in successive years the thoughts of young men." Anglo-Catholic too is St. Mary Magdalen, a fourteenth-century church restored in the nineteenth by George Gilbert Scott where, in vintage High Anglican manner, a portrait of Charles I, "King and Martyr," is displayed.

In modern times the various Christian denominations have been catered for by their own halls and colleges, although the non-Catholic institutions among them tend now to take students from a wider variety of backgrounds. Regent's Park College is a Baptist foundation which moved to Oxford from London in 1927. In 1957 it became a Permanent Private Hall of the university, with students taking the same degree examinations as other undergraduates. The same status is enjoyed by the Roman Catholic St. Benet's Hall, Greyfriars, Campion Hall, and Blackfriars (whose "bleak cool austere chapel" is mentioned in Jill Paton Walsh's novel *Lapsing*). Mansfield College was formerly a private hall for Congregationalists (now United Reformed), and Harris Manchester College for Unitarians. They became full colleges of the university in 1995 and 1996. The buildings of both, mainly from the 1880s–90s, are in neo-Gothic style and the chapel at Harris Manchester has glass by Morris and Burne-Jones.

Muslim places of worship include the Central Mosque in Manzil Way off Cowley Road and the Bath Street Mosque. The Oxford Centre for Islamic Studies, on George Street, is to move into new buildings on Marston Road which, as its website says, blend "the architectural features of the traditional Oxford colleges with the forms and styles of the classical period of Islam."

St. Frideswide

In Old English the name of St. Frideswide, patron saint of Oxford, was "Frithuswith," "Peace-Strong." The legendary histories have her bringing peace through miraculous cures and her prayerful life at the monastery built by her father, a local king, and named after her. But such serenity only becomes possible after some narrow escapes from a certain Algar, a villainous and impious King of Leicester, who has other ideas for her than life as a nun. Betrothed to Christ, she refuses Algar and he sends his men to take her by force. God blinds the villain's underlings—Frideswide prays successfully for them to be forgiven and their sight restored—but he will not take the hint and persists in pursuing her. Frideswide, warned by an angel, flees with two loyal nuns in a boat guided by an angel-boatman. Meanwhile, at the gates of Oxford, Algar too is struck blind; in William of Malmesbury's account (c. 1125) this causes him to repent and regain his sight, but in longer twelfth-century versions he remains "blind all the days of his life, always plotting and scheming to injure blessed Frideswide" (John Blair's translation in *Saint Frideswide: the Earliest Texts*). Safe in her holiness from his schemes, she stays for a few years in Bampton or Binsey—tradition conflates the two—before returning to Oxford and her monastery, where she dies on 19 October 727. (On this, her day, officials of the city and the university annually attend a service in the cathedral.)

The saint's cult grew up as miracles continued, and in 1180 what were believed to be her remains were reburied, with much ceremony, in a magnificent shrine: it was fitting that "so precious a pearl . . . should no longer lie hidden in the earth." A century later a new shrine was built, and survived until it was broken up during the Reformation. The bones were ejected in 1538 and Catherine Martyr, wife of the Protestant reformer and Regius Professor of Divinity Peter Martyr, was buried somewhere nearby in 1552. Her remains were in turn removed in 1556 after Catholicism had briefly regained power under Mary I. Finally in 1562 Canon James Calfhill imposed a strange compromise "by which the bones could be dealt with decently, while at the same time all foolish [Popish] superstition could be suppressed" (Blair's translation): the bones of Frideswide and Catherine Martyr were reburied, "mingled and confused" together, in an unmarked grave.

Fortunately some fragments of the shrine (carved with a variety of foliage including hawthorn, sycamore, oak, and maple) came to light in 1875 and 1985. They were sufficient to enable the partial reconstruction installed in the Latin Chapel of the cathedral in 2002. Here too, in the brightly colored glass of the east window designed by Benjamin Woodward, is Edward Burne-Jones's account (1859) of Frideswide's life. Algar and his followers march, heavily armed, while the saint hides in a bush and then a pigsty, heals the sick, and draws water from the well at Binsey. (The well is still to be seen in the churchyard there.) A bolt of lightning like a red lance hits Algar. In the final panel, at bottom right, the dying Frideswide's attendants kneel, united in devotion, their robes joining like one richly colored cloth. She dies in a room whose Pre-Raphaelite detail contrasts with the fragmentary state of the shrine and the sketchiness of the legends: there is a deep casement, itself with stained glass, and a hint of greenery beyond. There is a dresser and even, in the top right-hand corner, a pink flushable toilet.

St. Peter in the East and St. Edmund Hall

The earliest Christian sites in the city include the small, dark crypt of St. Peter in the East. The church above it has been the library of St. Edmund Hall since 1970. St. Edmund of Abingdon, ascetic and scholar, taught at Oxford in the late twelfth and early thirteenth centuries and was (for the time) an unusually unworldly Archbishop of Canterbury in 1234–40. His cult was popular in medieval Oxford and the hall named after him was founded at the end of the thirteenth century. Between the 1550s and the 1920s its Principals were appointed by The Queen's College; when it achieved independent collegiate status in 1957, it retained the name "hall" to honor its continuity with the medieval academic halls of which it was the last survivor.

St. Edmund, in Rodney Munday's bronze figure (2007) sits at the college end of St. Peter's graveyard (full of snowdrops in late winter) near where he is thought to have lived and taught. He is lean, austere, deep in his learned or holy book, but not unapproachable since you can sit beside him on his curved bench. Two other figures, among those carved by Michael Groser on the tower of St. Peter in the East, have become well known. The keen but kindly eyes, elongated face, and slightly enigmatic smile belong to Rev. Graham Midgley (1923–99), English tutor and at various times

Vice Principal, Dean, and Chaplain of St Edmund Hall. With him, on the east side of the tower, is his labrador, Fred. (Both are wearing dog collars.) Midgley edited Bunyan's poems and wrote a good book on eighteenth-century Oxford, but his best-known composition is likely to remain his epitaph for Fred:

> Beneath this turf the Dean's dog Fred
> Without his master, goes to Earth, stone dead.
> But on the tower, stone Dean and Fred together
> Enjoy the sunshine and endure bad weather.

Fred and other labradors patiently endured not only the weather but the essays on Milton and Pope and Dickens read aloud by generations of undergraduates in the Dean's rooms.

The Hall has a famously attractive small front quadrangle which serves as a natural meeting place and focus for college life. The buildings of the quad were put up at dates varying from the late sixteenth century to the twentieth. (The well is medieval but with a modern wellhead.) At the west end is the Old Dining Hall, begun in 1659, and at the east the small chapel, and above it the paneled Old Library, of 1680–2. The east window of the chapel contains glass by Burne-Jones and Morris; the more unusual altarpiece is Ceri Richards' *The Supper at Emmaus* (1958). The risen Christ sits in intense yellow light at the moment when the two disciples' "eyes were opened, and they knew him; and he vanished out of their sight" (Luke 24:31).

Tall modern buildings by Kenneth Stevens and Partners (1965–9) helped accommodate the huge increase in student numbers after college status was granted. Two of these buildings bear the names of A. B. Emden (Principal 1929–51) and Rev. John Kelly (Principal 1951–79), who did most to transform a small hall with a reputation mainly for rugby and rowing into a full-scale college. (They are also among Groser's "grotesques" for St. Peter's: Emden, bespectacled, at the southeast corner of the tower, and Kelly, smiling with squash racket, above the porch.) The sporting reputation remained, its vigor attested by the loud, opposition-drowning college cry of

"Haaaaaall!" Something of the informality of the smaller institution also survived, as may be suggested by the general habit of calling the college "Teddy Hall"—as people have since at least the 1850s.

New College: cloister and chapel

There is a feeling of deep seclusion in New College Cloister, even if you can often hear, in the distance, traffic, the clang of scaffolding, or the screech of bicycle brakes. The cloister (1400) is dominated by an immense evergreen holm-oak (or ilex), planted in the nineteenth century and achieving more modern celebrity in a scene from the film of *Harry Potter and the Goblet of Fire*. The walls are lined with larger-than-life fourteenth-century mitered or crowned stone figures once attached to the tower of St. Mary the Virgin. Most are somewhat worn, have slightly bowed heads, and contribute, especially in the dark corners, to a rather eerie atmosphere. They must have looked quite different up on the tower in the sunshine, but here even the Virgin looks threatening. Her substitute scepter is made of iron.

Secluded though the cloister remains, one of the main purposes of William of Wykeham in founding the college in 1379 was to train clergy and send them out to be "fruitful to the Church . . . the King and the Realm." They were to fill some of the gaps left by the Black Death. Wykeham (c. 1324–1404) was himself a great man in church and state, Bishop of Winchester and twice Chancellor of England. In 1382 he also founded Winchester College, beginning a close—indeed for centuries exclusive—connection between that school and New College. He is represented as a kneeling figure on the gate tower in New College Lane, on the Muniment Tower in the Great Quad, and in stained glass in the north aisle of the ante-chapel. His New College was officially named St. Mary's—it was "new" to distinguish it from Oriel, which had originally been called St. Mary's. One of its innovations was the stress both on teaching undergraduates and on providing accommodation for them in college. In keeping with this emphasis, Wykeham built a single Great Quadrangle (completed in 1386) with chapel, hall, library, and living quarters: a purpose-built educational and spiritual center. Before this colleges had resident fellows while students were scattered in halls. The New College pattern was soon widely followed.

The chapel has not survived unscathed into modern times. The reredos, part of George Gilbert Scott's campaign of 1877–81, displays what Geoffrey Tyack describes as "ranks of anaemic saints and prophets." Nevertheless, there are individually powerful elements. Late fourteenth-century misericords—the carved undersides of seats in the choir stalls—depict some remarkably human, dignified figures, as well as winged monsters, peacocks, hedgehogs, walled cities with portcullises and spires, a fight with dagger and sword, and two tumblers poised acrobatically on a man's head. The ante-chapel houses a more sober and affecting work, Sir Jacob Epstein's *Lazarus* (1947-8). The "eight-foot-tall body [is] still swathed tightly for burial and only the head turned wearily towards the light, with eyes still closed," notes Epstein's biographer June Rose; it displays "a quiet compassion and a restraint rarely seen in his work." Its cream Hopton Wood limestone blends well with the pale tones of its surroundings; Eric Gill used the same stone for his World War I memorial, also in the ante-chapel. (To this he added, in 1930, the moving tribute to three German members of the college killed fighting on the other side.)

Beyond the Great Quadrangle and the Garden Quadrangle of 1682–1707 is the garden. Herbaceous borders line a stretch of the thirteenth-century city wall with its bastions and ramparts. There are interesting views into St. Peter's in the East and St. Edmund Hall, a variety of large trees, and, most distinctively, a large artificial mound. Once it was more artificial than now: Celia Fiennes, in 1694, describes "a great mount in the middle which is ascended by degrees in a round of green paths defended by greens cut low, and on the top is a summer-house."

Jews in Oxford

In the twelfth and thirteenth centuries a Jewish community flourished around Fish or Great Jewry Street—what is now St. Aldate's. The synagogue was on part of the site of Christ Church. The Jewish cemetery was where part of Magdalen and the Botanic Garden are now. Restricted from practicing most other trades, Jews were involved mainly in money-lending and property-letting—services in particular demand as the number of students in the city grew. David of Oxford, who died in 1244, was one of the most successful financiers of his time. But here as elsewhere in England life was precarious: there were periodic confiscations, fines, taxes, arrests, and accusations of coin-clipping, kidnapping, and sacrilege. Jews were obliged to wear a strip of yellow taffeta to mark them out—ominously suggestive of the later yellow star. In the year of David's death, students rioted against Jews, ransacked their houses, and were imprisoned for some weeks but then released without charge. In 1268 a Jewish onlooker allegedly attacked and desecrated a cross as it passed in procession towards St. Frideswide's. The Jews of Oxford as a group were held responsible, imprisoned, and then forced to raise large sums to pay for a marble cross (no longer extant) near Merton College and a new silver crucifix for processional use.

In the run-up to Edward I's expulsion of the Jews from England in 1290 there were further impositions: a ban on letting houses to Christians in 1271, a ban on usury, and a poll-tax of threepence each in 1275. There was a new sequence of accusations, in many cases probably manufactured. In 1279 several prominent Oxford Jews were hanged for coin-clipping; Queen Eleanor's cook obtained the house belonging to one of the victims, Isaac de Pulet. In 1287 the whole, by now dwindling, community was incarcerated until payment was forthcoming. (Much of what is known was gathered by Cecil Roth [1899–1970], the first Reader in Post-Biblical Jewish Studies at the university from 1939, in *The Jews of Medieval Oxford*.)

Scholars had sought out Jews in Oxford, not only to persecute them or to borrow money, but in quest of Hebrew learning. Roth believed that Friar Roger Bacon, among others, probably had such scholarly contacts. And it was mainly in the context of learning that people of Jewish origin gradually re-entered Oxford in the centuries after the Expulsion. (Practicing Jews, however, were at least in theory banned from the country until the 1650s.) There were a few families of shopkeepers in the eighteenth century, and at least one early dentist or "operator for teeth." But only in the mid-nineteenth century did a full community re-emerge. Various buildings were used as its synagogue until a more permanent site was found in Richmond Road—consecrated in 1893, rebuilt (David Stern and Partners) and reconsecrated in 1974. Jewish students have often formed an important element in the congregation; non-Christians have been allowed to enter the university since 1871.

The Oxford Martyrs: "such a candle . . . as I trust shall never be put out"

In 1557 a Spanish friar, having inspected the Oxford colleges, declared the doctrine taught there "Catholic and correct." It was a suitable place in which to put on trial and to burn the Oxford Martyrs, three Protestant leaders in fact closely associated with Cambridge, where the new faith had many more adherents. (Protestantism was strong also in London.) Thomas Cranmer, as Archbishop of Canterbury from 1532, and especially during the reign of Edward VI (1547–53), had been one of the chief architects of reform, compiling the original English *Book of Common Prayer* (1549, 1552). Notable among his allies were Hugh Latimer, for a time Bishop of Worcester, renowned for his plain-spoken evangelical preaching, and Nicholas Ridley, Bishop of Rochester and then of London. All three were notorious heretics and traitors in the view of the Catholics who took power on the succession of Mary I in 1553. The public dishonoring and condemnation of the three in Oxford was intended to discredit the Reformation as a whole.

The former bishops were held much of the time in the Bocardo prison (demolished in 1771), which was part of, or close to, the north gate of the city, next to St. Michael at the North Gate. The door of their cell is on show in the tower of the church. ("Bocardo" either with donnish wit refers to the logical figure Bocardo—difficult to get out of—or is more homely slang for a privy.) John Foxe's narrative, in his *Acts and Monuments* (known more often as *Foxe's Book of Martyrs*) describes their suffering and proclaims their martyrdom. Latimer and Ridley, having refused to retract their beliefs, were burnt at the stake on 16 October 1555. The place of execution, Foxe tells us, was "Upon the north side of the town, in the ditch over against

Balliol College." As the two elderly men prepared to face their terrible and very public ordeal, Latimer is supposed to have encouraged his colleague, "Be of good comfort Master Ridley, and play the man: we shall this day light such a candle by God's grace in England as, I trust, shall never be put out." These words do not appear until Foxe's second edition of 1570, but whatever was actually said, there is no doubting the bravery of Latimer and Ridley.

Latimer expired quite quickly. Ridley's suffering was appalling: the flames took slowly. His brother-in-law tried to hasten his death by piling "faggots upon him, so that he clean covered him, which made the fire more vehement beneath, that it burned clean all his nether parts before it once touched the upper." Still he called "Lord have mercy upon me," says Foxe, "intermeddling this cry, 'Let the fire come unto me; I cannot burn.'" A cross on the road in Broad Street, opposite part of Balliol, marks the probable site of the burnings: nineteenth-century workmen found here some charred bone and the remains of a stake.

Cranmer, who would suffer in the same ditch a few months later, was forced to watch from the tower of the gatehouse next to Bocardo. In late 1555 and early 1556 Catholic theologians continued to try to wear down the former archbishop's resolve. Eventually he did sign several recantations; legally, this should have saved him from execution but the Queen was determined to punish this chief Protestant offender. (She may have been further goaded by Cranmer's involvement in the downfall of her mother, Catherine of Aragon.) In February 1556, after a spell in the greater comfort of Christ Church Deanery, he was "disgraded"—stripped of his ecclesiastical dignities—in the cathedral and sent back to Bocardo. Then, on 21 March, he was taken to the University Church and placed on a scaffold "opposite the pulpit." The occasion was planned as a Catholic propaganda victory in which the ex-heretic would publicly confess his errors before he died. But Cranmer had changed his mind again. He seemed at first to be sticking to the expected script, but then came to "the great thing, that so much troubleth my conscience . . . and that is the setting abroad of a writing [his recantation] contrary to the truth which I thought in my heart, and written for fear of death, and to save my life if it might be." He rejected everything he had recently "written or signed with my hand . . . And forasmuch as my hand offended, writing contrary to my heart, my hand shall first be punished therefore: for may I come to the fire, it shall be first burned."

The learned Doctors who had condemned Cranmer were, Foxe is delighted to announce, dismayed and disappointed. They "began to let down their ears [metaphorically, no doubt], to rage, fret and fume." Amid much shouting he was silenced, "pulled down from the stage" and led to the fire, still arguing with two angry Spanish friars. "And when the wood was kindled, and the fire began to burn near him, stretching out his arm, he put his right hand into the flame," as promised. He stood still and steadfast, "and using often the words of [St.] Stephen, 'Lord Jesus, receive my spirit,' in the greatness of the flame, he gave up the ghost."

Statues of the three bishops figure on the Martyrs' Memorial, built in 1841–2 to the design of George Gilbert Scott. Its aim at the time was, for campaigners led by Rev. Charles Golightly, to reassert the Protestant roots of the Church of England in the face of the Oxford Movement's claim to continuity with Catholicism. The inscription on the monument declared forcefully that the martyrs died "bearing witness to the sacred truths which they had affirmed and maintained against the errors of the Church of Rome." Yet its neo-Gothic style is more often associated with the Catholic architect Pugin and with Golightly's opponents; for David Hinton in *Oxford Architecture* it is an "extravaganza" with "the full array of ogee arches, crocketed pinnacles, miniature battlements, and foliate ornament." Its model was the "Eleanor crosses" commemorating Edward I's wife, and particularly the cross at Waltham in Essex. "Fervent undergraduates preach here on warm evenings," said John Betjeman in 1938 (*An Oxford University Chest*). They might now find it hard to be heard over the traffic.

The Oxford Movement

Its leaders were John Henry Newman and his friends Richard Hurrell Froude, John Keble (after whom the college was named), and Edward Bouverie Pusey (whence Pusey House). One of their main beliefs was that the Church of England was the "apostolical" descendant of the Roman Catholic Church and had veered too far in the direction of Protestantism. Nonconformist churches—the Methodists and Baptists and the like—were not true churches. Where Evangelicals put individual bible-reading at the center of their faith, the Movement stressed the works of the Church Fathers and the authority of the church. Increasingly it also promoted ritual and the decoration of churches. A series of *Tracts for the Times* advanced the views of the movement, giving rise to its other name, Tractarianism. Furious controversy raged in Oxford, the group's headquarters, and the country at large, and was increased in 1841 by Newman's Tract 90, in which he argued that the Church of England's Thirty-Nine Articles of belief were not irreconcilable with Roman Catholic doctrine. Adherence to the articles had been, since 1571, a condition of membership of the university, therefore excluding non-Anglicans. For some people Tract 90, and Froude's posthumously revealed devotion to the Virgin Mary, sounded like heresy or even treason. Newman went on to cause an even greater scandal by converting to Catholicism, with some of his followers, in 1845. He left Oxford and went on to become a Catholic priest and eventually Cardinal and probable future saint—he was recently declared Blessed. The Oxford Movement is often felt to have declined after Newman's departure, but Keble and Pusey remained in the Church of England and continued to influence its Anglo-Catholic wing.

To outsiders such conflicts are difficult to fathom: is God really so pernickety, so keen on details? But debate was at least conducted without the bloodshed which characterized similar differences of opinion during the Reformation.

Oriel College: religion and reason

The college grew from the 1320s around a house called, from its oriel window, La Oriole. Rebuilding in the reigns of James I and Charles I produced the present front quadrangle with, opposite the entrance, porch and canopied statues probably inspired by those at Wadham. The Kings are likely to be Edward II, official founder of the college in 1326, and Charles I. (Some find them crude: "two awkward statues like weathercocks," says Christopher Hobhouse in his 1939 book about Oxford.) But it was in the first half of the nineteenth century that what happened inside these buildings mattered most.

Fellowships at Oriel were awarded on the basis of tough competitive examination, balanced by recognition of intellectual potential as much as academic achievement. This policy resulted in the election of a series of remarkable men, particularly under Edward Copleston, Provost 1814–28, and in the early years of his successor Edward Hawkins. Between 1815 and 1819 Thomas Arnold was a fellow: the future headmaster of Rugby School, educational reformer, campaigner for Catholic emancipation, and liberal opponent of the Oxford Movement—or the "Oxford malignants" as he put it in the *Edinburgh Review* in April 1836. At Oriel Arnold overlapped with John Keble, later a leader of the Movement and author of the bestselling cycle of poems *The Christian Year* (1827). Arnold's friend Richard Whately, eventually Archbishop of Dublin, became a fellow, like Keble, in 1811. Whately in his Oriel days was a traditional "Oxford eccentric" who kept a supply of herrings in his rooms and taught while sprawling on a couch and smoking. He walked the streets not in cap and gown but in white coat and hat, and trained his equally white dog, Sailor, to leap from trees into the river to astonish (and no doubt splash) passersby. But in more sober moods he was prominent among the Noetics (from the Greek *noetikos*, "of the mind or intellect"), a group including Arnold, Copleston, and Hawkins dedicated to religious belief based on reason and debate and to university reform. (The next generation of fellows included, in the 1840s, Thomas Arnold's son Matthew and his friend Arthur Hugh Clough.)

John Henry Newman, elected fellow in 1822, came to regard the Noetics as dangerously liberal in their churchmanship. But he benefited from their debates and acknowledged, in his spiritual autobiography *Apologia Pro Vita Sua*, that Whately "opened my mind, and taught me to think and to use my reason." Newman's main achievement at Oriel was his pioneering reform of undergraduate teaching. Only a few of the fellows were required, as tutors, to teach for their colleges; their work was supplemented by private tutors or coaches, usually recent graduates. Newman was appointed tutor in 1826 and was joined the following year by Richard Hurrell Froude, who would become a staunch Tractarian ally. Newman sought to limit the privileges of the gentlemen-commoners—undergraduates of high social standing—and to oppose their frequently cavalier attitudes to learning and religion. He also insisted that both the academic and the moral wellbeing of students was the responsibility of the college tutors, not the private coaches. He saw his students in the evenings, he went for long walks with them, he met them in the vacations. The tutor should, he said, be the student's "moral and religious guardian," not "a mere academical Policeman, or Constable."

Provost Hawkins, however, became worried about the way such pastoral intimacy enabled Newman to influence the young men's religious beliefs. They disagreed on many religious and disciplinary matters; there was, as Newman remembered it, "a state of constant bickerings—of coldness, dryness and donnishness on his part, and of provoking insubordination and petulance on mine." In 1830 Hawkins stopped Newman teaching new students, and he ceased to be a tutor in 1832. But his and his colleagues' work contributed to the wider reform movement in the university and established Oriel, for some years to come, as a center of excellence rivaled only by Balliol, if later greatly outshone by it.

In what was once part of Newman's rooms in the front quad, Oriel preserves a small Newman oratory. It is reached up stairs from the seventeenth-century chapel, where one may imagine young Noetics and Tractarians wrestling in prayer. The oratory is behind the organ. Glass designed by Vivienne Haig and executed by Douglas Hogg in 2001 features Newman, words from his "Lead, kindly light" and places associated with him—St. Mary's, the church at Littlemore and Oriel. Here there is a sense of quiet devotion refreshing after the tracts, controversies and theories.

Newman and the University Church: "Who could resist the charm of that spiritual apparition?"

Marks on a broad column in the University Church of St. Mary the Virgin show where the scaffold was erected for Cranmer's condemnation. From the 1830s, St. Mary's was more directly involved in the religious controversy concerning the Oxford Movement. Newman became Vicar in 1828 and in 1833 John Keble preached the sermon which many thought sparked off the Movement.

At St. Mary's, Newman preached regular parish sermons, meant in theory for the relatively small local congregation but much attended by students who wanted to hear him. He also gave lectures in the Adam de Brome chapel (then walled off, as not since 1932, from the nave) and University sermons. Today these weekly term-time sermons, addressed mainly to an audience versed in theology, are the main survival of the connection which made this the "University Church." Before most of the colleges and university buildings appeared, St. Mary's was the most visible manifestation of the institution. Here until the seventeenth century Congregation (the governing body) and the Chancellor's Court met, students attended their degree ceremonies, and the university kept its books upstairs in the Old Library. Even the university fire-engine was stationed at St. Mary's until the 1850s in Congregation House, built in the early fourteenth century for university meetings and now a café.

During Newman's incumbency, members of the university came to St. Mary the Virgin as much for the way he delivered his sermons as for their substance. According to several accounts he scarcely moved when he preached, and looked down to read his text. Yet, asked Matthew Arnold in 1883, "Who could resist the charm of that spiritual apparition, gliding in the dim afternoon light through the aisles of St Mary's, rising into the pulpit, and then, in the most entrancing of voices, breaking the silence with words and thoughts which were a religious music—subtle, sweet, mournful?" Henry William Wilberforce described how

> The sermon began in a calm musical voice, the key slightly rising as it went on: by-and-by the preacher warmed with his subject; it seemed as if his very soul and body glowed with sternly-suppressed emotion. There were times when in the midst of the most thrilling passages he would pause, without dropping his voice, for a moment which seemed long, before he uttered with gathered force and solemnity a few weighty words. The very tones of his voice seemed as if they were something more than his own.

The Church continued to regard Vicar of St. Mary's as an important appointment. The incumbents have gone on preaching a variety of views from Newman's pulpit. Peter Cornwell, like Newman, converted (in 1985) to Roman Catholicism. His successor, Canon Brian Mountford, brought a questioning, liberal agenda much of which would have horrified Newman: a respect for unbelief, an emphasis on the virtues and possibilities of doubt and on what Christians can learn from art and literature, an openness to different traditions. (A new plaque in the church remembers, beneath a gold martyr's crown, "the martyrs of the Reformation, both Catholic and Protestant" who were connected with Oxford or Oxfordshire or were brought here to be executed.)

Another evident change has been the immense number of visitors to the church—roughly 30,000 a year by the beginning of this century. Many go up the tower, which gives them a spectacular view of Oxford and the church some useful income. They can also stand in the quiet chancel, with its plain windows, fifteenth-century stalls, and pale wall memorials, or in the much broader nave with its fine Victorian stained glass (some of it by Pugin). But perhaps the most striking feature is the porch on the High Street, probably designed by Nicholas Stone. The Virgin and child are framed by twisted "barley-sugar" columns. The heads replace the originals, which were shot off by a departing parliamentarian trooper in the 1640s. Religious controversy was never far away.

Newman at Littlemore: "patriarchal simplicity"

Littlemore, two and a half miles south of Oxford, was attached to the parish of St. Mary the Virgin. Newman and his mother and sisters, who were living nearby at Rose Hill and then at Grove House, Iffley, took an interest in Littlemore and especially the health, education, and religious knowledge of its children. Newman also lobbied Oriel to build a church there; St. Mary and St. Nicholas, designed by H. J. Underwood, was consecrated in September 1836. (A chancel and tower were added in 1848.) It includes a memorial to Newman's mother, Jemima, who laid the foundation stone of the church—shown unfinished in the memorial—but died in May

1836. He felt that she often misunderstood his religious views and that he had even "taken a false step by wishing her to be at Oxford" but, he told his sister, "can never repent it for the good she has done to Littlemore."

Increasingly Newman walked out to Littlemore to escape from his controversial and (he felt) friendless public life in Oxford. In 1841 he took out a lease on an L-shaped granary and stables which had been converted into cottages. The following year he and a few disciples moved in and embarked on a quasi-monastic life. He denied to his bishop that "monastery" was an appropriate description and even, Mark Pattison claims, slammed the door in the face of the Warden of Wadham, an interfering evangelical who "asked if he might see the monastery." Pattison, the future agnostic and Rector of Lincoln College, visited Littlemore as a would-be disciple in autumn 1843 and found himself, he recorded in his diary, exaggerating his own faith. He "felt so anxious for N.'s good opinion, and suffered my mind to wander miserably in my prayers."

Father Domenico Barberi recalled in *The Tablet* that

> This unsightly building is divided by a number of walls, so as to form so many little cells; and it is so low that you might almost touch the roof with your hand. In the interior you will find the most beautiful specimen of patriarchal simplicity and gospel poverty ... At the end of [the] corridor, you will find a small dark room, which has served as an oratory. In the cells nothing to be seen but poverty and simplicity—bare walls, composed of a few rough bricks, without carpet, a straw bed, one or two chairs, and a few books, this comprises the whole furniture ... A Capuchin monastery would appear a great palace when compared to Littlemore.

Here, having resigned as Vicar of St. Mary's in September 1843 and preached his last sermon, "The Parting of Friends," to a tearful audience in Littlemore church, Newman spent his time writing and praying. It was Father Barberi who received him into the Catholic Church here in October 1845. (He left to prepare for ordination as a Catholic priest soon afterwards.) The building, once known as the

Littlemore Cottages or the College, is now an International Centre of Newman Friends. Visitors are shown Newman's writing-table and other memorabilia. The Catholic church of Blessed Dominic Barberi opened nearby in 1969.

Barberi's Capuchin monastery might have looked even more like a palace compared with the best-known institution in Littlemore, the Oxfordshire County Asylum, where from 1846 "lunatic paupers" were kept in often overcrowded prison conditions. The present, more civilized Littlemore Hospital moved into buildings across the road from the original site in 1998.

St. Aloysius and Hopkins' "Towery city"

John Betjeman, as a pupil at the Dragon School in North Oxford, was already fascinated by churches and church architecture. In St. Giles' he came upon the Roman Catholic church of St. Aloysius, where, he recalled in an essay in *My Oxford*, in "a side chapel there was a relic of the True Cross [since removed], surrounded by candles, polished brass and jewels, which seemed to me very sacred and alarming, as, indeed, did the whole church with its apse of coloured saints and its smell of incense and many *dévoués* crossing themselves and looking back at us while on their knees." It rendered everything "plain and trivial back at school," he says in his verse autobiography *Summoned by Bells*.

St. Aloysius was intended to have a strong impact on a city which, in spite of Newman's example, remained mostly unpersuaded of the virtues of Catholicism. Since 1795 there had been a Catholic chapel in the poor eastern district of St. Clement's, but St. Aloysius, begun in 1873 and dedicated by Cardinal Manning in 1875, was nearer both to the center and to wealthier and more fashionable North Oxford. Manning preached to a full congregation including Oscar Wilde (of Protestant family but tempted, for a time, to convert) about the university's decline from medieval certainties to "become the intellectual minister to a hesitating and fragmentary world" (*The Spectator*, 27 November 1875). Gerard Manley Hopkins, a priest somewhat more diffident about lecturing his flock, was here as curate in 1878–9. His time at St. Aloysius was not wholly happy. He claimed that most of his parishioners were friendly, but felt that they "criticised what went on in our church a great deal too freely." On the other hand he saw in many of them "a stiff respectful stand-off air"—any attempt to joke with the church's Young Men's Association would have "put them to deep and lasting pain," he told his mother. He seems to have been overworked—when he left four new assistants were brought in—and felt some sense of exclusion from his beloved university. (Catholics had been allowed to attend the university since 1871, but were forbidden to do so by their own Church authorities until the 1890s. Hopkins, however, had been an undergraduate at Balliol in the mid-1860s, before his conversion.) "We are strangers in Jerusalem," the ex-Balliol and Merton Manning had declared in his sermon of 1875, "and to be strangers in our home is full of pain. We know its every street, and love its every stone."

Hopkins' mixed feelings about Oxford are apparent in his sonnet of March 1879, "Duns Scotus' Oxford," where the "Towery city and branchy between towers"—man and nature together—is simultaneously mourned and celebrated. The modern city, with its expanding suburbs, is not what it was: "Thou hast a base and brickish skirt there, sours/That neighbour-nature thy grey beauty is grounded/Best in." Once country and town were balanced— "coped and poised"—in this essentially rural place. Yet the poet still breathes the same air, lives among the same "weeds and waters," as his favorite theologian Johannes Duns Scotus (c. 1265–1308), a Franciscan friar who studied and taught in Oxford. It was he, "Of realty the rarest-veinèd unraveller" as the poem has it, who influenced Hopkins' response to nature as symbol of God and his search for *haecceitas* or "thisness." (Such complexities did not recommend themselves to the Protestant and humanist posterity who took the word "dunce" from Duns.) Scotus was also known for his promulgation of the doctrine of the Immaculate— sinless—Conception of the Virgin Mary, which the poet hymns at the climax of his sonnet.

Hopkins is commemorated in St. Aloysius by a holy water stoup given in his memory. The church pays more attention, understandably, to St. Edmund Campion, a Catholic martyr from Oxford to answer the Protestant Oxford Martyrs whose memorial can be seen from outside the church. He was a fellow of the recently-founded St. John's and impressed Queen Elizabeth with his eloquence when she came to Oxford in 1566. He was, according to Thomas Alfield's *True Report of the Death and Martyrdome of M. Campion* (1582), "a glass and mirror, a light and lantern, a pattern and example to youth, to age, to learned, to unlearned." He went to Ireland in 1570 and then to the Catholic college at Douai, where he was later ordained as a Jesuit priest. He came back to England as a missionary in 1580 and was captured the following year. He was hanged, drawn, and quartered at Tyburn on 1 December 1581 with two fellow-missionaries—traitors, as far as the law was concerned. A wall-painting at the west end of the church shows Campion standing on a cart, the noose round his neck. His look suggests both suffering and spiritual insight, the sense of a world beyond the terrible moment. (Campion Hall, a Jesuit permanent private hall of the university, was founded in 1896 and moved to its present buildings in Brewer Street in 1935.) A matching painting shows scenes from the life of the sixteenth-century Jesuit St. Aloysius Gonzaga. The church became the Oxford Oratory in 1993.

Keble College: a "peculiar nineteenth-century stare"

In Parks Road rise the tall, distinctive structures of Keble. As the naming after John Keble suggests, the college is "a sort of apotheosis of the Oxford movement, translated into architectural terms" (John Julius Norwich, *The Architecture of Southern England*, 1985). Over a background of deep red, William Butterfield's "designs run riot in contrasting colours of buff, yellow, blue and black, sometimes diapered, sometimes chequered, in horizontal bands, dotted lines or zigzags." Keble caused controversy at the time of its erection (1868–82) and has continued to divide opinion. "It can never look mellow," J. D. Sedding wrote in *Building News* in 1885:

No-one supposes that it ever will look less startling and raw than
its talented author took pains to make it ... Nature—who is a
soft-hearted creature—will try her best to throw her charitable
cloak over its crude walls; but Keble will be a nature-puzzling,
time-defying object till the crack of doom, and will stare with its
peculiar nineteenth-century stare straight into the eyes of eternity.

Norwich finds the style "at its most abandoned in the vast
Chapel." With its high pinnacles, on its grand, often windy quadrangle, it makes an impressive statement. High above the doors is
a Lamb of God in high relief, its fleece ribbed like some kind of
armor; many feet above that, St. Michael spears the dragon. Inside
are mosaics, stained glass, patterned tiles and brickwork, and textiles. It all seems rather somber apart from William Holman Hunt's
The Light of the World (1851–3), which is housed in a side-chapel.
Christ—calm, bright-haloed, and carrying a lantern—knocks at a
closed door: "Behold, I stand at the door, and knock: if any man
hear my voice, and open the door, I will come in to him, and will
sup with him, and he with me" (Revelation 3.20). Hunt worked to
achieve the quality of spiritual luminescence with the aid of "the
phosphor light of a perfect moon," gaslight, and candles. (He produced a second version for St. Paul's Cathedral in London in 1900.)
The painting has always inspired devotion in some viewers, groans
in others. For Thomas Carlyle it was "a mere papistical phantasy."
For others it was too sentimental or simply over-familiar. For the
painter it had deep personal significance: behind the frame, invis-
ible to the viewer, he inscribed the words "Non me Praetermisso
Domine," asking Christ not to pass him by.

Exeter College

The present Exeter chapel, consecrated in 1859 and restored in 2007,
replaced a seventeenth-century one. (The college itself was founded
originally in 1314 but almost all the surviving buildings are much
later.) Most architectural historians would, it seems, happily pull
it down. Exeter "could never leave well alone," laments John Julius
Norwich. The chapel, derived by Sir George Gilbert Scott from the

much larger medieval Sainte Chapelle in Paris, exhibits "unrelieved awfulness. Its great height totally overpowers the innocuous front quad, while its interior is an orgy of meretricious decoration that makes a sorry contrast with the cool restraint of its glorious exemplar." For Michael De-la-Noy in *Exploring Oxford* (1991), the style is "a sort of exhausting Victorian Byzantine." Peter Heyworth (*The Oxford Guide to Oxford*, 1981) joins the hunt: the chapel is "a restless agglomeration of special effects" including its "forest of vaulting ... mosaic and gold-leaf reredos framed in claustrophobic arches" and "stained glass, bright but without brilliance. It leaves one gasping for air."

Certainly there is much to look at—the heraldic shields over the stalls by G. F. Bodley, the large rosettes on the roof, the columns and capitals, the authoritative figure of the crowned Christ at the center of the sparkling gold reredos. Near the altar stands the large tapestry of *The Adoration of the Magi*, "one of Burne-Jones' most haunting and most somber designs, long figures still among the lilies," thinks David Piper in *Treasures of Oxford*. (It was executed by Morris & Co.; Burne-Jones and Morris were both undergraduates at Exeter, as was Tolkien, commemorated at the back of the chapel in a bust by his daughter-in-law, Faith Tolkien.) Perhaps the chapel is a little overwhelming; perhaps most worshippers and visitors are less sensitive souls than the commentators.

Manchip, the Master of Warlock College—a thinly disguised version of Exeter—has reason to dislike the chapel in Robert Robinson's *Landscape with Dead Dons* (1956). Someone stabs him in the back with one of his own dessert-knives when he is on the roof—he used to enjoy the view—and conceals the body by propping it up like one more statue. But there is not much room on the roof of the real Exeter chapel for stabbing people, and the statues are prominent but rather lower; Robinson said that he "borrowed the statues from Trinity."

Changing churches

Oxford church buildings have changed their size, shape, and function. St. Ebbe's was founded in the early eleventh century but rebuilt in the nineteenth; all that remains from the Middle Ages is the fine Romanesque doorway incorporated in the west wall. The fourteenth-century interior of St. Michael at the North Gate was remodeled after a fire in 1953. St. Philip and St. James in North Oxford, with its tall spire and "fanciful hips and ridges" (John Betjeman), is now the Oxford Centre for Mission Studies. All Saints, formerly the official City Church—St. Michael's succeeded it—has been the magnificent library of Lincoln College since 1975. St. Paul's in Walton Street thrives, in spite of its crumbling Ionic columns, as the Freud café.

At St. Cross church Dorothy L. Sayers' Lord Peter Wimsey, Balliol's most famous fictional graduate, marries Harriet Vane to the disgust of his snobbish, dreadful sister-in-law the Duchess. She judges it "an obscure little church in a side-street, very gloomy and damp-looking" (*Busman's Honeymoon*, 1937). It seems unlikely that she would regard its new role as the Balliol Historic Collections Centre with greater favor. (Next to the partly twelfth-century church is the graveyard where, buried, are Kenneth Grahame, Walter Pater, A. C. Bradley of *Shakespearean Tragedy*, and Kenneth Tynan, the theater critic.)

St. Peter-le-Bailey, a church designed by Basil Champneys to replace an earlier, nearby church demolished in 1874, still serves a religious function but as the chapel of St. Peter's College. St. Peter's—established on a fairly constricted site as a hall in 1928 and a college in 1961—has absorbed and adapted several other buildings including the church rectory (Linton House), Hannington Hall (built originally as part of New Inn Hall in 1832), and the former Central School for Girls in New Inn Hall Street. The classical Canal House (1827–9), headquarters of the Oxford Canal Company, became the Master's lodgings.

First intake of students at Lady Margaret Hall, 1879 (by kind permission of the Principal and Fellows of Lady Margaret Hall)

9 | **Privilege and Progress**
The Changing Face of
City and University

The population of Oxford went up from 49,000 in 1901, to 106,000 in 1961, and 151,900 in 2011. From the 1950s, people from Asia and the Caribbean began to settle, and by 2009 "19.6% of the population were estimated to be from black and minority ethnic backgrounds" (oxford.gov.uk). Also by 2009, following continued expansion by Oxford and Oxford Brookes Universities, an estimated 26 percent of "the working age resident population" were full-time students. Increasing numbers of them were postgraduates, whose numbers and importance were recognized by the foundation of the graduate-only colleges Nuffield (endowed 1937, built mainly in the 1950s), St. Antony's (1950), Linacre (1962), St. Cross (1965), Wolfson (1965), Green (1979, becoming Green Templeton following a merger in 2008 with Templeton College, originally the Oxford Centre for Management Studies), and Kellogg (1990).

Probably the greatest change, however, resulted from the extraordinarily rapid growth of the motor industry (see p.185–88). It was the main reason for the 43 percent increase in the population, from 67,000 to 96,000, between 1921 and 1939. Thousands of houses were built in the 1930s, and the areas nearest to the new industrial base—including Cowley, Rose Hill, and Headington—expanded quickly. In effect, a new city appeared east of the old one. Geography exacerbated the class separation between the two: the central university area lies between the eastern suburbs and the commercial center, railway, and bus stations. Blackbird Leys, where a large estate was built in the 1950s–60s, is about five miles from the center.

But the most famous example of exclusion on social grounds—the Cutteslowe Walls affair—happened not in East Oxford, but in a newly developed northern suburb. The walls were built in 1934 by the Urban Housing Company to separate its estate, off respectable Banbury Road, from the Cutteslowe council estate. The two walls, about eight feet high and with spikes on top, divided Wentworth Road from Aldrich Road, and Carlton Road from Wolsey Road; the council-house residents, cut off from the main road, were forced to make long detours on their way to work and school. There were protests, petitions, and legal rulings. In 1935 the trade union activist Abe Lazarus marched on the walls with men carrying pickaxes and sledge-hammers, and a brass-band to celebrate the people's victory, but was stopped by police. The City Council went ahead and removed the walls in 1938 but was forced to rebuild them after a judgement in the High Court. Eventually, in 1959, the Council was able to buy the strips of land on which the walls stood and, amid much cheering, to demolish them. (The streets still change name when they reach the site of the old barriers. A blue plaque at 34 Aldrich Road, erected in 2006, commemorates the demolition.)

Social problems, as in any city, remain, and Oxford has a particularly serious homelessness problem. Combating it are several hostels as well as the Gatehouse drop-in center at St. Giles' Parish Rooms, providing food in the early evenings, and the Crisis Skylight Café at the Old Fire Station which offers "on-the-job training and experience for homeless people." Simon House in Paradise Street helps recovering alcoholics. Giving aid to the world more widely, the Oxford Committee for Famine Relief began at a meeting in St. Mary the Virgin in October 1942. It campaigned successfully for food supplies to be allowed through the Allied blockade for the starving people of Axis-occupied Greece, and developed into the more famous Oxfam. The first Oxfam shop opened at 17 Broad Street in 1948.

"Packed with the potentially great": social division and the university

The history of Oxford University has been marked by internal divisions between rich and poor colleges and students. Christ Church and Merton looked down on "lesser" colleges. Wealthy gentlemen-commoners had privileges while servitors, in order to pay their way, waited on their wealthy fellow students at table or in their rooms.

Sometimes they even did their academic "exercises" for them; "the difference, Sir, between Servitors and Gentlemen Commoners," explains a Brasenose servitor in a comedy of 1704, "is this, we are men of wit and no fortune, and they are men of fortune and no wit" (Tom Baker, *An Act at Oxford*). Still in much later times "braying accents across the quad" (Dennis Potter, *Stand Up, Nigel Barton*, 1965) denoted the objectionably loud presence of the privileged.

Inequality gradually decreased following the university reforms of the nineteenth and twentieth century. By the 1950s academic ability was beginning to replace wealth, going to the right school, sporting prowess, or family connections as the main criterion for admission. The colleges were pressed further in this direction by the findings of the public Robbins Report of 1963 and the internal Franks Commission of 1966. There would be later charges of elitism and campaigns by the university to combat it. Debate about how to persuade members of some social and ethnic minority groups even to apply for admission has intensified since the replacement of grants for most students by loans, and more recently by huge increases in fees. But on the whole it remains a much more meritocratic place than for most of its history. The historic role of a small minority of black students—future politicians, lawyers, and writers from Africa and the Caribbean—has recently been revealed by Pamela Roberts in *Black Oxford*.

Students from grammar schools arrived in increasing numbers from the 1940s. But it was still possible to feel excluded. Joe, a northern grammar-school boy in Melvyn Bragg's novel *Crossing the Lines* (2003)—a keen debater before he comes to Oxford in 1958— finds himself "tongue-tied" by the speakers at the Oxford Union: "He knew ... that he could not dress like that or speak or perform like that to an audience which he believed to be almost mythically intelligent and critical and itself packed full of the potentially great. The speakers in their evening dress, the speeches full of knowing, anecdotal embroidery, classical tags, the place so clearly a forum for those who would rule over us unnerved and paralysed him." Joe and his friends abandon the Union for more congenial places, but social division remained rife even in the apparently safer setting of at least some of the colleges. Alan Bennett was in Cambridge for his interviews and exams in 1951, although he eventually went to Oxford instead. He was shocked by his first experience of loud, loutish, greedy, and self-confident public school boys at dinner in hall: "neat, timorous and genteel, we grammar school boys were the interlopers; these slobs, as they seemed to me, the party in possession" (*The History Boys*, Introduction). Some students, Sir Keith Thomas notes in his discussion of postwar college life, saw no such problems, and the socially mobile adapted to the situation, "often acquiring a new accent and a new style of dressing." But others "equated Oxford with snobbishness and social competition, and some of them left . . . with a permanent feeling of inferiority or resentment" (*The History of the University of Oxford*, volume 8). Certain differences between groups, in the years just after 1945, when servicemen returned to take up their delayed or interrupted studies, would have been difficult to remove. As Thomas puts it, "Ex-Majors with MCs, wives and moustaches had little in common with 17-year-old boys who carried green ration-books entitling them to extra bananas."

In 1899, long before the class make-up of the university had significantly changed, Ruskin College was established with the intention of opening educational opportunities for workers. "Knowledge," declared one of the founders in 1900, "must be used to emancipate humanity, not to gratify curiosity, blind instincts, and desire for respectability." The college, at first called Ruskin Hall, took John Ruskin's name for the sake of his social criticism rather than his writings on art. It moved from 14 St. Giles' to the corner of Walton Street and Worcester Place in 1903. The present building there, of 1912, was bought by Exeter College when Ruskin moved to its redeveloped second site in Old Headington, opened fully in 2012. It has remained an independent college, with links to trades unions and access to university lectures and libraries, open to students with few or no previous qualifications. Hardy's Jude needed an organization like this, as he looked out from the top of the Sheldonian across the "unrivalled panorama" of the spires, gables, chapels, and gardens of the fictional Christminster and realized "that his destiny lay not with these, but among the manual toilers in the shabby purlieu which he himself occupied, unrecognized as part of the city at all by its visitors and panegyrists, yet without whose denizens the hard readers could not read nor the high thinkers live."

"Very much still on probation at this University": Oxford women

"Inferior to us God made you," J. W. Burgon, Dean of Chichester, told women in a sermon preached in New College Chapel in 1884, "and inferior to the end of time you will remain. But you are none the worse off for that." (The Dean is better and more happily known for one line from his "Petra" describing the "rose-red city—half as old as time.") Burgon was worried about the decision to let female candidates sit in on some university examinations. He thought that "an ever-increasing body of marriageable and attractive young women" was dangerous for the men. On the other hand he claimed that the women were becoming too like the men. His contemporaries often expressed similar concerns: learning was bad for women's health and marriage prospects; they distracted the men or got in their way in lectures and libraries; they were behaving unnaturally; they were, for the student magazine *Isis* in May 1897, invading "Amazons."

To counteract the claim that they might be frivolous or distracting, women students often worked harder than men, were strongly discouraged from social contact with them, and were expected to dress demurely. For their pains they were often caricatured as dowdy, sexless, earnestly intellectual as girls were not supposed to be. Oxford men in novels continued to marry not their fellow students but the visiting sisters of friends. In the essentially male university of *Zuleika Dobson* everyone falls for Zuleika, the granddaughter of the head of a male college, who penetrates even the sanctum of the Duke's rooms in Trinity—the unusual and titillating sound of "the ascending susurrus of a silk skirt" is heard on his stair. Meanwhile the women's colleges are dismissed, in the novel, as comical "virgincules" where learning and beauty have allegedly yet to be combined. The inhabitants of the virgincules were often, into the mid-twentieth century, described patronizingly by male Oxbridge writers as "undergraduettes."

Acceptance of female students and dons would be hard won: as late as 1938 Vera Farnell, Dean of Somerville, felt she must warn the new intake, "You must seriously realize that you have to be careful how you behave. It isn't a joking matter. The women are very much still on probation at this University." But there was, as relations between men and women changed in society at large, gradual progress towards parity. Permission for dons to marry in 1877 resulted in a growing female presence—wives and daughters reinforcing the sisters and aunts—in university circles. Oxford High School for Girls was founded in 1875, the same year in which the Oxford Delegacy of Local Examinations introduced new examinations specifically for women over the age of eighteen. A greater step forward came with the foundation of Lady Margaret Hall and Somerville Hall in 1878. There were two halls because those campaigning for a new institution disagreed over its religious status: LMH, as it is usually called, was an Anglican foundation while Somerville was non-denominational. LMH expanded gradually on its present site by the River Cherwell and the University Parks, with elegant, mostly red-brick "Queen Anne" buildings by Basil Champneys and Reginald Blomfield, a "neo-Byzantine" chapel by Giles Gilbert Scott (1931–2), and eight acres of peaceful gardens. Somerville was established at Walton House, nearer the city center, and came to fill an area between Walton Street and Woodstock Road (see p.172–74).

At first LMH and Somerville provided only accommodation, while tuition by male university staff was organized by the Association for Promoting the Education of Women in Oxford. Also under the direct aegis of the Association were "home students"—young women either studying from home or living in hostels (soon including some foreign students, mainly from North America). The Society for Home-Students eventually changed its function and became St. Anne's Society in 1942 and St. Anne's College in 1952; the change was signaled by the increasing use of buildings on the site between Woodstock and Banbury Roads from the 1930s onwards. The hall dates from 1959. The most recent structure, at the front of the college on Woodstock Road, is the Ruth Deech Building of 2003–5 by Kohn Pedersen Fox Associates, named after

Baroness Deech—former student, law fellow, and Principal of the college, best-known as Chairman of the UK Human Fertilisation and Embryology Authority.

Two more women's colleges were established by the end of the nineteenth century, St. Hugh's in 1886 and St. Hilda's in 1893. St. Hugh's initially occupied a house at 25 Norham Road, near LMH. Later it moved to a much larger North Oxford site, with red brick buildings completed in 1916. The college has gradually annexed houses in Woodstock Road and elsewhere on its perimeter, as well as putting up such newer and larger structures as the orange-brown and glass Mablethorpe Building. Its extensive gardens, incorporating those of the Mount and the Lawn, local nineteenth-century houses, were established by Annie Rogers (1856–1937), classics tutor and campaigner for women's education. (In 1873 she had provocatively entered for an Oxford exhibition—a type of scholarship—and would have won it if she had been male. In the new "degree-level" exams, forty-odd years before women were entitled to actual degrees, she obtained a first in Latin and Greek in 1877 and in Ancient History in 1879.) St. Hilda's developed near the Cherwell around an eighteenth-century villa, extended in the 1860s and the 1890s, now Hall Building. Later additions include Garden Building (glass walls and timber frame, by Peter and Alison Smithson, 1968–70) and the Jacqueline du Pré Concert hall (see p.120–21).

Slowly but surely the women's colleges gained acceptance. They employed their own female tutors and fellows, who were paid considerably less than their male equivalents. (Lack of money remained the women's colleges' main problem for much of their history.) Women were allowed to take some of the same degree examinations as men from 1884, and all except for those in medicine and divinity by 1894. They could, with their chaperones, attend university lectures. A proposal to admit them to full degrees was at last accepted, after earlier setbacks, in 1920. (This step took even longer to achieve in Cambridge where, in spite of significant early progress, male opposition was more fierce and degrees for women were not granted until 1948.) Finally in 1959 the women's colleges were granted the same status as the men's.

Full equality had been delayed by the limitation to only five women's colleges. For most of the period, 1927–57, the university also restricted the number of female students to 840 in all. Some distinguished female speakers were invited to the Oxford Union, but women could not become full members until 1963; similarly guest participation in the Oxford University Dramatic Society had been allowable, but membership was possible only from 1964. While individual students often found their time in women's colleges immensely fulfillling, complete integration became possible only when all colleges became co-educational, starting with the admission of women by Wadham, Brasenose, Hertford, Jesus, and St. Catherine's in 1974. Most other colleges followed in 1979, and by 1994 all but St. Hilda's were mixed. These changes followed much debate, with some in the women's colleges in particular arguing the case for single-sex education. Finally St. Hilda's bowed to the inevitable and admitted men in 2008.

Somerville College

"Be of good courage. I have overcome the world," proclaims a window-inscription in the non-denominational chapel (1935) of Somerville College. Given how much they achieved in a male-dominated society, many graduates of the college might have taken this in an encouragingly secular sense. Somerville took the name and the determination of Mary Somerville (1780–1872), writer on science, mathematics, and physical geography. Beyond the discreet gatehouse (1933) in Woodstock Road, buildings in a variety of styles—the red brick and white-columned library is by Basil Champneys (1903)—are named in honor of the novelist Winifred Holtby, Baroness Thatcher (the Margaret Thatcher Conference Centre), and the Nobel Prize-winning crystallographer Dame Dorothy Hodgkin (1910–94). Hodgkin was an undergraduate, tutor, professorial fellow, and finally honorary fellow of Somerville. Unlike most of her contemporaries, she also managed successfully to balance motherhood and a career. In 1938 she was the first fellow of a women's college to have a child while in post. Other women who studied here include Vera Brittain, Iris Murdoch, Dorothy L.

Sayers, and, more briefly, Indira Gandhi, later Prime Minister of India.

Vera Brittain, in *Testament of Youth*, remembers the intense excitement of her first months at Somerville. "Having hitherto been thrown for speculative companionship chiefly upon my own society, I found cocoa-parties and discussions on religion, genius, dons and Third-Years far too enthralling to be abandoned merely for the sake of a good night's rest." For weeks she and her new companions went to bed after two in the morning, absorbed in "that urgent, hectic atmosphere, in which a number of highly strung young women become more neurotic and *exaltées* than ever through over-work and insufficient sleep." In *Gaudy Night* (1935) Dorothy L. Sayers, two years Brittain's senior at Somerville, addresses the problems of such a small, sometimes claustrophobic community of "highly strung young women" but demonstrates also how strong the women and their college could be.

Sayers' Harriet Vane has been separated from her time at "Shrewsbury" College by years of difficult experience in the outside world. She comes back first to a gaudy or reunion and then to investigate a campaign of poison-pen letters and poltergeist-like vandalism. She observes a gossip-, jealousy- and recrimination-ridden society of women "walled in, sealed down, by walls and seals that shut her out." One (female) character bitterly voices the traditional objections to such societies: "A woman's job is to look after a husband and children . . . I wish I could burn down this place and all the places like it—where you teach women to take men's jobs . . . No wonder you can't get men for yourselves and hate the women who can." Harriet develops a more balanced understanding of, and respect for, most of the Shrewsbury Senior Common Room. The level-headed Dean, Miss Martin, is "quite the sanest person I ever met." The Warden, Dr. Baring, possesses the vital ability to soothe crusty and affronted male academics. (Surviving or evading male domination and stereotyping is an important art for the women. One of the students has come to Oxford only to please her parents—she dislikes it, wanting to give up and become a cook instead—but Harriet counsels her that she must not let the side down. It would not be "fair to other Oxford women.") Harriet helps to expose the hatreds which threaten the life of an essentially healthy college—to restore it to its own ideal. The breadth of literary, often comic, and parodic references in the novel carries it beyond the narrow confines of the college, and the fact that Harriet bandies about such allusions with just as much wit and intelligence as Lord Peter Wimsey suggests the equality of the sexes. Her own independence of spirit, which makes her loathe as well as love Lord Peter and call him in only reluctantly to solve the crime, is a good advertisement for independent women more generally. When she eventually agrees to marry him, it is clear that she is entering a marriage of equals. And as John Dougill points out, "Wimsey apart, the key roles are taken by a female detective, a female criminal, and female suspects. By rewriting Oxford detection in this way, Sayers established the women's college as an idealized counterpart to that of the men."

Oxford science: making "particular enquiries"

Scientists including Boyle and Hooke conducted research in Oxford (see p.71), and from the seventeenth century there were Professors in a number of scientific subjects, some of whom gave lectures. But it was not possible to study natural science as part of a degree until 1850 and it was many years before it achieved any kind of parity with more traditional subjects. Scientific study faced entrenched bias, lack of funding, and inadequate facilities well into the twentieth century. G. C. Bourne reports in *Nature* in 1896 that students hear nothing of science "unless they make particular enquiries about it: and if they do, they are as often as not told that it will not give them the breadth of education necessary for their future careers." It was difficult to pursue serious science when, still as late as the 1920s and 1930s, "from the college enclave, research could be seen as an ungentlemanly and boorish Germanic notion, and postgraduate supervision as a Yankee device for inserting plebeians into a patrician university" (J. B. Morrell in the twentieth-century volume of *The History of the University of Oxford*). Vocational subjects from agriculture to engineering were the subject of even stronger prejudice. And applicants were further discouraged by their teachers' truism that they should choose "Cambridge for science, Oxford for arts." Until the early twentieth century this view accurately reflected the greater progress in scientific education and research at Cambridge, but it lingered much longer.

The initial enthusiasm of the founders of the University Museum in the 1850s and of the Clarendon Laboratory in 1872 was not fully followed through. Yet gradually Oxford became a major scientific center, partly as a consequence of the World Wars, when the importance of science was made unequivocally clear. Numbers of Oxford students reading for degrees in the natural sciences rose from about eight percent in the mid-1850s to 13.7 percent just before World War I, 19 percent in 1939, and 35 percent in 1970. The visible sign of the change was the expansion and continuing improvement of the university Science Area, off Parks and South Parks Roads, and nearby laboratories and institutions. The Radcliffe Science Library (formerly housed in part of the University Museum) had opened in 1901, the Electrical Laboratory in 1910, the Dyson Perrins Inorganic Chemistry Laboratory in 1916, the Dunn School of Pathology in 1926, Biochemistry in 1927. All of these were subsequently developed, expanded, or replaced, with the library extending under the lawn of the University Museum. Frederick Lindemann (Lord Cherwell), Professor of Experimental Philosophy—physics—between 1919 and 1956, made the Clarendon a major center for low-temperature physics and oversaw its move into a new building in 1939. The pace of construction quickened from the 1960s and 1970s, with new buildings for Zoology, Psychology, Computing, Theoretical Physics, and many other disciplines. As the Science Area filled up, some researchers moved south of Oxford to Harwell, where the Atomic Energy Research Establishment took over an RAF airfield in 1946, or, next door, the Rutherford Laboratory. Harwell and the Rutherford (now Rutherford Appleton) later became part of the much expanded campus recently renamed Harwell Oxford. Culham Science Centre began as an atomic research laboratory on another disused airfield. (The fusion energy experiment MAST is based here.)

Among the most notable Oxford scientists have been the Australian Howard Florey (Lord Florey), Professor of Pathology from 1932. With his colleague Sir Ernst Chain, who left Germany in 1933, he worked on the development of penicillin and shared a Nobel Prize for medicine with Sir Alexander Fleming, its discoverer, in 1945. In 1956 Sir Cyril Hinshelwood, who worked on the kinetics of chemical reactions, shared a Nobel Prize for chemistry. The crystallographer Dame Dorothy Hodgkin investigated the structure of penicillin, insulin, and vitamin B12. Her Nobel Prize for chemistry came in 1964. A later Nobel laureate, for physiology, in 1973, was Nikolaas Tinbergen, who worked in Oxford on both animal and human behavior from 1949. More recently the behavioral ecologist John Krebs spent much of his career in Oxford. (He became Principal of Jesus College in 2005, and Lord Krebs in 2007.) Some of the latest research can be followed on Oxford Science Blog (www.ox.ac.uk/media/science_blog) and Oxford Sparks—"online public science" (www.oxfordsparks.net/).

10 | The Oxford Brand
Commerce and Industry

"Untruthful! My nephew Algernon? Impossible! He is an Oxonian," declares Lady Bracknell in *The Importance of Being Earnest* (1895). Thirty years later Jay Gatsby makes the most of a more dubious claim to be what one character calls "an Oggsford man" in *The Great Gatsby*. And Toad, in *The Wind in the Willows* (1908), concedes in his boastful song that "the clever men at Oxford/Know all that there is to be knowed" even if "they none of them know one half as much/As intelligent Mr. Toad!" Oxford is itself, these examples suggest, a brand.

The recognition factor started from the university—Oxford University Press jealously defends its right to attach the word "Oxford" to publications—but it has extended beyond books to such products as Frank Cooper's Oxford Marmalade and the Morris Oxford. More loosely—literally, in this case—you could once wear "Oxford bags." (Harold Acton is supposed to have started the fashion in the 1920s with trousers 26 inches at the knee and 24 at the ankle.) There have been Oxford shoes, shirts, and armchairs. Undergraduates were said to speak with an "Oxford voice": D. H. Lawrence mocked it as maddeningly "languishing/and hooing and cooing and sidling through the front teeth" and attributed it not only to Oxonians but to anyone who can sound "so seductively superior, so seductively/self-effacingly/deprecatingly/superior." Once such tones had, like the so-called King's, Queen's, or BBC English, career and export value; it was probably worth hooing and cooing, when under consideration for a job, the fact that you were "up" at Magdalen or Merton.

Even before the university, the city was well positioned for trade. In the Middle Ages wool came in from the Cotswolds and went out again, either directly or as cloth. Wine came from Southampton or London. Corn, livestock, and timber were brought to market from

The iconic Morris Oxford, exported all over the world

the surrounding countryside, and horses were bought and sold in Horsemonger Street, the present Broad Street. Many citizens were leather-workers—cobblers, cordwainers, tanners, or saddlers; in the twelfth century, recent excavations in Merton Street have shown, there were also workers in horn. Stone was quarried at Headington and Wheatley, and ocher ("of a yellow colour and very weighty," says Robert Plot in *The Natural History of Oxfordshire*, 1677) on Shotover. Iron-free clay from Shotover was used to make white wares including pipes. Most of these industries suffered some decline from the late thirteenth century onwards, and especially after the Black Death; a westward shift in the wool trade was another hindrance, as was the increasing stranglehold of the university.

Oxford was also well known for its butchers, and its most famous exports in later times—according to a much-repeated quip—were sausages and parsons. The former would one day be the concern above all of John Wiblin, "Family Butcher, Bacon Curer, and Lard Refiner" of 31 St Giles', established in 1855, the proud "Maker of the Celebrated Royal Oxford Sausages." (Isabella Beeton's recipe for Oxford Sausages includes pork, veal, beef suet, lemon-rind, sage-leaves, and marjoram. An eighteenth-century version by Mr. Ayres of New College uses much the same ingredients and advises you to "work it up with 2 or 3 eggs as you see good.") The future parsons—long, indeed, the university's main product—brought some trade to the town. But the university fought hard to impose restrictions on who could sell what, where, and to whom; controls on the pricing of food and goods for scholars were imposed as early as 1214. In the nineteenth century, however, such regulation withered in the face of population growth, consumer demand, and the arrival of the canal, the railway, and the tourists. Shops began to appear in the suburbs. The Victorian and Edwardian city center had an extraordinary variety of shops, eating-places, and hotels—and public houses, already often the preserve of Morrells, the brewery established in St. Thomas' Street on the site of earlier breweries in the late eighteenth century. (Its main rival, Halls, began brewing in 1795.)

As in other towns, small shops in much of the city center were taken over or replaced by chain-stores in the course of the twentieth century. (This has not, however, been accompanied by the sort of destruction of the historic center found in some towns—fortunately you cannot knock colleges down.) Outside the city a different approach to shopping has been promoted at Bicester Village, the commercially successful outlet shopping center at the edge of Bicester. In a rather different field, Oxford scientific companies have prospered. Oxford Instruments was the first company to make superconducting magnets outside the United States. It was founded by Martin and Audrey Wood in 1959, operating at first from "study, spare bedroom, and ex-coal cellar" in North Oxford, then from a large garden shed, before graduating to a former stables and slaughter-house in Middle Way in Summertown, a boat-house at Osney Mead, and later more purpose-built factories and laboratories. (See Audrey Wood's book *Magnetic Venture*, 2001. Sir Martin and Lady Wood also founded in 1985 the Oxford Trust, promoting science education; it established Science Oxford and the Oxfordshire Science Festival.)

But the most evident industry in the city today is tourism, bringing huge crowds, congestion, and noise, but also international contacts, fame, and big money. According to Oxford City Council there are "approximately 9.5 million visitors per year, generating £770 million of income for local Oxford businesses." There are jobs, and no longer in the summer season only, in transport, guiding, information, hotels and hostels, catering and supply; selling souvenirs and ice-cream, kebabs, and gourmet meals; taking money and policing queues at the gates of the most popular colleges, chauffeuring punts, cleaning and repairing the battered streets.

Shopping in Victorian Oxford: tweed trousers, second hand classical books, and fancy pipes

The advertisements in the *Guide to Oxford* published in 1868 by Abel Heywood offer a snapshot of the goods and services available at the time. "Opposite Magdalen Church" you could buy a comprehensive selection of "parasols and umbrellas, stays and baby linen, chintzes ... table sheetings, damasks, blankets, flannels, &c ... mantles, bonnets, millinery, & French [artificial] flowers' from Elliston and Cavell," "Linen and Woollen Drapers, Glovers, Hosiers, Haberdashers, Silk Mercers, Shawl Men, Furriers, and Carpet Factors"; "Family Mourning—Funerals Furnished." (This early department store was eventually taken over by Debenhams, still on the same site, in the 1950s. The name Cavell and Elliston was kept until 1973.) Further clothing could be purchased or ordered from Hyde & Co. of 2–3 and 31–2 Queen Street, including ladies' riding habits, "liveries made to order on the most reasonable terms," flannel shirts, and "mechanics' clothing ... well made, from durable materials, suitable for working men." They particularly "Beg to call the attention of Clergymen" (Oxford was full of them, whether resident or visiting) to their "ALL-WOOL TWEED TROUSERS, in Black or Oxford Mixtures, made to order at 14s. 6d., giving the greatest satisfaction for their comfort and durability." The parsons could also get "Cassocks in Russell Cord" for 21 shillings or in black tweed for a substantial 30 shillings.

Spiers and Son, whose shop flourished in the High between 1835 and 1889—by 1868 they were also established in Oriel

Street—offered such "Useful and Ornamental Manufactures" as maps, writing cases, cutlery, "Gilt and Ormolu Furniture in medieval and other styles" (this was the age of the Gothic revival), and "Fancy manufactures in general, Articles of Taste & Vertu, &c.." (Verdant Green, the innocent undergraduate in Cuthbert Bede's novel of 1853, immediately runs up a large bill at Spiers'.) "Second Hand Classical and School Books" were sold by Joseph Thornton at 11 Broad Street and 33 High Street; Thornton's remained in Broad Street until 2002. Photographic Views of Oxford were available from Wheeler and Day of 106 High Street. "For a good cigar, go to Mayo's Havanna [sic] Cigar Depot, 13, Corn Market Street . . . Importer of Meerschaum and other Fancy Pipes, Cigar and Fusee Cases, &c." Alfred Grose dealt in tea, sherry, and port opposite the Town Hall. Finally the 1868 guide includes a several-page advertisement for the Shakspeare [sic] Hotel in Cornmarket, "newly erected and handsomely fitted up" and "replete with every comfort" including a ladies' coffee room and Turkish bath. Should potential clients doubt the efficacy of hot-air baths, medical testimony is extensively cited from such worthies as Dr. John Le Gay Brereton, "Introducer of the Bath in Australia." The hotel was replaced by a bank in 1877.

Other businesses which were thriving at this time included the upmarket "wholesale and family grocers" Grimbly Hughes, who had premises in Cornmarket from 1840 to 1961. Their name, proclaims an advertisement of 1923, "is a household-word in the district as symbolical of the very best in Provisions, Groceries, Confectionery, Wines, Spirits, Cigars, etc." (The later building on the site became a McDonald's.) Boffin the baker, confectioner, and restaurateur had been at 107 High Street since 1847. Boswell's, possibly established as early as 1738, made and sold trunks and cases at 49–50 Cornmarket; it developed its Broad Street premises in 1929 and still sells cases as well as toys, kitchenware, and cosmetics. Soon, in 1874, Frank Cooper's Oxford Marmalade would go on sale in its distinctive stoneware jars at 84 High Street; he started by selling the surplus from a batch made from Seville oranges by his wife Sarah Jane. (Production moved into the factory in Park End Street between 1903 and 1947—now the Jam Factory restaurant, bar, and arts center—then to Botley Road and, following a takeover, out of Oxford in 1967.) The Museum of Oxford displays a Cooper's cutter for slicing orange peel: what the manufacturers called, more grandly, a New Universal Marmalade Machine.

There were also, of course, many smaller businesses like G. Claridge Druce, pharmaceutical chemist of 118 High Street, who in a late 1890s *Handbook to Oxford* offers not only lantern slides of the Oxford area ("a Speciality, being made by the wet collodion process") but "Deodorized non-inflammable Paraffin for preventing baldness, promoting the growth of the hair, 2 shillings per large bottle." Clearly the High Street was a good place for ailing students, visitors, and townspeople, victims perhaps of the notoriously damp local climate: at no. 140 Jessop's Oxford Specifics offered "catarrh specific" and similar potions aimed at neuralgia, dyspepsia, rheumatism, skin problems, throat problems, and bronchitis.

As ever, some businesses failed as others flourished. Jane Welsh Carlyle would have shed no tear for the famous Angel Inn, at least as she found it in 1837. She judged the "bread and butter et cetera . . . first rate, and the silver forks in 'good' style," but discovered traces everywhere of religious and social "Cant": bibles and hassocks in all the rooms, waiters "all large elderly men" with "a sort of mazed abstractedness and sad gravity of look which gave one a notion they must . . . have been unsuccessful graduates," maids all "*myladies*" and curtsies. But many people were sad at the Angel's demolition to make way for the Examination Schools in 1877.

Trade more generally suffered at mid-century, as Alan Crossley, Chris Day, and Janet Cooper explain in their *Shopping in Oxford* (1983). Not only did population growth slow, but the university failed to keep pace with the size of the population; in 1801 it had represented a tenth of the people in the city, but in 1861 a twentieth. Tradesmen relied on the university to boost their profits with its termly influx of wealthy, extravagant, or simply needy students and its longer-term requirements for provisions and services. They suffered also in the 1870s agricultural depression but less, *Shopping in Oxford* thinks, than in most towns: university trade was still available—if reduced, tourism was developing, and North Oxford was growing.

Horizontal Cornmarket: an "increasingly faceless corridor"?

Cornmarket, the architect John Melvin feels, "imposes an overwhelming alienation on the individuals who are drawn along this increasingly faceless corridor." Once it had some character, provided in part by the Clarendon Hotel and the nearby Cadena Café. (Here W. H. Auden sat in the mornings when he was Professor of Poetry, talking to undergraduates. Michael Alexander, in "To W. H. Auden in Heaven, with Apologies," remembers him "crumpled," unpoetic, but generously available over coffee and the *Telegraph* crossword.) The hotel, an important coaching inn with "extensive stabling and loose boxes," originally called the Star, was demolished and replaced by a branch of Woolworth's in 1955. It stood on the site of the Clarendon Centre (built 1983–4), where, for Melvin, "we enter a sanitised and infantilised world" in which the senses and imagination are stimulated only by "the anodyne chain store." The Cadena, famous for its cakes and Palm Court orchestra, survived until 1970.

Things were better, as Melvin says, in the Edwardian Cornmarket, which was

> lined with shops displaying their wares in an inviting and tangible way that formed part of a lively public scene. Today the chain store and service provider have replaced the specialist shop. The engagingly detailed shop front has been superseded by ubiquitous plate glass.

The main aesthetic problem, he feels, is the replacement of verticality—up to the decorative gables visible in old photographs, down to the busy shop-front—with horizontality.

One improvement to the jammed, chaotic Cornmarket of the 1980s and 1990s, at least, has been the banishing of buses from the street. (It had been semi-pedestrianized—buses and taxis allowed—since 1973. Queen Street is also pedestrianized.) And there are, of course, some surviving more attractive buildings. Among those Melvin exempts from censure at the Carfax end are H. T. Hare's Midland Bank (now HSBC) and Tower House (1896–7), and at the

St. Michael's end, the 1914 building by N. W. and G. W. Harrison which is now Waterstone's: "a clever and well-informed exercise of dressing a steel-frame building in a city suit." Leading off Cornmarket are the fine restored sixteenth-century shops of the Golden Cross, and beyond that the Covered Market. Here, as not in Cornmarket or Queen Street, some specialist traders (slightly precariously) survive.

The Covered Market

In medieval and later Oxford, traders operated from stalls or shops in all four directions from Carfax. There were fishmongers in St. Aldate's and butchers at the Carfax end of High Street—further along which were poulterers, glovers, apothecaries, and at one time sellers of wood and straw and pigs. There was dairy produce in what is now Queen Street, while drapers, shoemakers, and cobblers operated in what became Cornmarket. (There were also, of course, people buying and selling corn, originally in the street and its hotels and at Carfax, later at the Corn Exchange of 1894–96 in George Street, now part of the Old Fire Station arts center.) Butter was sold from the Butter bench at Carfax itself. All this activity generated debris, dirt, and traffic.

In setting up the Covered Market, which opened in 1774, the Oxford Improvement Act (1771) sought to remove the dirtier and more unsavory trades from the streets, and to control and regulate them on one large premises. In theory all butchers, fishmongers, and greengrocers had to move in or stop trading. The market building at first consisted of three avenues, extending to four in the nineteenth century.

Market livelihoods are increasingly at risk from competition and high rents. But at the time of writing there are still butchers (with, for meat-eaters at least, magnificently varied wares on display), greengrocers, and a fresh fish shop. There are also florists, bakers, pie-shops, jewelers, cafés—including the long-established and traditional Brown's—clothes shops, Cardew's the tea and coffee company, and—mostly a more recent development—gift and souvenir shops.

Morris Cowley

The rise to success of William Morris (1877–1963), later Lord Nuffield, and the consequent transformation of Oxford from a quiet university city to a busy commercial and industrial one, seems in retrospect to have been irresistible. He set up his first business with £4 of capital when he was sixteen—bicycle repairs at his parents' terraced house at 16 James Street, in East Oxford. He went on to assemble and sell bicycles and moved into larger premises at 48 High Street. He built motorbikes and then, in 1904, went into cars. A small display at 21 Longwall commemorates his garage there (designated at the time 100A Holywell) in a former livery stable, selling, repairing, and hiring vehicles and drivers out to rich undergraduates among others. Morris also excelled as a racing cyclist, in 1900 winning seven titles on bikes he had built himself. (Even Morris was not, however, quite as precocious as the 21 Longwall display suggests, giving his birthdate as 1887.)

In 1912 Morris Garages moved to the vacant former Military College in Temple Cowley, a village southeast of Oxford. The new factory produced 393 Morris Oxfords in 1913 and 907 in 1914. Productivity was greatly increased by the method of buying in parts from other manufacturers and assembling them into Morris' own designs. Numbers fell during World War I, when the company mainly went over to producing mine-sinkers and grenades. (During World War II the by then much larger works assembled Crusader tanks and Tiger Moths, and repaired aircraft and other vehicles.) But after 1918 production recovered rapidly: 3,076 cars in 1921, 6,956 in 1922, 55,282 in 1925, 96,512 in 1934. There were two hundred employees in 1919, five thousand in 1925. *Autocar* in 1929 describes Cowley as "big and busy," houses and factory-space increasing everywhere, workers flowing in and out while "the cars flow out only—always moving—an orderly but irresistible torrent."

Development was speeded up when in 1926, on a ten-acre site across the road from the Morris works, the Pressed Steel Company of Great Britain opened with sixty American-imported presses and

580 employees. The production of all-steel bodies here replaced the more laborious business of fitting steel panels onto wood. The Pressed Steel factory was a separate company from 1930 but eventually joined the Morris works as part of BMC in 1965. Another important technical advance was the introduction of moving assembly lines in 1933. Advertising was also well organized. *Morris Owner*, a magazine published at Cowley, flourished from 1924 to 1951. There were publicity films and there were stunts like the intrepid journey of a Morris Cowley from Singapore to London in 1929. In Oxford a strong Morris presence was maintained at the garage and showroom in St. Aldate's (on the site of the present Crown Court); but Cowley remained at the center of the operation, as is suggested by a 1938 poster for "a special excursion to Oxford" which will include "a visit to the colleges" (small capitals) and "the Morris works" (large capitals). In 1930, in a successful bid to fight the slump, the price of a Morris Minor was reduced from £125 to £100. (The first "Bullnose" Morris Oxfords in 1913 had cost £175, a two-seater Morris Cowley £125 in 1915. Apart from a period when prices temporarily went up during the inflation of 1918–20, the most expensive Morris car before 1930 was the Oxford Six: £365 in 1929.)

Even Lord Nuffield's philanthropic donations could be seen as profitable publicity. "He gave ten thousand pounds away and he'd get twenty thousand pounds' worth of propaganda out of it," Norman Brown, a Pressed Steel worker in the 1930s and 1940s, told the Channel Four Television History Workshop program *Making Cars* in 1985. "I think he was a clever chap in that sense." His benefactions continued, however, long after their possible value for advertising the company. Over all, he gave away at least thirty million pounds, mostly to medical and educational causes. In Oxford he gave land and large sums of money from 1937 to set up Nuffield College, and left it more than three million pounds at his death in 1963. (He wanted a college for engineers but was persuaded to accept one concentrating on social studies.) He also gave generous amounts to St. Peter's, Worcester, and Pembroke Colleges; to the Radcliffe Infirmary and the Wingfield Orthopaedic Hospital (now the Nuffield); established a university medical school in 1936; and funded Howard Florey's work on penicillin.

The 100,000[th] Morris Eight was produced in 1936 and the millionth Morris in 1939. MGs—the name with such glamorous associations stood, improbably, for Morris Garages—were made in Cowley from 1927 and in Abingdon from 1930. There was, of course, a human cost to all this productivity. Work on the production line was grinding and often physically demanding. As new machinery replaced the simpler assembly methods, it also required increased skill and speed. Injuries—loss of fingers or hands, mainly—were frequent until at least the 1940s, and there were occasional fatalities. Whereas Pressed Steel recognized the Transport and General Workers' Union after a strike in 1934, William Morris remained fiercely opposed to the unions. Briefly he supported Oswald Mosley's Fascists, and is alleged to have said that he would pay agitators a one-way fare to Russia. He was patriarchal, not easy to work with, distrustful of committees, and, in his later years, of new ideas and practices. Only in 1956 did the company endorse full union rights.

Equality of pay for women, who were a substantial part of the workforce for much of its history, took longer to achieve. There was little progress until the Equal Pay Act of 1970 and subsequent equality of opportunity legislation. Some of the men, Jenette King told *Making Cars*, "did have this macho image that they felt, oh, well, they're great big men and they go home and they say to their wives 'Oh, God, it was terrible in there.' I mean, what's it going to be like when their wives find out that an eight-stone woman's doing the same job as them?" Kathy Moxham (Pressed Steel 1944–81) once got so frustrated with a sarcastic male colleague on the assembly line that she poured a gallon tin of glue over his head: "I said, 'Now, if you can't shut up, you're glued up.'"

In 1952 Morris merged with its old rival, Austin, to form the British Motor Corporation. There was continued expansion at Cowley in the wake of Alec Issigonis' successful post-war Morris Minor—first produced in 1948—and Mini (1959). (Issigonis first worked at Cowley in 1936 and was based in Birmingham from

THE OXFORD BRAND

1955.) But BMC, and the British car industry, were about to go into a steep decline. The company became part of British Leyland in 1968, which got into such difficulties that it was nationalized in 1974 and laid off 1,400 Cowley workers soon afterwards. Further changes followed, with Austin Rover taking over in 1982, and later the Rover Group, owned from 1994 by BMW. The production process was modernized, fewer workers were needed, and most of the works were demolished in the 1990s. Such local landmarks as the conveyor bridges across the bypass and Garsington Road disappeared. The Morris works have been replaced by a business park and shops, including a large Tesco. But on the Pressed Steel site there has been a great revival of car-building since 2001, when production of the new BMW Mini began. By 2012 nearly two million had been made.

Salters' Boats

River transport flourished in Oxford as well as cars. Salters' were established as boat-builders on the Thames at Folly Bridge by the brothers John and Stephen Salter in 1858. The company, whose history has been documented by Simon Wenham (in *Oxoniensia*, 2006) went on to build, sell, and hire boats from skiffs to punts, narrowboats, racing craft, and steam launches. In 1905 they launched, and tested on the Thames, the 105-foot paddle-steamer *Endeavour*, which the Baptist Missionary Society used on the River Congo.

Salters' own steamers had been taking passengers on Thames trips since the 1880s. In May 1888 the propeller-driven *Alaska* completed the first five-day round trip between Oxford and Kingston-on-Thames; Wenham notes that single fares were eighteen shillings, with extra charges for meals and hotels. Gradually more steamers (converted to diesel between the 1940s and 1960s) traveled this route; by 1898 there were seven, and by 1900 the Kingston service left twice daily. In 1956 the company owned seventeen such passenger-boats and until about 1960 was still carrying up to 350,000 people a year.

The crews on these boats—permanent employees supplemented by seasonal workers—lived onboard, were well fed, and socialized very actively with other crews. But their working day could run from six in the morning to ten at night, Salters' could not compete with the sort of wages offered at the Cowley works, and demand for their services decreased as road-transport increased. At the same time there was overcrowding on the river, causing long delays at locks. Some boats were arriving three hours late, by which time "people are going squirmy," as Bill Dunckley, who worked at Salters' for over sixty years, told Wenham. For all these reasons the Kingston service had to be abandoned in the 1970s.

The company went on building boats, and especially electric-propelled craft. (Its website now advertises a £39,995, 21-foot "Electric Weekender" and still on the other hand skiffs, punts, and a six-foot child's paddle boat for £1,695.) They also continue to hire out boats and to take passengers on shorter Thames excursions to Iffley Lock and to Abingdon and on "Public Jazz Cruises—Now with on board BBQ." The atmosphere is less inhibited than in the days of the second generation of Salters (John's three sons), faithful Methodists who banned alcohol and would not sail on Sundays. (Two of them, John and James, became Mayors of Oxford.) The current managing director, John Stephen Edward Salter, is the great-great-grandson of the original John. Another family boat business, Bossoms, flourished between the early nineteenth century and 1945. It then changed hands but Bossoms Boatyard and Marina have kept the name, the location at Medley on the Thames, and the tradition of craftsmanship.

Books

Already in the thirteenth century Catte Street was known for its bookbinders and scribes; printing in Oxford is first recorded in the late fifteenth century, and became more closely associated with the university from the 1630s. The presses themselves operated in the basement of the Sheldonian Theatre and then in the grand, purpose-built Clarendon Building next door, before moving into much larger premises off Walton Street in 1830. (On-site printing ended in 1989.) The influence of Oxford University Press and its ability to publish academic books have been much increased by sales of bibles, dictionaries, and English language-learning materials. Its most ambitious publication is the *Oxford English Dictionary*. Foremost among its editors was Sir James Murray (1837–1915), working at first in London and then from 1885 in a large iron hut or "scriptorium" in the back garden of "Sunnyside," his house at 78 Banbury Road in North Oxford. With a small team of assistants—extracting enough money from the Press was always a problem—Murray labored at the immense task of collating the examples of word-use sent in by hundreds of volunteer readers and arranged in pigeonholes. The first part of the dictionary was published in 1884 and the last in 1928; there were entries for 414,825 words. Murray, working on determinedly during his last illness, lived to edit as far as the letter T. Another team, under his co-editor Henry Bradley, was based in the Old Ashmolean Building, now the Museum of the History of Science. Later work went on in Walton Crescent, nearer the Press. With the language forever expanding, revision continues.

Benjamin Henry Blackwell opened a small bookshop at 50 Broad Street in 1879, and soon took over the surrounding properties. Today's shop incorporates the 10,000 square feet of the Norrington Room (1966)—skillfully extended beneath the Library Quadrangle of Trinity College—and is part of a larger group which even, in 1999, committed the once unthinkable deed of taking over Heffers, the famous Cambridge bookshop. (Cambridge sensibilities were spared by the retention of the name.)

11 | The Dark Side
Murder, Disease, and War

A maid was hanged at Greenditch [at the city gallows, on a site now part of St. Margaret's Road] ... for murdering her infant bastard.—After she was cut down and taken away to be anatomised, William Conyers a physician of St. John's College and other young physicians did in short time bring life into her. But the Bailiffs of the town hearing of it, they went between twelve and one of the clock at night to the house where she lay, and putting her into a coffin carried her into Broken Hays [a waste area which later became Gloucester Green], and by a halter about her neck drew her out of it, and hung her on a tree there. She then was so sensible of what they were about to do, that she said "Lord have mercy on me" &c.

Anthony Wood reports this horrifying tale of 1658. The second hanging so enraged local women that, in an act of pointless but understandable solidarity with its victim, they cut down the tree. And when the bailiff mainly responsible for the deed failed in his business as a cutler, "they did not stick to say, that God's Judgements followed him for the cruelty he showed to the poor maid." Another woman, Anne Green, hanged at Oxford castle in 1650, had been more fortunate: when she too revived, the eminent medical men who had been about to dissect or "anatomise" her protected her until a pardon was granted. (Iain Pears draws on Green's case in his novel of conspiracy-riven Restoration Oxford, *An Instance of the Fingerpost*, 1997. Wood is one of his narrators.)

Oxford, like any city, has always had its bloody incidents. Some of the earliest known were examples of ethnic cleansing. On St Brice's Day in 1002 King Æthelred II ("the Unready") ordered the extermination of Danes in England. They were, a later royal charter proclaims, "growing up like cockle amongst the wheat." A group of Danes in Oxford barricaded themselves into St. Frideswide's church. The townspeople burned the church; the charter announces its

MISS MARY BLANDY.

In Oxford Castle Goal, charged with the Cruel Murder of her Father,
Mr FRANCIS BLANDY, late of Henley upon Thames in Oxfordshire,
by Putting Poison into his Water Gruel, 1751.

Mary Blandy, alleged poisoner, in prison before her hanging

rebuilding with no trace of regret for the victims. In 2008 building work at St. John's College revealed the savagely hacked bones of about 35 young men who probably also died on St. Brice's Day. This group were almost certainly warriors, not local settlers; archaeologists found evidence of a diet rich in fish, unlike that of inland Oxford. (A Danish army took vengeance in 1009, burning the town.)

Later times had their fatal brawls between Town and Gown, their murders, and armed robberies. "Tales of Murder, Romance, Betrayal, Escape and Execution" are promised in a display at the Castle, in whose moat a number of dismembered skeletons have been excavated. They belong to hanged men, and a few women, whose bodies were dissected for anatomical purposes before being unceremoniously interred in the ditch. In 1297 the Manciple of Bull Hall and two "clerks" ran amok, rushing "through the streets with swords and bows and arrows before curfew, attacking any who passed by." Thomas Crosfield of Queen's College reports in his diary for 1633 that "Some unexpected accidents fell out in Oxford a little before Christmas: as of a smith and his wife near the Blue Boar that killed their prentice by running an hot iron into his belly." In 1544 two robbers with hammers and iron bars smashed their way into chests held at St. Mary-the-Virgin and made off with, among other things, the university's cash; in 1687 a more fearsome-sounding twelve armed robbers tied up members of the household of the Principal of Gloucester Hall and got away with most of the college plate.

In the following century a great talking-point was the trial and hanging in Oxford in 1752 of Mary Blandy, daughter of the Town Clerk of Henley. She had poisoned her father with arsenic, claiming to have thought it was a love-powder which would increase his affection for her. She wanted him to agree to let her marry Captain Cranston, a dubious character attracted only, it seems, by exaggerated accounts of the father's wealth. (He was in fact already married—invalidly, he maintained.) The powder was Cranston's idea. Blandy tried mixing it with gruel and with tea. Her attempts at concealment were amateurish: two servants were taken seriously ill; even her father realized what was happening and generously told her he forgave her. She was arrested soon after his death. Meanwhile Cranston, considered by many the real villain of the piece, had escaped to France.

The gallows are long gone, but a lesser instrument of punishment survives in the Pitt Rivers Museum: the stocks made in 1857 by Richard Humphries, who was handily both "Constable and Carpenter." He constructed them specifically for the benefit of a malefactor sentenced to six hours "in front of the Reading Room on the Footpath in College Lane," Littlemore. We do not know what crime had been committed; probably nothing much by modern standards. In 1870 Robert Hall, aged thirteen, was sentenced to fourteen days in Oxford Prison for stealing a leather strap. The previous year an adult offender, John Beckley, was sentenced to a year's hard labor for "embezzling 18 pounds." He already looks crushed and worn out in the photograph taken before the labor began.

The Civil War: besieging "the Mother Seat"

With London securely in Parliamentarian hands, Charles I made Oxford effectively his capital in the autumn of 1642. Its position in the middle of the country made it a good strategic choice. Charles came with soldiers, courtiers, and unceasing demands for money, weapons, food, and accommodation. Most of the colleges were loyal to the King and yielded up their plate to be melted down and minted, at New Inn Hall, as coin. Corpus Christi managed to hold out and keep its plate. Exeter College put up a struggle, but could not go against Charles' menacing third-person expression of surprise that "in a time when the Commonwealth of Learning is in such danger, and Colleges themselves not like to outlive his Majesty if he be destroyed in this Rebellion," there should be "such scruples against the assisting his Majesty with what will be taken from them by those who endeavour to oppress his Majesty." The King wrote this reply—angrily, one imagines—on the back of a letter from the college.

In 1644 a town document was similarly maltreated when the minutes of a City Council meeting were struck through, following the rejection of the councillors' petition against having to provide yet more money for the royal garrison and against the high-handedness of its commander. (The Mayor was jailed for a time.) The petitioners' frustration had boiled over after two years of food and fuel shortages caused by overcrowding of soldiers, refugees, and prisoners. There were outbreaks of plague, "camp fever," and, less than a fortnight before the latest demands, fire. Anthony Wood says that it began in a house in what is now George Street, "occasioned by a footsoldier's roasting a pig which he had stolen. The wind being very high and in the north, blew the flames southward very quick and strongly and burnt all the houses and stables" in much of the western part of the city.

Most of the undergraduates either went home or joined the royal forces. The rooms they vacated were taken by officers and courtiers. Soldiers and camp followers were billeted, or found themselves lodgings, in poorer parts of Oxford. Drills and parades happened in the quadrangles, the Parks, and Port Meadow. Gunpowder was produced at the Osney mills and kept in New College cloisters and muniment tower. Weapons were manufactured at Wolvercote or requisitioned from the citizens, whose loyalty to the royalist cause was often lukewarm compared with that of the university. Yet the court behaved almost as if there was no war. At Christ Church, the King's headquarters, there were court weddings and funerals in the cathedral. Queen Henrietta Maria held court at Merton; doors were made linking Merton with Corpus, and Corpus with Christ Church, for royal convenience. William Dobson, the main court painter after the death of Van Dyck in 1641, was present to paint the cavaliers in their finery. The King brought with him the organist George Jeffreys and the lutenist John Wilson. According to John Aubrey, court ladies wandered about and played their lutes in the grove at Trinity and came to "our chapel, mornings, half-dressed, like angels." Such conduct was not calculated to please old Ralph Kettell, President of Trinity since 1599. When Lady Isabella Thynne and "fine Mrs Fenshawe" decided to "have a frolic to make a visit" to him, "The old doctor quickly perceived that they came to tease him" and treated Mrs. Fenshawe to a lecture on morality: "I will not say you are a whore; but get you gone for a very woman." Aubrey does not say whether she was annoyed, laughed, or (unlikely, perhaps) was duly chastened. He thought that Kettell's death in 1643 was hastened by the Civil War, "which much grieved him, that was wont to be absolute in the college, to be affronted and disrespected by rude soldiers"—and fine ladies, perhaps.

The King and his commanders were aware, however, of the need to defend the city. Both townspeople and the remaining university people were conscripted, reluctantly, to build earthworks. (An embankment survives in the fellows' garden at Wadham.) Outside the East Gate, an extra wooden gate was put up on Magdalen Bridge. Cannons were positioned near all the entry-points to the city. Meadows outside the defenses were deliberately flooded. Eventually Oxford would be besieged twice, late in the spring of both 1645 and 1646. In both cases the King was elsewhere—on the first occasion he left with an army but on the next, as defeat came nearer, disguised as a servant called Harry. In 1646 Sir Thomas Fairfax told Parliament that it was essential now to capture this "the Mother Seat to hold up the spirit of the Enemy." They took him seriously, supplying him with "1,200 wooden spades and shovels, 300 steel spades and 500 pickaxes . . . 200 sets of horse-harness and twenty carriages for provisions . . . 500 barrels of gunpowder, 1,000 hand grenades . . . 30 tons of bullets, 40 tons of match and 200 scaling-ladders" (David Eddershaw, *The Civil War in Oxfordshire*, 1995). Woodstock had surrendered to Parliament in April and Banbury Castle in May; Oxford eventually followed suit after drawn-out negotiations on 20 June, when Fairfax accepted the capitulation at Christ Church. The garrison was allowed to march out and disperse over a period of several days. Fairfax, aware of the risks as his own men came in from their camps in Marston and Headington, earned the gratitude of later generations by sending guards to protect the Bodleian Library.

War, disease, and "filthy and noxious . . . ditches"

Oxford colleges are temples of youth—and of its loss. The lists of war dead are long and the college chapels are also full of memorials to learned young victims of accident and disease. University College Chapel ends its list of 1914–18 dead with 22 young men "Accepted for Matriculation"—would-be students who did not even live to start their studies, including the poet Charles Sorley, killed aged twenty at the Battle of Loos in 1915. There were, of course, hazards for non-students too. In the nineteenth century agricultural accidents were fairly common, as were drowning in the river or canal, or having your clothes catch fire. A report on local mortality for 1849 includes people caught by threshing machines, falling on scythes, and run down by carts. Modern transport also had its problems: on Christmas Eve 1874, in snowy weather, a train which had just left Oxford on its way to Birkenhead was derailed near Kidlington, and 34 passengers were killed. A wheel of a dilapidated carriage added at Oxford had collapsed. Most of the coaches overturned and the front one was crushed.

Plague visited periodically. In the fourteenth century New College was built on land which became available because most of its inhabitants had died in the Black Death. One of the worst outbreaks of infectious disease was at the so-called Black Assize of 1577, when up to three hundred people died of "gaol fever" (probably typhus). At the assize court held within the Castle precinct at Shire Hall (on the site of County Hall in New Road), Rowland Jenkes was condemned to lose his ears for selling Popish books or, according to a slab in County Hall, for scandalous words uttered against the Queen. Many of those at Jenkes' trial, among them the High Sheriff and other senior officials, were dead within six weeks. Some attributed the outbreak to a curse uttered by Jenkes. The surviving authorities, more practically, moved the assizes further away from the prison—the suspected breeding-ground of the disease—to the Town Hall.

Later came cholera, which killed 86 people in 1832, 44 in 1849, and 116 in 1854. Most of the victims lived in the lower lying parts of the town: the parishes of St. Aldate, St. Clement, St. Ebbe, and St. Thomas, where working class housing had grown in the early nineteenth century. Wells were flooded by burst cesspools and polluted by sewage from higher land. There were open drains and flooded cellars; at a coroner's inquest in 1849 the jury "were struck with the filthy and noxious state of the ditches on the north and west end of Jericho Street." (An open sewer ran down from the Radcliffe Infirmary through Jericho and into fields.) The authorities responded with attempts to ensure that cholera sufferers' clothes were burnt and that patients were isolated from their communities. In 1854 Dr. Henry Acland, physician to the Radcliffe Infirmary and university Reader in Anatomy, set up a "House of Reception or Isolation" in a converted shed and tents at the edge of Port Meadow. Acland and his predecessors at the time of the earlier outbreaks conducted conscientious enquiries into the probable causes of the disease. They measured changes in temperature and ozone levels and looked at the occupation, age, and gender of those who died and those who survived. They also, encouraged by the findings of Dr. John Snow in London, gave some thought to the possibility that cholera was water-borne, but considered the evidence as yet uncertain. Improvements in the city's water supply would eventually, by the 1870s, greatly reduce the risk of disease.

Anthony Wood: "a most egregious . . . Blockhead"?

Anthony Wood, who styled himself more distinctively "Anthony à Wood," is the most notable recorder of Oxford buildings, customs, institutions, and people. He compiled such vast, detailed volumes as *The History and Antiquities of the University of Oxford* and *Athenae Oxonienses* (biographical data on Oxford writers). His information came from the archives of the university, the colleges, the churches, and the Bodleian Library, from information submitted by other scholars, and from oral testimony. And he was himself one of the city's more colorful and quarrelsome inhabitants; both his uninhibited attacks on others and theirs on him qualify him for a place in this chapter.

Wood was depressive by nature, especially after 1670 when deafness, "the first and greatest misery of his life . . . made him exceeding melancholy and more retired." (In his *Life and Times* he wrote of himself in the third person.) But, after a childhood in Oxford and Thame disrupted by the Civil War and the death of his father, he had found his vocation in the 1650s. Having read William Dugdale's *The Antiquities of Warwickshire* (1656), a work by which his "tender affections, and insatiable desire of knowledge, were ravished and melted down," he decided to do for his city what Dugdale had done for Warwickshire. In the process he contrived to make many enemies. Those he called "snivelling saints" attacked him for keeping company with Catholics—friends, owners of manuscripts, patrons. (The Vice-Chancellor himself searched Wood's house in Merton Street and had him swear the official oaths of allegiance to crown and Church.) He quarrelled with John Fell, Dean of Christ Church, who supervised and altered the translation into Latin of *History and Antiquities* (1674): it was "Full of base things put in by Dr Fell—to please his partial humour [biased disposition]—and undo the author." Warden Ironside of Wadham "gave me roast meat and beat me with the spit" (metaphorically, violent though the times were). "He told me that my book was full of contumelies, falsities, contradictions and ... frivolous stuff." The Warden was offended particularly by Wood's naming, in print, of clergy and the noble patrons who had advanced them in the Church. Wood vented his spleen in private: Ironside was "a fool, puppy, child."

In 1694 Wood even succeeded in alienating the good-natured John Aubrey, who had supplied him with many a fact—almost wholly unacknowledged—from his own fruitful research. Wood not only appropriated the material but physically maltreated Aubrey's manuscripts, including some of his *Brief Lives*. He cut out pages and an index, refused to return papers, tried to blame Aubrey for libellous statements in his own *Athenae Oxonienses*, and after 25 years of friendly collaboration "speaks ill of [Aubrey] and bespatters me wherever he goes." Fortunately Aubrey did not see Wood's retrospective re-imagining of his first meeting in Oxford in 1667 with this "credulous," misinforming, sponging, "shiftless person, roving and maggoty-headed, and sometimes little better than crazed." Wood himself was perhaps somewhat crazed when he wrote this account: suffering the stress of his much more dangerous disagreement with the 2nd Earl of Clarendon. In *Athenae* Wood had mentioned the "corrupt dealing"—he advanced men for payment—of Clarendon's late father, Charles II's Lord Chancellor the 1st Earl. This was undoubtedly true, but it was not a politic thing to say about one of the great officers of state. The younger Clarendon felt strongly enough to take the matter up with Wood's university. The Vice-Chancellor's court eventually—in 1693—fined him £40, expelled him from the university, and had a copy of the offending volume publicly burnt on "a fire of two fagots" outside the Sheldonian. He went on working and defending himself, however, and in 1695, the year of his death, applied for and obtained a royal pardon.

It may seem apt that his coat of arms—to be seen on the small memorial to "Antonius Wood Antiquarius" in Merton ante-chapel—incorporates a snarling black wolf. Thomas Hearne, his fellow historian, summed him up in the same sort of robust terms Wood was fond of bestowing on others: he was "always looked upon in Oxford as a most egregious, illiterate, dull blockhead, a conceited, impudent coxcomb." Perhaps he was a coxcomb, perhaps he could snarl like a wolf, but he was far from illiterate and never dull (in either Hearne's sense "stupid" or the modern "boring").

"The likeliest progenitor of unlikely events and persons": Oxford in crime fiction

"Haunts of ancient peace were all very well, but very odd things could crawl and creep beneath lichen-covered stone," we are told in Dorothy L. Sayers' *Gaudy Night*. Oxford in fiction is, famously, a much more dangerous place than Oxford in fact. Colleges have been peopled with corpses by generations of crime writers, from Michael Innes' *Death at the President's Lodgings* (1936), to Robert Robinson's irreverent *Landscape with Dead Dons* (1956), and Antonia Fraser's *Oxford Blood* (1985).

Colin Dexter's *Inspector Morse* novels (1975–96) often use Town as well as Gown settings: bodies are found in a pub parking lot at Woodstock, in Park Town, floating in the Cherwell, hanging in a ter-raced house in Jericho. Morse dances with his pathologist at a ball in the Town Hall until, inevitably, they are both called away to a crime-scene; he is admitted to the John Radcliffe Hospital in *The Wench Is Dead*; not unconnectedly, he drinks beer or whisky, usually contriving that Sergeant Lewis should pay at the White Horse in Broad Street, at the Turf, Trout, and Mitre, and anywhere else he can. He patronizes the bar at the Randolph Hotel where, in *The Jewel That Was Ours*, a woman dies and the "Wolvercote Tongue" is stolen. (He might shudder, and Lewis look blank, at the claim of the current Macdonald Randolph website that its Morse Bar "screams elegance.") In the course of his investigations Morse also meets some devious, arrogant, and murderous dons, but part of him still strongly identifies with the university where he was once a bright if unsuccessful undergraduate. (He had an ill-advised love-affair.) His learning, eccentricities, flashes of brilliance, and pedantry, his passion for crossword-solving and Wagner, make him very like the traditional caricature of an Oxford academic.

The settings in *Morse*, whether Town or Gown, tend to become rather more picturesque in the television versions. And in their sequel, *Lewis*, there is even more focus on quadrangles and golden stone. (Lewis and Hathaway are to be seen especially often in Merton Street and Magpie Lane.) But there are other, less postcard-like university settings. Dorothy L. Sayers, while keenly aware of ancient haunts and lichened stone, is primarily interested in the tense relationships between the small group of women forced together in the Senior Common Room of Shrewsbury College, as focused by the semi-outsider's perspective of Harriet Vane (see p.123–24). Guillermo Martínez, in *The Oxford Murders*, takes us not only to such traditional settings as Merton but to Cunliffe Close near Summertown, the tennis club in Marston Ferry Road, and the Mathematical Institute in St. Giles'.

Edmund Crispin's *The Moving Toyshop* (1946) involves the investigation of a murder but cannot be said entirely to belong to "the dark side." Its main characters—the poet Richard Cadogan and the detective and Professor of English at St. Christopher's College, Gervase Fen—are essentially comic figures. There is an academic element in the humor—frequent playful literary quotation, crimes patterned on Edward Lear's limericks; the source of the title in Pope's *The Rape of the Lock* is announced at the end with a flourish. But there is also farce not unlike that of the Ealing comedies of the time. There are frantic chases through the college, the streets, the Sheldonian, and the Parks. More and more people join in, including twelve intoxicated guests, most of them uninvited, at a tea-and-madeira party in New College. Pursuers cram into Fen's chaotically driven and "extremely small, vociferous and battered sports car," *Lily Christine III*; they run, cycle, and punt, and there is a climactic fight at Botley Fair. At one point, in pursuit of their investigation, Fen and Cadogan each take one side of George Street in order to search for "beautiful blue-eyed girls" who own small, spotted dogs; Fen at once runs into difficulties when discovering that in order to tell the color of someone's eyes you must peer into them closely. The farcical elements operate, of course, as part of Crispin's parody of the conventional crime-novel. In his world nothing is what it appears to be, from the apparently disappearing Iffley Road toyshop of the title onwards. (Cadogan finds the victim strangled there, is coshed by someone, and when he comes to finds that the toyshop is now, and has always been, a grocer's. All is explained much later.) St. Christopher's is both next door to, and modeled on, the real St. John's. Oxford residents will know that New Inn Hall Street is too short to have a number 229. There is much self-reference, aptly for the literary preoccupations of Professor Fen. He enjoys, in mid-investigation, thinking up such titles as "Fen steps in," "The Return of Fen," "A Don Dares Death (A Gervase Fen Story)," "Murder Stalks the University," and "The Blood on the Mortarboard. Fen Strikes Back"; he is, he explains to Cadogan, "making up titles for Crispin." (And Crispin is itself made up—the pseudonym of Robert Montgomery, taken from Michael Innes' detective novel *Hamlet, Revenge!* Innes, in turn, was the pseudonym of the Oxford don J. I. M. Stewart.)

"None but the most blindly credulous," says Crispin in an introductory note, "will imagine the characters and events in this story to be anything but fictitious. It is true that the ancient and noble city of Oxford is, of all the towns of England, the likeliest progenitor of unlikely events and persons. But there are limits."

World War I

Most male undergraduates, dons, and college staff of fighting age volunteered for the armed services in 1914. The number of undergraduates resident in Oxford steadily decreased until, in 1918, there were about twelve percent of the 3,000 men present before the war. Women's colleges continued to function; some students engaged in part-time war-work in Oxford, but a number left, mainly to volunteer as nurses. Vacated buildings were soon filled: there were Belgian refugees in Ruskin College and Serbians in Wycliffe Hall, soldiers and members of the Royal Flying Corps in various colleges, and military hospitals at Littlemore Hospital, the Examination Schools, and Somerville—the students moved into part of Oriel College. In New College Gardens more makeshift tents were used for treating soldiers with shell-shock. Vera Brittain, very soon to leave Oxford to nurse with the Voluntary Aid Detachment, took part in a concert for the patients in the garden of Somerville on 28 May 1915 and noted in her diary

> A lot of them were sitting outside & others were in beds all round or sitting in the windows in their pyjamas. The combination of the lovely garden, the music & the wounded soldiers made me feel about as sad as I could feel. Men are so pathetic when they are weak & ill, & I think it hurts more to see them trying to hobble about than before they can walk at all. It all seemed so terribly wrong—to see those fine well-built men crippled & invalided, their strong capable bodies rendered temporarily, at least, useless, all for the sake of no one quite knows what.

She could imagine all too easily her brother and the man she intended to marry among the wounded. And she thought of "all who never come back, whose crushed & broken bodies lie lifeless on the fields of Flanders, past all the loving redemption which is given to these & such as these at Somerville." Her menfolk would be among those who did not come back.

Roughly eighteen percent of the Oxford University men who joined up—including those who had graduated before the war—died: about 2,700 out of 14,700. Corpus lost a quarter of those who served, almost all of them commissioned officers and so particularly exposed in trench-warfare. J. M. Winter, in his article for *The History of the University of Oxford*, points out that the percentage rises to 31 for those aged nineteen or twenty when the war began; seventy percent of Oxford-educated men who were killed (sixty percent nationally) were under thirty. Many local people, of course, also died while serving in the Oxfordshire and Buckinghamshire Light Infantry. They, and the dead from the Oxfordshire Yeomanry, are commemorated in the Military Chapel of the cathedral. Another memorial, in the cloister, tells us that the Oxford Diocesan Guild of Church Bell-Ringers lost 120 men. The Soldiers of Oxfordshire Museum, which opened recently in the grounds of the Oxfordshire Museum in Woodstock, focuses especially on the "Ox and Bucks" and the Queen's Own Oxfordshire Hussars.

War dreams and war: 1918–45

After the war many servicemen, and some women, returned to their interrupted university studies. Some found the transition from the horrors of war to academic study difficult. Harold Macmillan could not resume his studies at Balliol because to him Oxford "was a city of ghosts." Brittain did come back, but found herself "lost and bewildered, amid a crowd of unfamiliar ex-schoolgirls in a semi-familiar Somerville." Later she suffered "dark hallucinations"—the delayed stress of her experiences made her think that her face was changing, she was growing a beard, becoming a witch. Robert Graves (who, like Siegfried Sassoon, had briefly been a patient at the hospital in Somerville) would, in mid-lecture, "have a sudden very clear experience of men on the march up the Béthune-La Bassée road; the men would be singing, while French children ran along beside us, calling out 'Tommee, Tommee, give me bullee beef!' . . . Or in a deep dug-out in Cambrin . . . there would be a sudden crash and the tobacco smoke in the dug-out would shake with the concussion and twist about in patterns like the marbling on books" (*Goodbye to All That*). These "day-dreams" did not stop, Graves says, until 1928. But he found he could identify with Anglo-Saxon literature in a way his lecturer could not: "I thought of Beowulf lying wrapped in a blanket among his platoon of drunken thanes in the Gothland billet; Judith going for a *promenade* to Holofernes's staff-tent; and *Brunanburgh* with its bayonet-and-cosh fighting." It made sense in a way that the eighteenth-century poetry he was expected to read, with its "drawing-room and deer-park atmosphere," could not.

Brittain campaigned for peace; she studied modern history at Somerville in 1919–21 in the hope of understanding how the war had happened, why nobody had stopped the slaughter. Many Oxford undergraduates, hopeful of preventing another war, supported the League of Nations, whose great advocate, Gilbert Murray, was Professor of Greek. And at the famous debate in 1933 the Oxford Union voted by 275 to 153 that "this House will in no circumstances fight for its King and Country." For *The Daily Express* on 13 February that year, it was "a contemptible and indecent action," a victory for "the woozy-minded Communists, the practical jokers and the sexual indeterminates of Oxford." (Any Nazi readers would no doubt have agreed. Tradition maintains that the vote helped persuade Hitler that Britain would not fight him—or could not win.) But J. M. Winter reminds us that this was not, "as so much of the popular press claimed at the time," a vote against war but "against the shrill patriotism of the popular press of 1914, against the language of 'dulce et decorum est pro patria mori,' against the persecution of conscientious objectors: in sum against the stance of an earlier generation which spoke an older language about honour, duty and empire."

Some remained simple patriots but, on the whole, as Winter notes, "when Hitler made war unavoidable in 1939, stoicism, not enthusiasm, was the response of Oxford and the nation." Bravely or stoically, over two-thirds of the available undergraduates volunteered for action in 1939 before the introduction of conscription. (In the event joining up was, for many, deferred until 1940.) For most of the war students took abbreviated courses and had the right to return later. Again buildings changed their function: the Ministry of Transport took over much of Merton, and the Potato Marketing Board was based in St. John's. The intelligence corps of the War Office was in Oriel, and from 1942 there were Foreign Office codebreakers in Mansfield. St. Hugh's became the Combined Services Hospital for Head Injuries. At the Clarendon Laboratory scientists worked on radar and—in the lead-up to the development of the atom bomb—atomic energy. Thousands of evacuees from London were settled in homes in Oxford; up to 20,000 arrived in September

1939, although some soon went back at least until the Blitz began in 1940.

John Wain gives an impression of the strange situation of the students who were able to undertake longer courses—people, like him, declared medically unfit for military service, and the larger group invalided out by injury: "With our artificial legs, our glass eyes, our deflated lungs, our asthma, our heart disease, we limped about, discussing Shakespeare and Milton among the skirling of huge lorries running in four-wheel drive" (*Sprightly Running*, 1962). Rationing made, especially in the women's colleges, for such fare as dried eggs or (at St. Hugh's, as remembered by Margaret Potter and cited in *Oxford Today*, 1989) "slices of grey national bread and bowls of cocoa-flavoured dried milk powder which could be eaten in lumps or diluted into a drink." And conditions remained spartan even after the war. Roy Foster, who came up to Wadham in 1947, "was informed by the porter a) that there was a cold water tap on the landing . . . b) that the scout would bring a jug of hot water at about 7.45 a.m . . . ; c) that the bath facility was in a separate, single-storeyed building behind the college library; it had about 12 massive baths, duck-boarding on the floor and owls in the rafters."

Fortunately, Oxford was not bombed. Air-raid shelters had been prepared, the largest of them in a basement of the New Bodleian, but only one bomb fell locally—between Cowley and Littlemore, without casualties. Hitler is said to have been keeping the city as a showpiece for Nazi-occupied Britain; it is easy to imagine the invaders appropriating, and strutting vaingloriously through, university ceremonies and processions.

12 | Surroundings
Beyond Oxford

Beyond and before

There is much to be seen in William Camden's "fertile country, and plentiful" of Oxfordshire, its plains "garnished with cornfields and meadows, the hills beset with woods . . . and well watered with fishful rivers" (*Britannia*, 1607), even if the woods and fish have declined a little since Camden's day. Other landscapes are also within reach, from the Vale of White Horse to the higher hills of the Chilterns and Cotswolds and the wetland of Otmoor, now mainly a nature reserve with reedbeds, teal, and lapwings. It was apparently less pleasant when, in the 1930s, John Betjeman noted "The sullen presence of Otmoor, that unexpected fen," brooding over its "damp, alarming district."

Some important local settlements preceded the growth of Oxford. The main Roman town in Oxfordshire was at Alchester, near Bicester, where recent excavation has shown that the Second Legion built a fort as early as 44–5 CE, soon after the Roman invasion; the fort was succeeded by a walled town. Dorchester-on-Thames, too, was originally a walled Roman market town. It became the seat of a Saxon bishop and for a time was effectively the capital of Wessex. "Now it sits aside from the stirring world, and nods and dreams" as Jerome K. Jerome's three men and dog pass on slowly up the Thames. What remains is the Augustinian abbey church, begun in 1170 and notable for its early fourteenth-century stained glass; since the Dissolution of the Monasteries it has served as the parish church.

Jerome's men row on past Abingdon—"quiet, eminently respectable, clean, and desperately dull"—with its abbey remains including gatehouse and long gallery, to Oxford. There they turn back, rapidly abandon the "bally old coffin of a boat" they have hired, and board

The River Thames and St. Lawrence's church, Lechlade (Ballista/Wikimedia Commons)

a train for London. They might more boldly, like Percy Bysshe Shelley and his friends in 1815, have continued upriver. Shelley's party, having started from Windsor, rowed on through the more peaceful stretches beyond Oxford, as far as they could, to Inglesham (a few miles downstream of the source). They stayed nearby at Lechlade, just inside Gloucestershire, where Shelley admired the early sixteenth-century spire of St. Lawrence's church and wrote "A Summer Evening Churchyard, Lechlade, Gloucestershire." In the still twilight, death seems "mild and terrorless as this serenest night."

The "hundred little towns of stone"

West of Oxford, towards the Cotswolds, and along the Thames and its tributaries the Windrush and Evenlode, are the "hundred little towns of stone" of Hilaire Belloc's "The Evenlode." Eynsham (pronounced "Ensham") had a powerful Benedictine abbey, founded in the early eleventh century with the greatest of Old English prose writers, Ælfric, as its first abbot, and rebuilt a century later. The buildings did not long survive the Dissolution of the Monasteries; much was re-used locally in this village full of interesting stone houses. But the illustrated plaques of the Abbey Heritage Trail, set up in 2005 with "cairns" of abbey stone, guide one along streets and though graveyards, green spaces, and parking lots, round the extensive former monastic precinct. The church of St. Leonard probably began, at the north gate of the complex, as a chapel for the villagers.

Near Eynsham is Stanton Harcourt, with nineteenth-century manor-house and fifteenth-century tower from its predecessor, where Alexander Pope finished translating his *Iliad*. The memorials in the church are celebrated by Simon Jenkins in *England's Thousand Best Churches* (1999):

> There are Harcourts military, political and judicial, Harcourts Gothic, Renaissance and Baroque, Harcourts in marble, alabaster and brass, rampant and recumbent, mourned by cherubs, angels, bedesmen, wives and offspring. Stanton Harcourt is a monument to the art of monument.

A few miles northwest of Eynsham, surrounded by peaceful farmland and reached down a deep, muddy track, is North Leigh Roman villa. It achieved its fullest development in the early fourth century and was abandoned in the early fifth. Traces of nearly seventy rooms have been excavated. Evidence of tessellated and mosaic floors were found in a number of the rooms in 1815–16, but only the geometrical mosaic from a large reception or dining room survives intact, seen through the windows of its protecting hut. And further west is Minster Lovell, with the ruins of the fifteenth-century manor-house and dovecote of the Lords Lovell by the fast-flowing Windrush.

Woodstock is another fine stone town with lanes, cottages, a small eighteenth-century Town Hall, and the sixteenth- and eighteenth-century Bear Hotel. The present location results from displacement, in the twelfth century, from the site of the royal Manor of Woodstock. The manor would later be replaced by the spectacularly larger Blenheim Palace.

Blenheim Palace

> The entrance to the park is a triumphal-arch . . . On the other side of a lake, and sufficiently above it, you see a long range of colonnades, towers, cupolas, and fine trees, with a magnificent stone bridge thrown across a narrow part of the lake, leading to a stupendous column, 150 feet high, bearing a colossal statue of John Churchill, first duke of Marlborough.

Thus Louis Simond, a French émigré visiting from America in 1811, describes the sweeping first view of the grounds at Blenheim. In 1705 Parliament (encouraged by Queen Anne) had granted Marlborough the royal Manor of Woodstock and £240,000 of funds to put up a grand new building. They recognized his victory over French and Bavarian forces in a battle the previous year near Blindheim (anglicized as Blenheim, pronounced "Blenim") in Bavaria. The Manor, often rebuilt, had been surrounded by Henry I's park for exotic animals in the 1120s and is supposed to have been the setting for Henry II's liaison with "Fair Rosamund" Clifford. Here, in legend, he built a labyrinth to protect her, but her enemy Queen Eleanor found a way through it and poisoned her. The last of the remaining buildings on the site were demolished by 1720.

Much at Blenheim directly celebrates Marlborough's military success at the Battle of Blenheim and in a series of subsequent engagements during the War of the Spanish Succession. On the corner towers of the building cannonballs are surmounted by inverted—defeated—fleurs-de-lys which in turn are crowned or pressed down by ducal coronets. A huge bust of the once seemingly invincible Louis XIV, which was captured by Marlborough at Tournai, is attached to the south front. Inside, the state rooms are hung with tapestries showing the victories, commissioned by the Duke in Brussels from Judocus de Vos. They present him as a dignified, commanding figure, his and his subordinates' gestures measured and elegant; bloodshed, amid delicate colors and in well-furnished rooms, is rendered as civilized triumph. And from the house there are views up to the 134-foot monument, or "column of victory" (1727–31)—it seemed, pardonably, 150 feet high to Simond. (Originally the aim was to glorify the nation, but the formidably determined Sarah, First Duchess of Marlborough, made Blenheim increasingly a monument to her husband, whose statue accounts for the top 34 feet of the column.)

Not only such individual features but the immense scale of the place is intended to salute the victory; no other non-royal secular house in Britain is called "palace." (At first it was Blenheim Castle, however.) If you could defeat Louis XIV, perhaps you could out-do, or at least rival, Versailles. From the beginning, the ambitiousness of the project caused friction between the Marlboroughs, the architects, and the government. The Duchess was at the heart of these disputes, particularly during her husband's absence at war and final illness, and from his death in 1722 until hers in 1744. She wanted to build a monument of worthy grandeur, but at the same time would have preferred a plainer and more comfortable place to live in: "I never liked any building so much for the show and vanity, as for its usefulness and convenience." (Visitors often commented on the

lack of convenience. In 1717 Alexander Pope found it "inhospita-
ble . . . a house of entries and passages . . . very uselessly handsome.
In a word, the whole is a most expensive absurdity, and the Duke of
Shrewsbury gave a true character of it, when he said, it was a great
quarry of stones above ground.") The Duchess struggled on to complete what she called this "chaos which nobody but God Almighty
could finish," hampered by her own strong views and those of the
main architect at Blenheim, Sir John Vanbrugh, by complex political intrigue and her fall from her position as Queen Anne's favorite,
and by money problems. Marlborough also fell from office under
the new Tory administration in 1711 and funds for the unfinished
house were stopped for several years. The Marlboroughs' political
position improved when George I became King in 1714, but work
at Blenheim was not resumed for some time—until the couple
finally decided to finance the project themselves.

Vanbrugh's plans for the palace were often grander, or more
romantic, than the Duchess'; unlike her he wanted, for instance, to
keep the picturesque old Manor. Inevitably his style is celebrated
or denigrated as "theatrical": he was a playwright with no architectural training. The Duke liked him, while the Duchess would have
preferred Sir Christopher Wren; Wren's former assistant Nicholas
Hawksmoor did work at Blenheim, adding his practical experience to
Vanbrugh's ambitious plans and taking a more conciliatory attitude
to the Duchess. Vanbrugh resigned after a dispute with her in 1716,
brought to a head by the fact that he not only wanted to preserve the
Manor but was living in it. Hawksmoor, however, returned to work
at Blenheim in 1722. During the Vanbrugh/Hawksmoor partnership much of the palace was completed, including such fine rooms
as the Great Hall, with its high oak doors, ceiling by Thornhill (the
Duke in classical garb shows Britannia his battle plans), and superb
view of the monument. Their Saloon, now the State Dining Room,
has wall and ceiling paintings by Laguerre—hired by the Duchess
to replace the more expensive Thornhill. (Thornhill charged £978 to
paint his ceiling alone, Laguerre £500 for walls and ceiling.) On the
walls, between Corinthian columns, appear representatives of various nations: it was a room "daubed," Thomas Hearne maintained,

"with abundance of persons of different countries, Atheists, Infidels, and Heathens being mixed in order to please Buffoons and good fellows." Laguerre also included himself and Marlborough's stout, "good fellow" chaplain Dean Barzillai Jones.

Hawksmoor, after his return, was responsible for the 180-foot Long Gallery on the west front, which later became the Long Library. Rysbrack's statue of Queen Anne at one end, commissioned by Duchess Sarah in 1738, ignores quarrels with the late monarch in order to reassert the original royal involvement in rewarding her general. At the other end of the library is the great organ of 1891 which, a notice tells us, has over 2,300 pipes. Hawksmoor worked also on the chapel, a room dominated by the rather cold splendor of Rysbrack's memorial (1733) to the First Duke and his sons. There are figures of the laureled victor and his family, their allies History and Fame, and, beneath, Marshal Tallard surrendering in 1704. At the end of the nineteenth century the 9th Duchess, forced to contemplate the massive memorial from a facing pew with the altar on her left, "often wondered whether the architect had wished to suggest that allegiance to John Duke [of Marlborough] came before allegiance to the Almighty."

The memorable impression Blenheim made on Louis Simond, and still makes on visitors now, owes much to "Capability" Brown. Vanbrugh's magnificent bridge was, before Brown's alterations, quite out of proportion with its surroundings. "The bridge," mocked Horace Walpole in 1760, "like the beggars at the old Duchess's gate, begs for a drop of water, and is refused." Brown, whose transformation of the grounds was achieved between 1763 and 1774, flooded the valley and widened the River Glyme, replacing the small lake east of the bridge and canals west of it with a much larger lake. The bridge, partially submerged after careful strengthening, remains a forceful presence but an elegant rather than an overbearing one. Brown also, in his usual manner, landscaped the park with slopes and trees artfully designed to suggest a natural pattern, and removed the by then unfashionable formal gardens of the Great Parterre.

Later elements essential to Blenheim today date from the time of the 9th Duke, who succeeded to the title in 1892 and died in 1934.

He employed Achille Duchêne to restore the north courtyard, which Brown had replaced with grass, to its stone Baroque spaciousness: a parade-ground humanized by the slopes and lake beyond, statues in niches and warm, ocher-yellow stone which glows even in rainy weather. Duchêne also brought back formal gardens, developing the Italian Garden (1908) east of the palace, and the Water Terrace (1925–30), with its fountains and statues, to the west. These and the many other improvements by the 9th Duke were made possible by his marriage to the immensely wealthy eighteen-year-old American business heiress Consuelo Vanderbilt in 1895. The marriage settlement brought the Duke an income of about $100,000 a year. The money, he made no bones about admitting, was the sole reason for the marriage. In her autobiography, *The Glitter and the Gold* (1953), Consuelo Vanderbilt Balsan—she and the Duke separated in 1906 and later divorced—describes what she saw as the horrors of her life in the hidebound and hierarchical British aristocracy of the time. Grand dinners were often ineffably tedious, and etiquette required the wearing of sixteen different dresses during a four-day visit to Blenheim by the Prince and Princess of Wales. On more private occasions, according to the ex-Duchess, dinners were served "with all the accustomed ceremony," but once the staff had delivered a course and retired Marlborough

> had a way of piling food on his plate; the next move was to push the plate away, together with knives, forks, spoons and glasses—all this in considered gestures which took a long time; then he backed his chair away from the table, crossed one leg over the other and endlessly twirled the ring on his little finger. While accomplishing these gestures he was absorbed in thought and quite oblivious of any reactions I might have. Eventually, he would come out of his trance and begin, slowly, eating, usually complaining that the food was cold! ... As a rule neither of us spoke a word. I took to knitting in desperation and the butler read detective stories in the hall.

More enjoyable was the company of the Duke's cousin, Winston Churchill, whether because of his "American blood"—his mother was the American socialite Jennie Jerome—"or his boyish enthusiasm and spontaneity, qualities sadly lacking in my husband." Churchill, nephew of the 8th Duke, was born at Blenheim on 30 November 1874. A permanent exhibition shows Churchill memorabilia, letters from Harrow and Sandhurst, his wartime siren-suit, and photographs: from the already genially pugnacious seven-year-old in sailor suit ("A future First Lord of the Admiralty," notes the label) to the elderly post-war Prime Minister leaving Downing Street in a car with a smile, a trademark cigar, and his miniature poodle Rufus. Paintings by Churchill here include one of the Great Hall. Recordings of some of the great speeches play, and next door are the bed he was born in, his baby vest and curls, and more of his paintings.

Churchill often stayed at Blenheim and took inspiration from his ancestor, the 1st Duke, whose life he wrote. The palace also had a more personal importance to him. "At Blenheim I took two very important decisions: to be born and to marry. I am happily content with the decisions I took on both occasions." Churchillian though this statement is, Clementine Hozier did have some say in the second decision, and he was even somewhat nervous before proposing to her in the small Temple of Diana (1773) in the grounds. A plaque at the temple records the occasion, on 11 August 1908.

There is much for visitors to see and do in the grounds of Blenheim: the rose garden, the cascade, lakeside walks, and—reached by mini-train, passing fantastically gnarled old oaks—the butterfly-house, adventure playground, garden center, and maze. One improvement since the nineteenth century is that sightseers are no longer pursued by staff desperate for remuneration. In *The Adventures of Mr Verdant Green* (1853–7) visitors are charged half-crowns by successive guides who show them the paintings, the rose garden, and the mountainous memorial in the chapel where sparrows nest. Simond, too, complains about the succession of rapacious guides, including a gardener on a donkey who "came after us . . . to direct our admiration to certain spots (all tame enough), and get his 2s. 6d" and—the seventh guide—"a coxcomb of an upper servant, who hurried us through the house." Having shelled out nineteen shillings altogether, Simond notes that "the annual income of the Duke of Marlborough is estimated at £70,000" (*Journal of a Tour and Residence in Great Britain*, 1815).

Buscot Park

The house at Buscot, in wooded countryside between Faringdon and Lechlade about eighteen miles southwest of Oxford, was built in 1780–3. Just over a century later it was bought by Alexander Henderson, a successful stockbroker who became Lord Faringdon. He began to give the grounds their present form, including Harold Peto's water-garden of 1904, a channel threading through pools from the house to the Big Lake.

Inside the house, with fine views out to the gardens and the two lakes (Big and Little), is the Faringdon art collection, begun by the first Lord Faringdon and continued by the next three generations of his family. The collection is rich in Regency furniture—black and gold Egyptianizing couch and *torchères*, mahogany side-tables by Robert Adam—but has a great range of paintings, furnishings, and sculpture from other periods. There are Old Masters, an eighteenth-century state bed, Pre-Raphaelites, Sickert's portrait of the 2nd Lord Faringdon coming down the steps at Buscot, and contemporary glass. Rembrandt's Pieter Six, a fair man in black, looking down, meditative, a little abstracted, contrasts with Rubens' Marchesa Veronica Spinola Doria in the same room, grander in shiny gray, gold-brocaded silk and large feathery ruff. Reynolds provides a fashionably wistful countess and Gainsborough some cows, no less graceful in their way, in a wooded lane at evening (oil and watercolor on brown tinted paper). More attention has been paid to the Pre-Raphaelite pieces upstairs, especially Rossetti's *Venus Verticordia*—turner of hearts—and *Pandora*, both in colored chalks. The model for Pandora was Jane Morris, William Morris' wife and Rossetti's lover and muse. (The three had met in 1857 when the painters were working on the Oxford Union murals.)

Perhaps the most distinctive room at Buscot is the Saloon, whose walls are entirely taken up with Sir Edward Burne-Jones' *Legend of the Briar Rose*. Four paintings accompany lines by William Morris describing scenes from the story of Sleeping Beauty. Burne-Jones sold them to the dealers Agnew's for £15,000 and the future first Lord bought it from them in 1890. (Burne-Jones then adapted the sequence to its setting by adding further rose bower panels between each painting.) The main challenge for the painter was to represent a deeply sleeping court—not dead, not dozing. The blossoming briar-roses which have penetrated the whole castle suggest the life, light, and spring which are about to return, but their thorns remain to be cut through by the armored prince who stands at one end of the room, sword in hand. Quintessentially Pre-Raphaelite, he looks more likely to swoon than to fight. But his somewhat vapid appearance prevents him, the only one awake, from taking away too much attention, too much magic, from the enchanted sleepers.

In *The Garden Court* the young women, in dark blues, greens, and purples, seem rather carefully arranged—as they might be by magic. They could look too obviously like the artist's models, artificially posed, but they seem to me more like dancers who are still now but will be ready at the next note to leap into life—a balletic version of "sleeping lions." (Tchaikovsky's *Sleeping Beauty*, of course, makes thoughts of ballet inevitable.) In *The Council Chamber*, by contrast, the King on his throne will take more rousing—he is weighed down by a crown like the miter of an Orthodox priest, a very long white beard, heavy robes, and age. His attendants seem somewhat more comfortable, but the knights or guards in *The Briar Wood* look more deathly, with a touch of the traditional pallid, martyred St. Sebastian. Sleeping Beauty herself, however, in *The Rose Bower*, seems more plausibly asleep, although lying on her bed slightly as if on a bier. She will revive, but the prince still has a long way to come, from the opposite end of the room, before he can reach and kiss her. The larger theme is "the quest for ideal beauty in an apathetic world" (Fiona MacCarthy in her life of Burne-Jones).

Kelmscott Manor: utopian rubble-stone

Close to Buscot and Lechlade, near the Thames, is another place of Pre-Raphaelite pilgrimage: Kelmscott Manor, William Morris' country home from 1871 until his death in 1896. The building itself, a substantial gray house of the sixteenth and seventeenth centuries in what Morris describes as "well-laid rubble stone of the district," suited his love of vernacular architecture. He enjoyed features such as the roof-slates, "'sized down'; the smaller ones to the top and the bigger towards the eaves, which gives one the same sort of pleasure in their orderly beauty as a fish's scales or a bird's feathers." He liked to think of the house as growing "up out of the soil and the lives of those that lived on it." It closely inspires the "many-gabled old house" and garden with superabundant roses, loud-singing black-birds, and wheeling swifts, which is the utopian destination of the Thames journey in his *News from Nowhere* (1890). (Morris and friends had earlier traveled to the manor by boat from Kelmscott House, his home in Hammersmith.)

The contents of the house celebrate Morris' work, that of his associates—especially Rossetti, who lived at Kelmscott for a time, Burne-Jones, and Philip Webb—and his distinctive taste in tapes-tries and furniture. Here are ceramics and embroideries, charcoal studies by Burne-Jones, paintings by Rossetti, green-painted furni-ture by Madox Brown, and the early seventeenth-century bed slept in by Morris. (It came with the house.) The hangings were made and designed by his daughter, May Morris; she embroidered the pelmet (wool on linen, 1891–3) with his poem "The wind's on the wold . . ." He is buried in the village churchyard.

Another place near Faringdon which appealed to Morris' love of solid craftsmanship was Great Coxwell Tithe Barn. This substan-tial structure—about 150 feet long and 48 feet high—was built at the end of the thirteenth century and was part of a grange or farm complex owned by the monks of Beaulieu Abbey in Hampshire. It has walls of Cotswold rubble-stone and a magnificent, complex roof structure. The oak posts are original, but the rafters have been restored or replaced in deal. For Morris it was "the finest piece of architecture in England . . . unapproachable in its dignity, as beauti-ful as a cathedral, yet with no ostentation of the builder's art."

"Several different plays somehow fused together": Lady Ottoline Morrell at Garsington Manor

Lady Ottoline Morrell entertained writers, artists, fashionable Londoners, noteworthy Oxford dons, and promising young under-graduates at Garsington Manor, southeast of Oxford, between 1915 and 1927. She was married to Philip Morrell, Liberal MP and a member of the branch of the Oxford Morrell family which had gone into law rather than brewing. She helped the careers of young artists, was painted by Augustus John and Duncan Grant, and can now be appreciated, Miranda Seymour argues, as "a trailblazer in fashion, the bohemian ancestor of all that is most adventurous in modern design" (*Dictionary of National Biography*). Maurice Bowra, in *Memories 1898–1939*, says that "Lady Ottoline was noteworthy by any standards. She was tall and even stately, with bright copper-coloured hair and a heavily powdered face, and she wore clothes remarkable for their brilliant colours and original design . . . She had a prominent, large nose, a jutting chin and a highly expressive mouth. She spoke with a curiously nasal tone ["a kind of cooing nasal hiss," says Anthony Powell] and at intervals shot out a red tongue and licked her lips with it." She was an obvious target for mockery, most famously as Hermione Roddice in D. H. Lawrence's *Women in Love*. (She was remarkably forgiving of such mockery and in her later years won the affection even of those who had once ridiculed her.) In her presence, visitors were usually more respectful: "For the most experienced in salon life, Garsington represented moving into the firing-line; for a nervous undergraduate, an ordeal of the most gru-elling order," remembered Powell.

According to Bowra

The fascination of Garsington lay partly in not knowing whom you would find there. There were the painters of the then younger gen-eration—Mark Gertler, sombre and serious, but supremely honest and devoted to his art; Stanley Spencer, torn between apocalyptic visions of . . . the Day of Judgement and domestic duties, such as giving the children their baths . . . Then there were the writers—Aldous Huxley, gentle and humane and omniscient; W. B. Yeats, shocking the more serious-minded by his stories about spooks; . . . Lytton Strachey, with his red beard and long spidery legs, talking in a falsetto voice; and, less commonly, Virginia Woolf, remote, beautiful, and ethereal, but flashing suddenly into keen comments on human foibles.

Less distinguished guests dreaded saying the wrong thing. "It was like acting in a play," says Powell, "or rather several different plays somehow fused together—in which you had not been told either the plot or your own cue."

A later owner of the house, Leonard Ingrams, started the annual Garsington Opera Festival in 1989. Performances, often exploring such unfamiliar repertoire as Haydn's operas, took place in the gardens. In 2011 the festival moved to the Wormsley estate, near Watlington, where a "pavilion" for 600 spectators is erected and taken down each season in the deer park.

White Horse Hill: "wave on wave of the mysterious downs"

Thomas Hughes, the author of *Tom Brown's Schooldays* (1857), came from the village of Uffington in the Vale of White Horse, then in Berkshire but since 1974 in southwest Oxfordshire. Tom describes "a land of rich pastures, bounded by ox-fences, and covered with fine hedgerow timber, with here and there a nice little gorse or spinney" where "the villages are straggling, queer, old-fashioned places, the houses being dropped down without the least regularity, in nooks and out-of-the way corners, by the sides of shadowy lanes and footpaths, each with its patch of garden." Above it all is White Horse Hill, whose top is "a place to open a man's soul and make him prophesy, as he looks down on that great Vale spread out as the garden of the Lord before him, and wave on wave of the mysterious downs behind; and to the right and left the chalk hills running away into the distance" with the Ridgeway—the ancient track—"keeping straight along the highest back of the hills."

The stylized galloping horse, trenched into the soil and then filled with chalk, was for centuries believed to commemorate Alfred the Great's victory over the Danes at Ashdown in 871: "There England rear'd her long-dejected head," as Henry James Pye patriotically averred in *Farringdon Hill* (1774); "There Alfred triumph'd, and invasion bled." But archaeological evidence has now shown that the horse is almost certainly late Iron Age, like "Uffington Castle," the grassy hill-fort above it. Presumably it was a tribal or clan emblem—probably of the Atrebates—or a territorial or religious marker. Conceivably it was sacred to the horse-associated Celtic goddess Epona.

Beginning in the seventeenth century, and continuing until the late nineteenth, people from the surrounding villages met every seven years to "scour" the horse and to take part in such sports as pig-racing and rolling cheeses down the hill. (Hughes' *The Scouring of the White Horse* was published in 1859.) The aim of the scouring was, as Thomas Baskerville put it, "to repair and cleanse this landmark, or else in time it may turn green like the rest of the hill, and be forgotten."

The Ridgeway leads west, between fields, from White Horse Hill to an earlier monument, Wayland's Smithy: a Neolithic chamber-tomb built in two stages. A first barrow, of about 3500 BCE, was replaced about a century later by a much larger one (180 feet long) and edged with sarsen stones. Legend makes it a place for supernatural happenings: Wayland, the magical smith of Germanic stories, would allegedly shoe your horse if you left him a groat on one of the stones. But here, often with no sound but the rustling from the clump of beeches which marks the site, the atmosphere seems more deeply numinous than even a mythical blacksmith could make it. No doubt it was part of a whole sequence or pattern of monuments leading on towards the sacred sites further west: West Kennet Long Barrow, Avebury, Silbury Hill, Stonehenge.

Stowe and Rousham: Grecian and "Kentissimo"

Northwest of Oxford is the mansion at Stowe in Buckinghamshire—late seventeenth-century, developed in the early eighteenth century and more fully to Robert Adam's designs in the 1770s. The house was bought by the founders of Stowe School in 1923, and the very extensive park was taken over by the National Trust in 1989. Here, where William Kent was one of the designers and Lancelot "Capability" Brown head gardener, are vistas of temples, statues, woodland, and the "Grecian Valley." The Temple of British Worthies (1735) displays busts of those "gallant spirits [who] founded constitutions, shunned the torrent of corruption, battled for the state, ventured their lives in the defense of their country, and gloriously bled in the cause of liberty" (*The Beauties of Stowe*, 1753). In other words there is an eclectic grouping of figures congenial to Stowe's Whig owner, Lord Cobham: Alfred the Great, Elizabeth I, Shakespeare, Milton, Hampden, the then living Alexander Pope.

Kent also worked on the house, and especially the gardens, at Rousham, designing winding paths with carefully managed views of the River Cherwell and such structures as the arcaded Praeneste and the two "eyecatchers"—one "ruin" adapted from an old mill, the other, with arches, specially built. For Horace Walpole it was all so splendidly Kent that it was "Kentissimo."

From an earlier period comes Chastleton House, in fine limestone with surviving seventeenth-century woodwork, furniture, and decorations.

"Our tree yet crowns the hill": Arnold, Clough, and the Oxfordshire countryside

"Maidens, who from the distant hamlets come/To dance around the Fyfield elm in May"; "the skirts of Bagley Wood where the gypsies pitch their tents"; "Hinksey and its wintry ridge"; "the warm, green-muffled Cumnor hills"; flowers picked in "Wychwood's distant bowers." Matthew Arnold's poem "The Scholar-Gipsy" (1853) is full of such references to the hills and villages west of Oxford. (Like White Horse Hill, most of these places used to be in Berkshire.) The landscape comes from the long walks taken in the 1840s by Arnold, his brother Tom and his friend and fellow poet Arthur Hugh Clough. None of them found it at all easy to keep at their academic work. They were therefore attracted to a story they came across in Joseph Glanvill's *The Vanity of Dogmatizing* (1661) of an Oxford student who left his friends and his studies, went to live with the gypsies and learned their secret ways.

Arnold's Scholar-Gipsy leads a solitary life in the deep country, searching always for truth. Students, hunters, harvesters, glimpse him in the fields and hills but he avoids all but the briefest of human contact. He looks back, for a moment, as he climbs up to Cumnor in the snow, at "the line of festal lights in Christ-Church hall," but goes on until he finds "some sequestered grange" where he can sleep in the straw. He is single of purpose, not part of the baffling, fluctuating world where people are "Light half-believers of [their] casual creeds": the contemporary world of the religious doubt explored in Arnold's "Dover Beach." At a more personal level, the wanderer does not suffer the conflicting desires of Arnold the Oxford dandy who also wanted to live up to the earnest moral example of his father Dr. Arnold; or of Arnold the rejected lover of "Marguerite," an "unsuitable" girl he met in Switzerland before he went on to become a Victorian public figure—schools inspector, prolific prose writer, Professor of Poetry at Oxford.

So undistracted is the wanderer, so unworn with care, that perhaps he has not died. He went from the world before he had "spent, like other men, [his] fire"; he has become, through lack of human cares, a happy equivalent of the accursed Wandering Jew or Flying Dutchman. Clough, more mortal, died at forty-one in 1861. Several years later Arnold wrote "Thyrsis" in his memory, returning to the landscape of the earlier poem and its opposition between aspiration and failure. Now change, in the tradition of poetic elegy, is everywhere. Sibylla the innkeeper and her sign have gone from South Hinksey; fields once full of "old, white-blossomed trees" and thick with cowslips and purple orchids have been ploughed. Clough/Thyrsis, too, is absent, and in his friend's opinion he had already gone astray: Thyrsis left the countryside and "his piping took a troubled sound/Of storms that rage outside our happy ground." Neither poet really liked the other's work: Clough's satire, social concerns, and open religious skepticism were not for Arnold—at least not in verse—whose poems were mostly lyrical. In the course of their somewhat difficult relationship, it had perhaps been the rambles from Oxford which brought the two men closest to each other.

Thyrsis is gone, and he will miss "the high Midsummer pomps," the breaking and swelling "musk carnations," "gold-dusted snapdragon," jasmine and rose, and "the full moon, and the white evening star." But the signal-elm is still there: while this tree stood, the friends had said, the Scholar-Gipsy could not die. (The real tree, an oak on Boars Hill, is still standing, hollow now.) Thyrsis quested, like the Scholar-Gipsy, and his brief "jocund youthful time" is still associated with "this rude Cumnor-ground." The poet will go on undaunted: "Our tree yet crowns the hill,/Our Scholar travels yet the loved hill-side."

Further Reading

T. H. Aston, general editor, *The History of the University of Oxford*, Oxford University Press, 1984–94.

Jeri Bapasola, *The Finest View in England: the Landscape and Gardens at Blenheim Palace*, Blenheim Palace, 2009.

Judy G. Batson, *Her Oxford*, Vanderbilt University Press, 2008.

Humphrey Carpenter, *The Inklings: C. S. Lewis, J. R. R. Tolkien, Charles Williams and their Friends*, Harper Collins, 1997 (first published 1978).

Humphrey Carpenter, *OUDS: a Centenary History of the Oxford University Dramatic Society 1885–1985*, Oxford University Press, 1985.

John Dougill, *Oxford in English Literature: the Making, and Undoing, of the 'English Athens'*, University of Michigan Press, 1998.

Christopher Hibbert, *The Encyclopaedia of Oxford*, Macmillan, 1988.

Stephanie Jenkins, *Oxford History*. www.oxfordhistory.org.uk.

John Melvin, *The Stones of Oxford: Conjectures on a Cockleshell*, Papadakis, 2011.

Jan Morris, *Oxford*, third edition, Oxford University Press, 2001.

Jan Morris, *The Oxford Book of Oxford*, Oxford University Press, 1978.

Jennifer Sherwood and Nikolaus Pevsner, *Oxfordshire*, Penguin, 1974.

Annie Skinner, *Cowley Road: a History*, revised edition, Signal Books, 2008.

Geoffrey Tyack, *Oxford: an Architectural Guide*, Oxford University Press, 1998.

Geoffrey Tyack, *Blue Guide: Oxford and Cambridge*, sixth edition, Blue Guides, 2004.

University of Oxford: www.ox.ac.uk.

Anthony Wood, *The Life of Anthony Wood in his Own Words*, ed. Nicholas K. Kiessling, Bodleian Library, 2009.

Index